DIVERS
AND
CAMERAS

A complete textbook for students, instructors and
advanced underwater photographers

By

Joe Strykowski

Illustrations by Ernie Duerksen

DACOR CORPORATION

DIVERS AND CAMERAS

Copyright © 1974 by
Joe Strykowski

DACOR CORPORATION
161 Northfield Rd.
Northfield, Illinois 60093

Library of Congress Catalog Card Number: 73-93201

Printed in the United States of America

CONTENTS

APPENDIX

FOREWORD

It was pre-ordained that having become totally captivated with the underwater world — we should make the development of fine diving equipment our life's work.

Even in those earliest days — when I could slip away for a few hours of peaceful exploration in the world below I was thoroughly confounded by the perplexing problems of underwater photography which seemed to nullify my considerable shore-side photographic talent.

As a consequence I began to lay hands upon any photographic book remotely related to underwater photography. My disappointment mounted as my collection of odd-sized books and pamphlets grew entirely out of proportion to the amount of information to be distilled therefrom.

In many cases, I felt as though I was paying for the privilege of viewing the author's personal photographic album.

And I soon discovered I was not alone in my desperation. Hardly a week went by without a request for recommendation for a concise and comprehensible book on underwater photography.

Once again we turned to Joe Strykowski. He had done a number of assignments for us — none more critical perhaps than the thousands of feet of 16mm film he had exposed in slow motion study in the research and development of our "TURBO-FIN".

His highly popular underwater photography course received glowing testimonials. Former students were gaining all kinds of awards.

His wizardry in taming complicated technical jargon into crisp and understandable material was well evidenced in the success of his earlier books, notably "DIVING FOR FUN."

Having this moment finished reading the manuscript of "DIVERS AND CAMERAS" I have only one thing to add.

The art of underwater photography today is a most precise and demanding one requiring knowledge and experience. Within the following pages is concentrated a king's ransom in underwater photographic knowledge — written in a style which is not only easy to read, but fun.

The would-be underwater photographer having absorbed this knowledge has but to gain experience to challenge our leading submarine photographic specialists. There are no shortcuts to professionalism . . . only practice, practice and practice.

Sam Davison, *President*
Dacor Corporation

". . . I have opened the way . . . it remains for others to follow me, to open up new paths, and to arrive at a definitive objective."

Louis Boutan, 1893
"LA PHOTOGRAPHIE SOUS-MARINE"

Chapter I.

DIVERS AND CAMERAS

In the dawn of his emergence, man soon learned he could communicate most effectively by scratching picture stories in the sand or on the walls of his cave.

In so doing, man had indeed developed a language. He had bridged the chasm of ignorance by communicating with visual symbols. Man, the visual communicator, had emerged!

Furthermore, due to his mind's ability to retain visual impressions, man discovered that he possessed a natural and virtually limitless storage capacity for these visual impressions from which he could summon — at will — most any of the impressions registered by his mind. And down through the ages as man's quest for knowledge led him from one marvelous technological achievement to the next — he attempted to record each important occurrence visually. But he also discovered there was an apparent limit to the credibility of eye-witness descriptions, sketches and paintings.

The public was justifiably skeptical and suspicious. They were unwilling to accept their fellow man's visual records as irrefutable proof. And man, the visual communicator, understood the problem and quite agreed. All too frequently, he found that his visuals were inaccurate and unintentionally distorted the things they represented . . . because what he sought to do was beyond his physical capability.

Testifying to his creative genius, man succeeded in devising the camera, an instrument through which all the details of yesterdays could be captured faithfully and permanently in visual impression. Almost concurrently with the development of the camera, man the diver having penetrated the sea and observing her wonders longed for some visual record to take back to his land-bound brothers.

Louis Boutan was such a man. His excursions underwater were necessarily of such brief times that he realized if any serious undersea research effort was to be mounted, the scientist would have to be able to make photographs underwater.

Boutan, a professor of zoology at France's Arago Marine Station, is credited with making the first successful underwater photograph in 1893. The extraordinary achievement involved using a wet plate camera in a watertight copper housing whose sum underwater weight was 400 pounds! The

monster camera required the lift of a fifty gallon wood barrel to offset its negative buoyancy.

The feat is even more incredible when one considers that time exposures of as long as 30 minutes were often required to make a photographic image.

The inventive Professor Boutan also devised the first underwater flash system.

An air-filled barrel provided the oxy-

gen for an alcohol lamp kept watertight by a glass dome. The dome also served as the flash reflector. At the appropriate moment, Boutan ignited the flash by squeezing a rubber bulb which blew powdered magnesium into the flame.

It is proper and just that this dedicated undersea explorer be recorded by history as the "Father of Underwater Photography".

While significant contributions were made by a number of early experimenters, underwater photography really became practical with the advent of self contained underwater breathing apparatus. Scuba provided the underwater photographer with the freedom of movement needed to effectively use the newly-developed miniature cameras as easily underwater as he could at the surface.

It is in the nature of man to accept the challenge thrown down by the unknown. It is for this reason he explores the outer reaches of the limitless space surrounding our planet and plumbs the deepest ocean depths.

And the exquisite thrill of being the first human to see a new horizon belongs to each diver no matter that he dwells in the heart of the largest megalopolis. Even so, this fascinating unexplored territory is rarely more than one hour's drive from where he makes his home.

Three quarters of our earth's surface is covered by oceans, seas, lakes, quarries, rivers and streams which have hardly been penetrated, much less explored.

It is little wonder then that scuba diving, the most challenging of sports, should have such strong attraction for man. And correspondingly, it is just as natural that those of us who enjoy the sea's bounty should wish to record the great underwater adventure so that it may be shared, albeit vicarious-

ly, with our less fortunate brothers who cling to the shore.

Though the adventure can only be fully experienced through the diver's eyes, the next best thing is the photographic story.

The diver also has an important responsibility to the community. He is the first to know about the insidious effects of pollution and overfishing, for example.

The non-diving public has only one view of the undersea world . . . the image and message they perceive through the efforts of the underwater photographer.

The public through these efforts are only now beginning to appreciate the vast potential of the sea and the need to conserve and protect its great bounty.

As man's activity in the deep sea expands into its even deeper reaches it becomes increasingly important that the role of the underwater photographer be expanded.

Only through the efforts of the subsea cameraman can the public view the world beneath the sea . . . and the importance of the public's attitude toward the world's oceans cannot be over-emphasized.

The late John F. Kennedy, in a 1961 message to the Congress, best summarized our relationship to the sea. "Knowledge of the oceans is more than a matter of curiosity . . . our very survival may depend upon it." In the final judgment — the world's population has the fate of the oceans in its hands.

The underwater camera is one of the oceanographers most important research instruments. It is capable of recording endless reams of scientific data aiding the researchist in programs

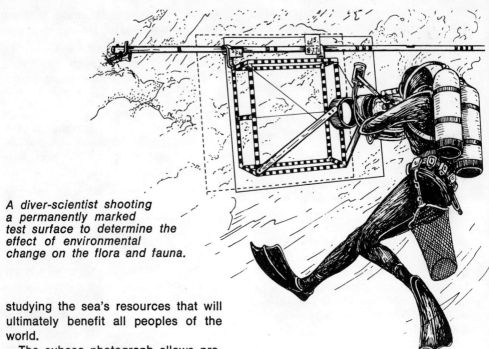

A diver-scientist shooting a permanently marked test surface to determine the effect of environmental change on the flora and fauna.

studying the sea's resources that will ultimately benefit all peoples of the world.

The subsea photograph allows precise analysis by the undersea scientist in the comfort of his laboratory, yielding detail which would probably have escaped even the most attentive of deep-sea observers.

Indeed many significant scientific contributions have been made by underwater photographers who were focusing on a particular subject and didn't even notice the wealth of detail the camera lens was including at the time the shutter was tripped.

The work of the undersea cameraman will continue to yield new knowledge which will help man to more fully understand the last unexplored frontier. This book was not written to make scientists out of divers, but to provide divers with the practical knowledge necessary to increase their photographic skills and enjoyment.

The art of underwater photography is an exacting one requiring skill, training and practice if the photographer is to become proficient. The good photographer is systematic, orderly and neat. He understands it is the sum of all the small details coming together when the shutter is pressed which determines the extent of the photographer's ability. It is only on this — his finished product — that the final judgement is passed.

"Luck" does not exist in the photographer's vocabulary. Only one thing is certain. When the photographer armed with knowledge and skill releases the shutter on his camera certain predictable results are obtained. The subsea photographer's motto could well be "STOP! LOOK! and THINK!"

The serious student of photography must be patient and not demand immediate perfection. He must instead build his ability on experience, gaining knowledge from practice and mistakes.

No one can be a successful underwater photographer until he thoroughly understands the fundamentals of photography. Hopefully, *Divers and Cameras* will provide those fundamentals, ample justification for its existence. Its purpose: to cultivate a better understanding of the art of underwater photography by presenting basic principles, current techniques and new developments.

Hopefully, the reader will find the chapters not merely theoretical; but aimed at teaching the art of creative underwater photography by providing practical applications of the mechanics of photography.

For more intensive study on any photographic subject included within these pages, a detailed bibliography can be found in the back of this book. Also many monthly photographic magazines are very useful in keeping the photographer abreast of the latest developments.

If the prospective undersea photographer finds such work worthwhile and is able to adapt to the demanding requirements he is certain to find the opportunities for future success are boundless.

Underwater photography is very different from what it was only a few years ago. Production housings were almost unheard of and those that were available were not very versatile. The Nikonos was not even a dream. The diver was a master of ingenuity, however. Mother's pressure cooker, rubber sheets, wood and virtually any conceivable building material was enlisted in the home construction of camera housings.

I have fond memories of filming reef fish with Bermudian Bronson Hartley's 16mm Bolex housed in a pressure compensated wooden box. The housing was pressure-compensated by a rubber balloon, which, when squeezed by increasing ambient pressure, would force air into the housing cavity.

But underwater photographic equipment has changed radically, becoming in the process better designed, more compact, better balanced and easier to use.

As a consequence, more and bet-

ter work is being done all the time and any diver can make outstanding underwater photographs provided he takes the time to learn the basic fundamentals.

A DIVER FIRST

To be an underwater photographer you must first be a *good* diver. While I've seen some fine pictures made by snorkelers, I'm afraid that they are certainly the exception.

Scuba equipment is absolutely necessary for all but the most casual flirtation with the art of subsea photography.

Becoming a trained certified diver is not nearly as difficult as it sounds. It only requires comfortable swimming ability, good health and a desire to enjoy one of the most fascinating sports available to man. Virtually every YMCA or scuba dive shop can put you in touch with a certified scuba instructor who will quickly demonstrate how to go "diving for fun."

But even experienced divers may have to be re-educated in the diving techniques required in underwater photography. If the diver is not constantly alert, it's quite easy to become so engrossed in picture making that he may lose track of his diving buddy — or unintentionally drift down progressively deeper — or be carried

with a current a considerable distance from his boat.

In the final analysis, the undersea

photographer combines all the qualities of any good diver: maturity, good judgement, discipline and a healthy respectful attitude for the aquatic environment.

Underwater photography can be as simple or complex as surface photography. The range of equipment available to the diver today includes virtually the entire spectrum of photographic equipment — from simple box camera to the most sophisticated photographic systems.

In most cases the quality of the finished photograph reflects a corresponding quality of camera equipment. Usually!

Occasionally excellent work is done by inexperienced photographers with rather primitive equipment. Ernie Duerksen, whose fine illustrations compliment this book, borrowed a cheap box-camera in a plastic housing immediately upon becoming a certified diver and headed for the clear waters of Mexico. His photographs were amazingly good. Ernie had a little something extra working for him, however. He is a trained artist and when he puts the camera viewfinder to his eye the photographic composition comes together naturally.

And having a super camera is no guarantee your results are going to be good either. Many years ago I had an opportunity to use a camera belonging to the great Lamar Boren, who likely has forgotten more about undersea photography than most of us can ever hope to learn. I had brashly commented that with his "super camera" anyone could make outstanding pictures.

Needless to say, I had abundant reason afterwards to wish that I had eaten the film rather than expose it.

Find a simple camera and housing that fill your present needs and learn all its potential before you graduate to complex camera systems.

And don't be misled. Anyone can make top quality pictures. Whether you can depends only on your imagination — your skill in recognizing good photographic compositions. The opportunities are limitless and the possibilities for specialization even underwater are considerable.

OPPORTUNITIES

Presuming that you are dedicated enough to develop your photographic skills to the point of being capable of making sharp negatives and prints of sufficient contrast and tone suitable for publication, you are well on your way to making underwater photography not only fun, but profitable.

Never before in the history of the publishing business have so many market opportunities existed for the underwater photographer. And they continue to increase.

The likelihood of your photographs being published are even greater if you have a talent for writing because the publishers prefer stories that are illustrated with top quality photographs.

And the undersea photographic opportunities are by no means limited to photo-journalism.

Underwater photography has become an indispensable tool to the marine biologist who through the study of fish life-cycles, habit patterns and population density esfimates may very well one day evolve the best scientific approach to assure adequate food for the world's population.

Free-swimming deep divers will provide important research data through underwater photography, a job that is done poorly now thru unmanned camera systems. Since they are controlled from the surface robot cameras bring back only a small percentage of useful data for the number of pictures exposed.

COMPETITIONS

Perhaps your interests are not commercial. You may enjoy participation in photography contests to match your photographic skills against those of other underwater photographers.

Never before in the history of underwater photography have there been so many opportunities to do so. Details of photography contests are listed regularly in the diving publications.

PRESENTATIONS

Some underwater photographers are neither interested in competition nor in selling their photographs. They enjoy the challenge of presenting slide programs to audiences. The programs may be educational, thought provoking . . . or simply entertaining.

The point is whatever your interest in underwater photography, the opportunities are truly boundless!

SUMMARY

Above water, almost anyone can make passably good photographs. But within these pages the student of subsea photography will find the basic principles and techniques through which consistently high calibre photographs can be made.

Make no mistake! Underwater photography presents the cameraman with perhaps the worst possible conditions. In most cases the diver-photographer is dealing with limited visibility, low light levels, dirty water and moving subjects.

Divers and Cameras will show you how to get the most from your camera through an intensive study of the sea environment, the phenomena of light, optics, flash, exposure meters, technique, macro photography and cinematography.

By serious attention to the chapters on composition and technique the student will be able to do more than just make a well exposed, well focused picture — he will be able to make a creative and aesthetic photographic statement. And this is the real pleasure of underwater photography.

"As it was hard to hold the camera still when diving, I used a wooden tripod, which I must say showed a regrettable tendency toward higher things and places."

Hans Hass,
"Diving to Adventure"

Chapter II.

THE UNDERWATER WORLD

Man stands at the land-sea interface faced with the problem of adapting physiologically and psychologically if he is to successfully penetrate the new dimension.

The differences between the land and sea are significant, yet the diver-photographer need only respect those differences to fully enjoy his new home.

This book presupposes that the reader is already a trained diver and consequently well acquainted with the physical aspects of the sea environment. The following material points out specific aspects of the undersea world which are possibly of even greater significance to the diver who is also an undersea photographer.

PRESSURE

Ask any diver to name the greatest single difference between the land and the undersea environments and almost certainly his answer will be *pressure*!

The density of water is approximately 800 times that of air, a fact not lost on divers who must take great pains to equalize the pressures within the body's air-containing spaces as they go deeper underwater.

The pressure which concerns the diver is that exerted by the water surrounding him at any given depth and is the sum of the pressure of the atmosphere (14.7 p.s.i. when measured at sea level) and the water itself (.445 p.s.i. per foot of depth in sea water, or

.432 p.s.i. in fresh water.)

The great pressure exerted by water is a result of its density. When one considers that average sea water, for example, has a density of 64 pounds per cubic foot when compared to the density of air (0.08 pounds per cubic foot) the reason for the dramatic difference in pressures becomes immediately apparent.

The increased water pressure affects the subsea photographer in a number of ways. Every diver must "clear" his ears on descent but frequently the *diver-photographer* finds himself descending with both hands full of photographic gear and his middle ear spaces demanding to be equilibrated with the increasing water pressure.

As a result the undersea photographer is forced to bypass the most positive method of equalization — the Valsalva maneuver — because it requires the use of the fingers to pinch off the nostrils.

He is compelled to practice other methods of stretching open the eustachian tube so that his hands are free for his photographic equipment.

Among the "no hands" clearing methods are yawning, swallowing, wiggling the jaw from side to side and simply forcefully "snorting" through the nose into the mask.

In still another way the diver-photographer must learn to function without the use of his hands. Should his mask accidentally flood with water while his hands are full of cameras and strobes, he need only tilt his mask straight up at the surface and exhale through his nose. The air will build up in the mask and force the water out. He may have to rock his head forward to drain the residual water into the bottom of the mask to see how much water remains. It only requires a few moments of practice.

Perhaps to an even more significant degree, is the undersea photographer's equipment imperiled by the water pressure. All underwater photographic equipment must be not only waterproof, but pressure-resistant. Housings to protect cameras from the environment range from simple molded plastic housings costing only a few dollars to super-sophisticated camera systems whose costs are in the tens of thousands.

Whether production or home-built, the housing must have the capacity to withstand the pressure stresses of your depth range of diving activity. An improperly constructed housing can be a definite hazard in deep water. Should it implode under pressure, the camera would obviously be ruined and it is quite possible the diver could be seriously injured.

WET SUIT COMPRESSION

The diver's wet suit is constructed of foam neoprene, an excellent insulating material because it places a barrier of air (in the form of millions of tiny air bubbles) between the diver's body and water. Unfortunately, these air bubbles are also compressed as the diver goes progressively deeper. The greater the compression of the suit, the less buoyancy it provides.

The diver-photographer may become so involved in picture-taking, that he may be unaware of his gradually increasing depth. The obvious danger is that the diver may be overwhelmed by nitrogen narcosis before he realizes his dangerous oversight, a deadly mistake.

BUOYANCY

While we're on the subject of the pressure-buoyancy relationship this would seem a likely place to discuss some of the other problems caused by buoyancy.

The specific gravity of a substance can be defined as its density compared to that of water, which is arbitrarily fixed at 1.0. It follows then, that any object whose density (specific gravity) is less than that of water will float, while one whose density is greater will sink.

In order that the diver-photographer enjoy complete mobility under water, he must maintain a delicate balance between positive and negative buoyancy. It is called neutral buoyancy; rather a utopian state, at best, only a trade-off between the two states. While this apparent weightlessness does provide ample freedom of movement to enable the diver to move easily through three dimensions, it is not without its drawbacks.

The weightless diver is at the mercy of any water movement. This can be a minor nuisance making it somewhat difficult to hold the camera steady, or it can be downright dangerous in a heavy surge close to the surface dashing cameras and photographer into sharp and unyielding coral reefs. If the water conditions make it difficult to hold the camera steady almost certainly will your photographs be ruined due to blurring.

The undersea camera should be slightly "heavy" (negatively buoyant) so that it can hang by a neck strap freeing the hands for light meter readings, changing flashbulbs, or whatever.

To minimize movement, the underwater photographer can stabilize himself by locking his fins into the coral, shipwreck, rocks or whatever happens to be handy and jamming his elbows tightly into his sides and bracing the camera tightly against the face mask. If both hands are not needed, get a hand hold on any nearby solid object.

If you're contemplating building your own housing, be sure to spend enough time calculating its buoyancy. If you're using Plexiglas[1] which has essentially the same specific gravity as water, you need only determine the displacement and weigh the camera (loaded with film) and everything else going into the housing to determine its state of buoyancy. Keep the housing as small as possible and it will be easy to establish relative neutral buoyancy. Remember, a camera which is excessively buoyant will place uncomfortable and tiring stresses on the wrists and forearms when photographing for extended times.

On the other hand, if the camera equipment is excessively negative, it is best to cement a small piece of styrofoam to the housing to offset the excess "heaviness". Also, it is a good idea to secure a small inflatable float (the marker buoy type) on the underside. There it is out of the way but can be inflated quickly to float the camera to the surface if for some reason it becomes necessary to ditch it.

Some experienced undersea photographers control their state of buoyancy by exercising breath control. Good photographers above or underwater generally hold their breath for only the *moment* the shutter is released to steady the camera and eliminate the possibility of exhaust bubbles obscuring a shot.

Holding your breath for that *moment* underwater is fine for experienced underwater photographers, but if you're just getting started in undersea photography, be very careful to avoid serious lung overexpansion.

A buoyancy compensating vest is a worthwhile investment. It allows the diver to make corrections in his buoyancy by partially inflating it orally. Remember to *vent* the vest as well as your lungs on ascent!

While I personally don't like to use heavily weighted tripods underwater, I must admit they have been successfully used by several subsea cameramen.

Obviously, heavy tripods or weighting yourself extra heavy can only be done sensibly when your submarine studio lies directly below a boat.

DEPTH

Considering the present alarming trend among many sport divers of descending beyond the recommended maximum depth for sport diving, it is worthwhile to speculate about a potential hazard of the sea environment. For want of a more scientific name, let's call this hazard the "lure of the abyss". "Lure of the abyss" is a diving malady with no scientific substance of which I am aware. However, since it certainly has affected me and a considerable number of talented underwater men with whom I have discussed the problem, I feel there is some basis in fact. Not infrequently, when a diver-photographer has descended a deep coral wall, for example, into his maximum safe depth in clear water there

---

is a compulsion — a mighty strong one — as he peeks over the coral shelf down into the twilight zone of the sea, to flip over the ledge and descend into the source of that midnight sea. It is almost hypnotic — and if the diver isn't very careful, he may engage in a dangerous flirtation — just to descend only a few feet more to see what amazing subject matter for his lens lies only a few feet deeper.

Certainly nitrogen narcosis can be blamed for some — perhaps all — of the lure of the abyss. But why, when diving over a flat shelf of the same or deeper depth, does not the same compulsion occur?

A number of skilled divers have already died in the sea's deep reaches. Perhaps their deaths have been explained away too easily.

HYPOTHERMIA

Normal *skin* temperature is considered to be 93°F. Any time the unprotected body is exposed to water temperatures lower than 70°F, it will suffer heat loss through direct conduction faster than the body can produce it.

Hypothermia, a malady which may be responsible for a number of diving accidents in cold water, occurs when the body is incapable of producing heat fast enough to balance heat loss.

A drop of only 5°F in skin temperature will make the diver uncomfortably cold. Another 2°F temperature drop will cause shivering, a principal symptom of the onset of hypothermia. As the cold reaches the brain, reasoning power and judgement are quickly diminished despite the fact *the victim doesn't realize anything is wrong.*

If the victim doesn't remove himself or is not removed from the water, it is possible the downward slide of the temperature in the vital organs will lead to collapse and death. Wet suits

only delay the process since heat loss continues even with the suit.

Even if not serious enough to threat-

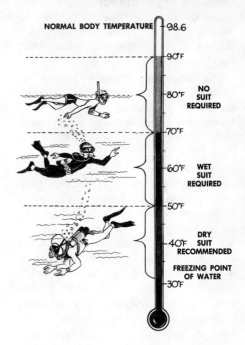

en life directly, significant heat loss may cause loss of the tactile sense, dexterity, and coordination even to the degree of making it impossible for the jaws to grip the mouthpiece in addition to seriously impairing the diver's ability to reason. The loss of body heat by conduction alone is approximately 25 times faster in water than in an equal volume of air.

Coupled with the fact that over 3,000 times as much heat is required to warm a given volume of water compared to the same volume of air, it is quite clear that underwater heat loss is a significant problem.

EQUIPMENT ALSO AFFECTED

The reduced temperature can also cause equipment problems. Condensation will form inside the camera housing if it is closed inside a warm house then taken into cold water.

Quite a bit of moisture can collect inside the camera housing, fogging the lens and quite possibly damaging the camera. The warm water vapor trapped in the housing this way, cools rapidly and forms moisture through condensation. If possible, avoid closing the housing in a warm humid room and always *tape* a packet of one of the commercial desiccants (silica gel) inside the housing to absorb the condensate. Make certain the desiccant is *taped* out of the path of the lens or any of the controls.

THERMOCLINE

A thermocline is the dividing plane between two layers of water of different temperature. The diver-photographer will have no trouble detecting the presence of a thermocline. He will certainly feel the sharp temperature discontinuity as he swims into it. And quite likely, he may even see it. The thermocline, because of its density difference from the layer of warmer water above it, can accumulate undersea particulate which may form an undersea curtain thereby reducing the penetration of sunlight.

SOUND

Try an experiment in sound! Blindfold a diver on shore and instruct him to listen carefully for a sound and point as close to the source of that sound as he can. Then have someone about 25 feet away rap against a scuba tank with the back edge of a diver's knife. The overwhelming odds are the blind-folded diver will point directly to the scuba tank. Try the same experiment underwater. The same diver will probably be 180° off!

Sound travels at a speed of 1,090 feet per second in air. In the vastly denser water environment however, sound travels at 4,800 feet per second,

almost five times as fast.

When the eardrum is exposed to water it no longer functions as it does at the surface. The direction of a sound's source is interpreted by the brain by calculating the time lag between the sound reaching one ear and then the other. In air, this system works beautifully, of course. At five times the speed of sound in air, however, underwater sounds simply travel too fast to be tracked effectively.

Unless you're able to afford one of the rather expensive underwater communication systems, you'll be somewhat handicapped in communicating with your diver-model . . . at least in the beginning.

As you gain more experience (particularly if you work consistently with the same model), you'll not find it such a serious handicap after all. You will develop a silent rapport through mutually understood hand signals and through carefully laid plans during the *pre-dive* briefing. One husband-wife photographer-model team I know have committed the entire deaf-dumb alphabet to memory and are able to carry on quite lengthy conversations underwater.

SOUNDS ATTRACT

One of the benefits of sound underwater is the attraction that the humming noise produced by movie cameras seem to have for fish, particularly sharks and barracuda. This "benefit" is considered by some as a mixed blessing at best.

The camera motor noise is amplified in the air space of the housing and seems to fascinate undersea crit-

ters. This fact may produce some real close-up opportunities for the subsea cameraman.

WATER RESISTANCE

As already stated, the density of water is about 800 times that of air. This factor in addition to the body heat loss conspire to cause fatigue. We tend to speak of diving as a "lazy man's sport" with the intent that if movement underwater is at a slow and easy pace the air supply lasts much longer and the onset of fatigue is delayed considerably.

The density of water, however, resists the diver's movements and this resistance increases incredibly with the slightest increase in speed.

If the diver attempts to double his speed, his energy expenditure multiplies by a factor of eight. Eight times the energy to double your speed — a very costly trade-off — considering

the penalty paid in high carbon dioxide levels and exertion.

The underwater photographer, because of his bulky underwater cameras and strobe lights, greatly increases his resistance in the water and is particularly vulnerable.

SALINITY

In the continuing process of weathering, aging and erosion, salts are formed which are ultimately carried to the oceans where they remain in solution at a predictable concentration: approximately 35 parts per thousand in average sea water.

These dissolved salts cause sea water to be electrically conductive, a fact which raises hell with most metal equipment. Uncoated aluminum is particularly vulnerable to the galvanic action of the sea water.

Immediately, after use in salt water, all equipment should be carefully washed with fresh water, especially *easy-to-pass-over* parts like the small set screws that hold control knobs to their shafts.

Any electrical equipment to be used underwater must be carefully maintained to prevent shock or possible electrocution.

DURATION

The subsea photographer is not permitted the luxury of his shore based counterpart; that of unlimited time to set up for a particular photograph. The undersea scenario is in a constant state of movement — its inhabitants are reluctant to remain motionless and pose. In natural light photography, the intensity of available light changes from moment to moment. The subsea photographer must know in advance what his shots are to be if he is to use his underwater time to his best advantage. The ability to "see" a good picture, compose it, adjust the camera's controls, and release the shutter must become second nature and require only moments of time.

The diver-photographer probably gets more down-time from his air supply than the average diver because the very nature of his work requires that he move slowly or that he indeed remain motionless if he is to capture a particular fish on film, for example.

Nevertheless, he is severely handicapped particularly in deep photographic missions because his available air supply dwindles in inverse proportion to the increase in depth-pressure.

SAFETY

If you are an experienced diver, you know that it is impossible to overemphasize safety underwater. The need for teamwork between the sub-

sea photographer and his buddy can't be stressed enough. When you are filming you want to concentrate completely on your photography and not worry about whether you're drifting down-current from your boat, how much air you have left, if something big and toothy is sliding unnoticed

up behind you. A good buddy must be *reliable* and *alert,* not the type that will swim off sight-seeing when you're concentrating on filming. He should be a good diver with an interest in helping you accomplish your goal. In the final analysis, "It is far better to have him and never need him, than to need him and not have him."

". . . it seemed very dark to me. The solar rays seemed to be extinguished by successive graduations, until its vague transparency became nothing more than drowned light."

Professor Aronnax
"Twenty Thousand Leagues Under The Sea"

Chapter III.

PHENOMENA OF LIGHT

The very word "photography" may be translated into ". . . to draw with light." It follows then, that a "photographer" is one, "who paints pictures in light"!

The aspiring underwater photographer must first develop an understanding for the nature of light and once grasped, he will comprehend how light makes a photograph. And it is this knowledge of how light can be controlled which will enable him to make good pictures.

LIGHT IS ENERGY

The first thing you must remember is that light is a form of energy.

Light travels through space in the form of electro-magnetic waves. It is composed of small particles called photons. These waves of photons travel at the mind-boggling speed of 186,000 miles per second! There are many different wave lengths of light which correspond to different kinds of light. Although each of the colors of the rainbow has a different wave length, they can all be combined to form *white light*.

THE SPECTRUM

Conversely, white light (sunlight) can be resolved into the different colors.

When sunlight is made to pass through a glass prism, it is separated into a band of colors called the *spec-*

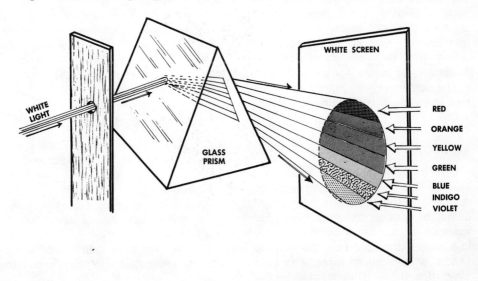

WHITE SCREEN

WHITE LIGHT

GLASS PRISM

RED
ORANGE
YELLOW
GREEN
BLUE
INDIGO
VIOLET

trum. Red, orange, yellow, green, blue, indigo, and violet are only the colors of the *visible* spectrum. Violet has the shortest wave length and red, the longest. The difference between red (the longest *visible* wave length) and violet (the shortest) is only .00012 of an inch. It is said that within this short visible spectrum are 1,000 distinct hues. Incidentally, to commit the spectrum to memory you need only remember "ROY G. BIV". Not at all original, but quite effective.

Still shorter than the violet are the invisible ultra-violet rays and longer than the red rays are the infra-red rays. Though invisible, these colors are of importance in photography.

LUMINOSITY

Consider the relative brightness of different colors! You will readily agree certain colors appear brighter than others. This quality is termed a color's luminosity. Luminosity may be defined as the degree of light intensity a color possesses.

Consequently, hunters wear orange or red outfits so to be distinguishable from the natural colors of the forest. Surprisingly though, of the colors of the visible spectrum, yellow has the most luminosity which means that it appears brightest to the eye. Green, interestingly, runs a close second but would be a poor choice of color for hunters — or divers, for that matter.

The luminosity of colors to either side of yellow or green diminishes radically.

REFLECTION

If you think about it, everything seen by your eyes (excepting sun light or light-emitting objects, e.g. light bulbs) is through reflected light. For example, if you see a candle burning in a chapel, the light from the burning candle is transmitted directly to your eyes. If a statue is illuminated by the candle light, you see the statue by means of the candle light falling on the statue and being reflected to your eyes.

Anytime light strikes a smooth polished surface at an angle, the light will be reflected making the same angle perpendicular to the mirror as the incoming (incident) light.

Consequently, the angle of reflectance is always equal to the angle of incidence. If light strikes an object whose surface is rough or irregular, however, the light waves reflect at different angles and become disorganized and no reflected image can be seen.

ABSORBTION

Any good photographer knows a smooth, white surface makes the best screen for the projection of a movie film or transparency because all colors will be reflected equally.

Try projecting a color slide against a rough black surface, for example, and you will quickly learn that dark surfaces tend to absorb much more light than light-colored surfaces. For example, black would make a poor projection screen since it absorbs from 95 to 99% of light, reflecting only a tiny percent.

For the same reason, people living in hot tropical climates favor white clothing — which is highly reflective and consequently cooler — to dark clothing — which absorbs the sunlight and converts it to heat.

COLORS ABSORB AND REFLECT

Each of the *pure* colors of the spectrum is produced by monochromatic light, that is — light waves of only one frequency.

The colors seen by our eyes, however, are usually combinations of at least two pure colors.

In the spectrum illustrated, white light is separated into its component colors.

Now, if you hold a red handkerchief in the violet end of the spectrum and pass it slowly through indigo, blue, green, yellow and orange, it will not appear red at all. It will appear to be black! The red handkerchief appears black because it absorbs violet, indigo, blue, green, yellow and orange. And since it reflects nothing it appears black.

Hold it before the red, however, and it returns to red! It appears red because it reflects and *does not absorb* red.

Correspondingly, the other colors will appear black when held before the other six colors and only reflect their true color when held in their respective zone on the spectrum.

If a yellow glass is held before the spectrum only the yellow light would be transmitted, and all the other colors are absorbed. Transparent objects — like window glass, for example — are termed "colorless" since all colors are freely transmitted through it.

The obvious conclusion? As light falls on an object, some light will be absorbed and some light reflected, and these factors determine the color you see!

REFRACTION

Light is beautifully predictable. It always travels in a straight path as it passes through a substance of uniform density, like air. It will continue traveling in a straight path even though it passes into a substance of a different density (air to water, for example) provided it enters the second substance at a right angle to its surface.

When light rays pass obliquely from a substance of one density into a substance of a different density, they undergo a change in velocity *and* direction. This phenomenon is termed "refraction of light."

The degree of refraction depends upon the angle which the incident (incoming) ray makes at the surface of

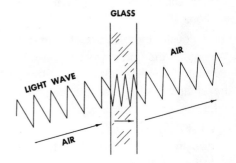

the refractive substance and secondly, the relative density — which establishes the refractive powers of the two substances.

DISPERSION

As we have already seen, a ray of white light is composed of the seven colors of the visible spectrum. That white light can be resolved into these colors is due to the fact that each of these colors is refracted to a different degree. This phenomenon of light is called dispersion and is a major consideration in the design of any photographic lens.

DIFFUSION

At the noon hour, the sun has climbed to its apex in the heavens and hangs there directly overhead. On a reasonably clear day (free of cloud cover or haze, etc.) this means that most of the light reaching you is direct sunlight.

But the sun occupies this lofty position only a short time and the closer it is to the horizon, as at sunrise and sunset, the greater the distance it must travel through the atmosphere to reach you.

As the rays of sunlight travel through the atmosphere, they must pass through clouds, fog, haze, smoke, smog and water vapor. Here, small particulate tends to absorb, reflect, diffuse and scatter the light in all directions.

Obviously, the closer to the horizon the sun, the greater the distance through the atmosphere the light must travel and the greater the degree of diffusion and scattering.

What light does reach us in this way is now mostly diffused light. It is the diffusion of light and the scattering of light rays occurring when the sun is close to the horizon which causes the incredibly vivid colors we frequently see at sunrise and sunset.

As the sunlight penetrates the atmosphere, green, blue, indigo, violet and some yellows are scattered, permitting only the red (which has a longer wave length) and fragments of yellow rays to pass through. The result may very well be a spectacular yellow-orange glow lighting up the horizon.

Conversely, when the sun is high overhead, less atmosphere and correspondingly less scattering particulate must be penetrated. Only the blue rays (which have shorter wave lengths) are scattered which is why skies are generally blue. At the same time, the green and red rays penetrate the atmosphere and combine to make the sun appear yellow.

COLOR TEMPERATURE

As has already been seen — light has color. The color quality of a particular light source is determined by a correlation which exists between the light source and its temperature.

At a casual glance, the light from the sun and the light from electric lights appears the same — almost white. But the color quality is really quite different.

The electric light bulb emits light — or is said to be luminous — because it is hot. And the hotter the source of light, the whiter the light emitted.

This phenomenon of light is called *color temperature* and is measured as Kelvin temperature after the great Irish physicist, Lord Kelvin.

Color temperature is a measurement of a light's whiteness. The *higher* the color temperature, the *colder* its light. The *lower* the color temperature, the *warmer* the light.

As a result, light with a low color temperature will have a red-yellow cast while light with a higher color temperature will be bluer. All colors are rated in Kelvin degrees to correspond to a given temperature which establishes a standard measurement of the colors of light.

Later, in the chapter titled "Film and Filters for the Twilight World," we will discuss the importance of color balance. This important aspect of photography is insured by selecting color films whose Kelvin color temperature corresponds to that of the light source.

PHENOMENA OF LIGHT UNDERWATER

Having investigated the characteristics of light in air, we are ready to explore the behavior of light underwater.

The diver-photographer soon discovers there are significant differences in the manner in which light behaves in water. These apparent differences exist not because of any change in the

"The photographer can function as long as there is light; his work—his adventure —is a rediscovery of the world in terms of light." Edward Weston

physical laws which govern light, but because the properties of water are quite different from those of air.

And if the beginning underwater photographer would effectively control light underwater — he must first understand the complex nature of light in this new environment.

SUNLIGHT

As we have already learned, long before it reaches the water, sunlight is scattered, refracted, and diffused while passing through the atmosphere. As the sun's rays penetrate the air-water interface, the amount of light actually entering the water depends on a number of factors, not the least of which is the brightness of the sun. The brighter the sun, the greater the amount of light entering the water.

The angle at which the sun's rays strike the surface likewise determines the amount of light entering the water. The amount of natural light available underwater depends not only on the intensity of the sun and the conditions of the sky — but also, as we shall learn, to a great extent on the time of day, the conditions of the surface, and a number of other considerations.

SURFACE CONDITIONS

While occasionally we are blessed with one of those "flat, calm" days . . . they are rather rare. And just as surely as a perfectly calm day permits the greatest degree of light penetration, an extremely rough, choppy surface reflects as much as half of the sun's light. Breaking waves can also

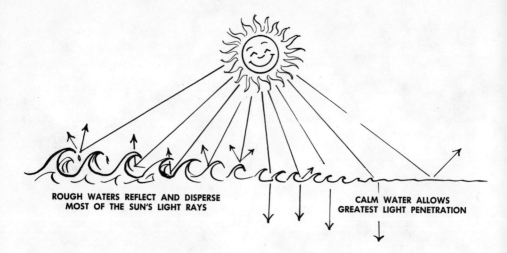

ROUGH WATERS REFLECT AND DISPERSE
MOST OF THE SUN'S LIGHT RAYS

CALM WATER ALLOWS
GREATEST LIGHT PENETRATION

significantly reduce the light penetration. The wave action of rough surface water tends to bend the entering light so that the light is reflected by the different surfaces . . . altering its direction and diffusing it. It is for this reason and the absorbing of light that the tips of breaking waves appear to be "white-caps." Small wave action, fortunately, does not appreciably reduce the penetration of light.

REFLECTION

Light will reflect off any smooth surface, be it a mirror . . . or the ocean's surface, a fact which places severe limits on the time available to the subsea photographer for natural light photography.

Under the best of conditions, some light will always be reflected by the water's surface . . . the amount reflected being determined by the surface conditions . . . and the angle of the sun.

ANGLE OF THE SUN

Still one more factor contributing to the reduction of light intensity is the angle of the sun as measured from the vertical. Since more and more of the sun's direct rays are reflected back into the atmosphere as the sun's angle decreases, it follows that the least

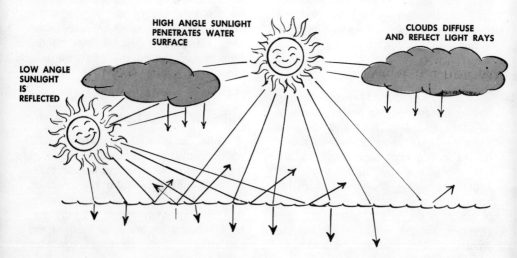

HIGH ANGLE SUNLIGHT
PENETRATES WATER
SURFACE

CLOUDS DIFFUSE
AND REFLECT LIGHT RAYS

LOW ANGLE
SUNLIGHT
IS
REFLECTED

light loss occurs when the sun is as close as possible to directly overhead (90° to the horizon at 12:00 noon) presuming a clear sky, and the water surface flat and calm.

Even under such optimum conditions at least 2% of the sun's rays will be reflected. And as the sun arcs closer to the horizon (as early in the morning or late in the day) the amount of light loss due to reflection increases dramatically.

Consequently, what light does penetrate is mostly soft and diffused which not only lacks the intensity of direct sunlight, but because of its diffused nature produces little in the way of contrast, impairs color rendition and generally precludes natural light photography.

Theoretically, it would seem that the natural light photographer will find his best lighting underwater is between the hours of 10:00 AM and 2:00 PM.

More about this later.

CRITICAL ANGLE

When the sun is very close to the horizon, the water surface offers a highly reflective surface which tends to reflect all light rays back into the atmosphere. This phenomenon also applies to light originating underwater.

Remember! Reflected light makes the same angle perpendicular to the reflecting surface as the incident (incoming) light. When the incident (incoming) angle of light strikes the water surface (above or below) at any angle less than 48.6°(measured from the vertical) all light will be totally reflected. This phenomena is termed the "critical angle."

REFRACTION

Put on a mask — hold your hand in front of your face and submerge. You will see immediately that objects underwater appear larger and closer

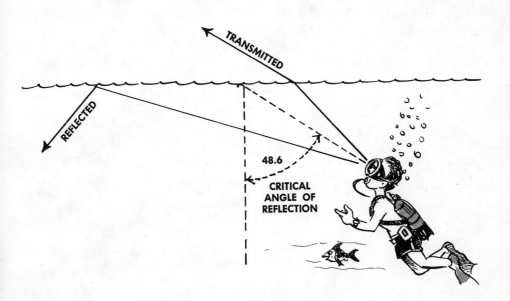

SIZE

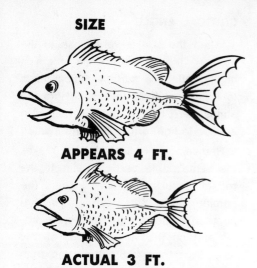

APPEARS 4 FT.

ACTUAL 3 FT.

than they really are, a phenomenon caused by the difference between the refraction of light rays in air and in water. Any transparent substance which is capable of transmitting light has an "index of refraction".

The index of refraction of any transparent substance is a measurement of the bending of light as it enters from a substance of a different density.
Note:

As the sun moves closer to the horizon, it is apparent that it is this "bending" of sunlight which requires that such light rays that do penetrate must travel even further through the water to illuminate an underwater subject at a given depth. And the closer to the horizon the sun, the greater the distance such "bent" or *refracted* light must travel to reach the sea floor.

WHY THE MAGNIFICATION?

In water, the sun's rays are refracted because of the different densities of air and water. Light travels slower in water than in air (135,000 miles per second in water compared to 180,000 miles per second in air). As the refractive index of water is 1.33, objects seen underwater appear to be proportionally larger in a ratio of one to one and a third (1:1.33).

That the refractive index of water is four-thirds (4/3) that of air accounts for the one-third magnification of underwater objects.

Of particular importance to the underwater photographer is the fact that underwater, objects which appear magnified to the diver's eye will appear magnified to the same degree to the lens of the underwater camera!

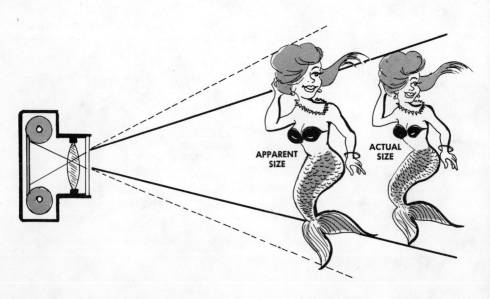

APPARENT SIZE

ACTUAL SIZE

The camera is encased in a water-proof, pressure-proof housing with a *flat,* transparent port — and light must travel through the water, the housing lens port, the air space between the lens port and the lens before it reaches the film.

"APPARENT DISTANCE"

This bending of the light rays as they pass through the lens port from the water, in effect, causes an increase in the focal length of the lens. The lens, therefore, behaves as though its focal length were 1.33 times greater than it actually is.

The area covered by the diver's eye and the camera's lens are consequently reduced. In terms of the effect on underwater photography, the camera subject takes up a greater space (the picture angle becomes narrower) in the water than on land. Subjects correspondingly look 25% closer than their actual distance.

Divide the refractive index of air (1.00) by that of water (1.33) and you have .75. As a result, underwater, photographic subjects appear to both eye and lens to be only three-fourths (¾) of the actual distance away. Since the camera sees the subject at the same distance as does the diver's eyes, the underwater photographer must set the "apparent distance" between the subject and camera on the lens distance scale and *not* the measured distance. If he actually measures this distance, his underwater distance setting must only be ¾ of that distance.

It is the *flat port* of the housing which causes this magnification distortion and it can be largely overcome with the use of a spherically curved or dome lens port.

ATTENUATION OF LIGHT

Everyone has seen that light energy *decreases* as the distance it must travel *increases.* If, on a dark night, you walk away from a campfire, it will be immediately apparent that the further from the fire you are the less intense will be the light. Likewise, if a diver swims *away* from the source of light energy, the light will eventually become invisible.

This phenomenon is termed attenuation and it generally describes a lessening in intensity of light's brightness . . . a characteristic of light, incidentally, which occurs more rapidly underwater than in air.

As the diver quickly learns, the intensity of natural light penetrating the water diminishes with each additional foot of depth. This lessening of the sun's intensity underwater is brought about because the water has absorbed the light and converted the light energy into heat energy . . . a characteristic of light's behavior underwater termed *absorption* and the equally important phenomenon of *scattering.*

ABSORPTION

It is misleading and an oversimplification to say that the intensity of light decreases with increasing depth. The colors of sunlight as we know have different wavelengths and are not absorbed uniformly. As a result, light (whether natural or manmade) produces different color balances at different depths, a phenomenon called selective absorption.

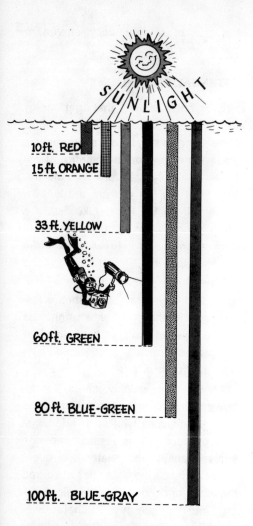

SUNLIGHT

10 ft. RED
15 ft. ORANGE
33 ft. YELLOW
60 ft. GREEN
80 ft. BLUE-GREEN
100 ft. BLUE-GRAY

SELECTIVE ABSORPTION

Red, the least penetrating color (and the longest wave length), will lose all its intensity and be absorbed within the first 10 feet of depth. Orange will probably disappear at about 15 feet as its wave length is selectively absorbed, and yellow — a highly luminous color at the surface — is completely absorbed by 33 feet. Generally, beyond this depth only blue-green or blue-gray light is present to any significant degree. This is why natural light color photographs made in this depth range usually resemble black and white photographs which have been tinted with blue-green ink.

While much of this light is absorbed by the water and converted to heat energy, some light energy is *scattered* in water.

SCATTERING

Were you to dive in the purest of distilled waters, you would still find that water scatters light energy.

Microscopic-sized particles of plankton, bottom sediment, mineral or decomposing plant life are suspended in the clearest looking waters. This bright particulate, depending upon whether its concentration is light or heavy and the size of individual particles is large or small, tends to reflect and scatter light as it travels through the water.

Indeed, mid-ocean layers of plankton have been discovered so dense that sunlight could not penetrate them. Thus scattered, light appears omnidirectional and diffused which unhappily, reduces photographic detail and contrast, and tends to make subjects look "foggy".

Air has 2,000 times the transparency of water, a factor which makes it apparent that the farther light energy must travel through water the greater the reduction of light's intensity and the degradation of the quality of its color. And the longer the light path — the total distance light must travel to the subject and from the subject to the camera lens — the greater the loss of light intensity and photograph quality.

"BLURRY" WATERS

Occasionally a diver operating in a "blue hole" experiences a visual disturbance underwater called "blurring".

The "blurring" phenomenon is caused by the non-uniform mixing of waters which have slightly different indexes of refraction. Occasionally, there may be an intermediate layer of water which is different in temperature — not unlike a thermocline — or salinity, as compared to the water above and below it. The imperfect mixing of waters of different densities and different refractive indexes causes the "blurring" phenomenon.

VISIBILITY

Underwater visibility has been defined as the maximum distance (vertical or horizontal) at which an object can be clearly distinguished.

As mentioned earlier, water is 2,000 times *less* transparent than air, a distinction which makes apparent the monumental differences between vision in the air environment and underwater.

The range of visibility is highly variable, extending from conditions of absolute zero visibility in some rivers and harbors to hundreds of feet in the crystal waters of some Caribbean reefs. Generally, conditions of the best visibility are to be found in the crystalline blue water of the open sea as opposed to harbors or inshore waters where exposed to heavy concentrations of particulate in suspension. Lee shores offer better visibility than do windward shores. Visibility improves when the sun forms a 90° angle to the horizon and the water is clear. Due to the greater penetration of the sun's rays, late morning and early afternoon are optimum undersea photographic periods.

"No photographer is as good . . . . . as the simplest camera."

Edward Steichen
"The Family of Man"

Chapter IV.

CAMERAS

Light makes the picture! Press the camera's shutter release and the shutter opens. For a fraction of a second, light streams through the lens and forms an image on the film . . . and a photograph is made.

The camera is really just a device which gives the photographer precise control over light and this, basically, is the story of photography.

Too often, people who are casually interested in underwater photography — or surface photography for that matter — tend to be put-off by the perplexing vocabulary of the photographer. "f"-stops, exposure index, vignetting, depth-of-field, chromatic aberration, etc. . . . are all important words in the photographer's vocabulary. To the would-be underwater photographer, however, such "professional" words and phrases serve only to intimidate and chagrin. Too often those who are frightened away by its apparent complexity are people who could make good use of photography — not only by doubling their underwater pleasure in recording memorable dives on film — but by turning it into a profitable hobby . . . or career. With this in mind, the purpose of "Divers and Cameras" is to impart a working knowledge of underwater photography and initiate the novice sub-sea photographer into the art and science of underwater photography.

Hopefully, the reader will find the terminology easy to digest.

THE CAMERA

Virtually any camera can be installed in a housing and taken underwater. And almost any one of them will take good pictures if the diver-photographer knows how to use it. It is a common mistake for the novice to become so hung up on sophisticated equipment and gadgets, he loses sight of the fact the camera merely *takes* the picture. It is the talent and artistry of the man that *makes* the photograph. The camera is a wondrous machine — but it cannot think. The photographer must think for it. He must compose the scene and adjust for differences in distance and light intensity. The diver-photographer carries two indispensable photographic tools underwater with him — his brain and his eyes. As has been proven many times, when these tools are not used effectively the photographs taken with a Hasselblad may well look as though they were made with a two dollar box camera. Use these tools well, however, and the box camera can produce a work-of-art.

While the cost and complexity of camera equipment varies widely, all cameras are quite alike and the selection of a camera is largely a matter of personal preference.

There is no single "ideal" underwater camera, though the amphibious 35mm Nikonos II almost approaches that status because of the availability of the incredible variety of underwater gadgets and conveniences that extend its versatility.

If you already own a good camera perhaps the most reasonable solution is to build or buy an underwater housing for it. There are a number of production housings available to accommodate most any popular camera. Bear in mind, however, these housings don't come cheap and the camera must warrant the expense. Don't buy a two-hundred dollar housing for an old 35mm camera which may only be worth $25. It happens all the time!

Ultimately the selection can be distilled down to the photographer's finances and needs. Before selecting an underwater camera from the almost infinite range of possibilities, the advantages and disadvantages of each should be carefully weighed.

In the final analysis, the neophyte must get a camera-housing combination and *use* it. If you want clear, sharp photographs, you must become intimately familiar with your equipment. The best insurance for successful photographs is a knowledge of the camera or, more to the point, what is going on inside it.

THE PINHOLE CAMERA

Perhaps the easiest place to begin is with the simplest of all cameras — the pinhole camera.

Any camera is basically a light-tight box with a hole in one end and a light-sensitive film at the opposite end. Light enters the small hole and forms a real image on the surface of the film. Despite the lack of a real lens, some surprisingly beautiful photographs have been made with a "pinhole" camera. If you'd care to try a fun photographic experiment, build a pinhole camera. It will only take a few minutes.

Find a conventional cigar box and spray the inside with any *flat* black paint to eliminate reflection. Find the center of one end and drill the pinhole (use a 0.02 in. diameter jeweler or hobbist drill) or heat a #10 sewing needle and punch the hole. Cover the hole with a piece of black tape. Now, you need a completely darkened (light-proof) room. Tape a strip of 35mm film, emulsion side up, to the inside of the box at the end opposite the pinhole. Tape the box shut to avoid light leakage. You are now ready to make a "no-lens" photograph.

While on the subject of pinhole cameras, we'll drop one more crazy experiment on you just for fun.

An even simpler pinhole camera can be made in just several minutes by cutting some black cardboard to the shape and dimensions illustrated and

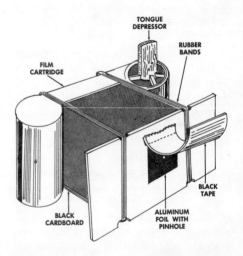

taping and rubber-banding the whole arrangement to an instant load 126 film cartridge. Cut a one inch hole in the center section and tape a 1½ inch square piece of aluminum foil over the inside of the hole. Use a #10 sewing needle to make a hole in the center of the foil.

Rubber bands will reinforce the cardboard and a winder can be made from a medical tongue depressor (ask your family doctor for one). Add a strip of black tape and you're ready to take pictures.

While you must calculate an exposure time, the pinhole camera does have great depth of field so you don't have to worry about focus. Take the camera outdoors, place it on a solid surface, aim it at a stationary object, and remove the tape covering the pinhole. Try Tri-X for an exposure time of 60 seconds. Replace the tape and again remove the film in a darkroom and process.

Before you get too excited about the pinhole camera, however, it is only fair that you be made aware of its serious shortcomings.

First, while it does have good depth of field, the subjects are *not* in sharp focus. Secondly, it has low light intensity which means extremely long exposure times are necessary. Third, the illumination tends to fade from the center of the photograph to the edges.

Although surprisingly good photographs have been made with pinhole cameras, the vast photographic improvements gained with the addition of even the simplest lens are obvious.

CARTRIDGE LOAD "BOX" CAMERA

If a simple lens is substituted for the pinhole it will produce a much more satisfactory image.

Now, replace the black tape with a shutter mechanism and you have made two very important refinements which will prove quite useful to the photographer.

The lens permits vastly greater amounts of light to pass onto the film than does the pinhole. The shutter controls the precise amount of time in which light will pass through the lens . . . this being fixed at 1/90th of a second for the simple cartridge load 126 camera. The combined action of the two serves to provide a photographic image much sharper than could possibly be attained with the pinhole.

If the diver is only casually interested in photography and wants to be able to take an underwater snapshot occasionally, he will find the Kodak Instamatic camera in an uncomplicated Plexiglas housing just about foolproof. It utilizes an instant loading film cartridge and requires no focusing.

Because of its fixed-focus lens everything is reasonably sharp from a point about six feet in front of the lens to infinity. The simple lens has a pre-set aperture set for average lighting conditions.

The Kodak Instamatic has provisions for flash attachments and flash synchronization which, along with the wide range of films available and close-up lens attachments, do increase its capability. And the advantages of the Instamatic camera — Plexiglas housing are obvious. It is comparatively inexpensive, easy to use, very rugged, and will take surprisingly good pictures when the photographic conditions are good.

On the other hand, the photographer — with the exception of choice of a faster or slower film — has little control over the amount of light entering the camera. This translates into loss of close-up shots, fast-moving subjects, or subjects in highly-lighted or poorly-lighted conditions.

In other words, the simple box camera does a great job when used for its designed purpose — taking good snapshots when the conditions are suitable for the camera's limited capability.

POCKET INSTAMATICS

An entirely new line of equipment is being produced which may further revolutionize an already revolutionary industry. It centers around a new sub-miniature camera, appropriately named the "Pocket Instamatic", which is at least equal in quality (photographically speaking) to the present 126 cartridge Instamatic. The models available range from a fast lens, range-finder coupled, electronic shutter model down to box camera simplicity, and it actually produces a standard print (3½ x 4½ inches) which is bigger than the standard print size from a 126 negative.

The Pocket Instamatic may very well replace the bigger Kodak Instamatic now that some enterprising manufacturers are mass producing relatively inexpensive housings for it.

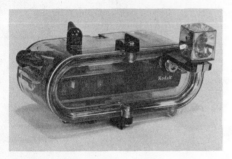

Conversely, the serious photographer who desires a greater degree of flexibility in selecting subjects, determining exposure and focus, and controlling light must choose from the more expensive range of adjustable cameras.

And before he can expect to even equal the photographs he made with the almost "foolproof" box camera, he must have a good knowledge of the basic components of the adjustable camera and fully understand the function of each.

HOW THE CAMERA WORKS

Before continuing, a´ review of the essential parts of a camera and the function of each of these parts might be in order. The cut-away camera illustrates the component parts of any adjustable camera. First, we must begin with a light-proof box — (A) the camera body. The film advancer (B) consists of two spools separated by a track that allows the film to be wound from spool to spool advancing it frame by frame, after properly positioning it for exposure.

The lens (C) is an optically shaped glass which gathers the light rays reflected from the subject, bends and projects them in the form of a sharp image on the film (D) — a light-sensitive substance on a plastic base, which records the visual image of the subject.

The viewfinder (E) is an optical sight or frame used for composing the picture and aiming the camera. The shutter (F) is a spring-driven mechanism that controls the exact time during which the film is exposed to the light admitted by the aperture (G). The aperture is an adjustable hole which controls the precise amount of light reaching the film when the shutter is open. Focus (H) determines image sharpness of far and near subjects and is controlled by adjusting the distance between the lens and the film plane. This adjustment is made generally by turning the lens in or out.

Before the would-be photographer can hope to make consistently high quality photographs, he must acquire a comprehensive knowledge of the interrelationships between all these components and how they work collectively to precisely control the light that makes the picture.

Perhaps the next logical considera-

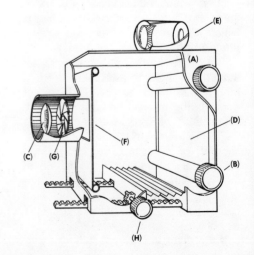

tion in choosing a camera is the selection of film size.

FILM SIZE

One of the most important factors in the choice of a camera is the size of film it uses. This largely determines the overall quality and sharpness of the photograph. Generally speaking, the larger film format cameras provide higher quality print enlargements by virtue of their larger negatives. The following chart will give you some idea of the overall dimensions of the most commonly used films.

Film Type	Frame Size	
110	13mm x 17mm	cartridge
135 (half frame)	18mm x 24mm	magazine
126	28mm x 28mm	cartridge
135 (full frame)	24mm x 36mm	magazine
120	2¼″ x 2¼″	roll

As you can see, the film format of each film varies considerably.

The Pocket Instamatic 110 film size provides a surprisingly good image when projected as a slide or made into a standard print. It is an ideal compact camera for divers who want an inexpensive camera for occasional surface and underwater snapshots.

The Kodak Instamatic does provide a larger format. As with the 110 film size, though, the small negative size does not permit quality enlargements due to excessive graininess and poor resolution.

In both standard and Pocket Instamatics, the film cartridges snap in and out easily making reloading a breeze. This is not much of a benefit underwater, where the maximum of 20 exposures per cartridge is something of a nuisance.

The Kodak Instamatic offers a complete range of equipment, underwater housings and accessories. While it lacks the controls of the adjustable camera and couldn't be considered a professional — or, for that matter, a serious amateur's camera — it should more than satisfy the needs of the occasional snapshooter.

The half frame (35mm) format lies somewhere between the Kodak Instamatic and the full-frame 35mm camera — more versatile than the former and more economical than the latter. The only desirable aspect of this format, in my opinion, is its ability to produce 72 photographs using a 36 exposure roll of any standard 35mm film.

While I have made some good enlargements from half-frame negatives, the quality of the image in prints enlarged from half-frame negatives cannot compare to full-frame 35mm.

Full-frame 35mm is by far the most widely used film format in the underwater world. It is used as extensively in the ranks of professionals as it is with serious amateurs and for a number of good reasons.

The camera, even in its underwater housing, is compact, mobile and versatile. The film size provides excellent projection characteristics and sharp, fine grained negatives which can be enlarged substantially without appreciable degradation of image quality. It offers an incredible variety of interchangeable lenses as well as a wide selection of film types from which to choose.

And it offers a capacity of up to 36 exposures when equipped with a standard camera back. Bulk film loads and special interchangeable backs can increase its capacity to as many as 250 exposures per film load.

There are a number of underwater photographers who shoot exclusively in the 2¼ x 2¼ inch format. The advantages of the large format include a photographic image whose dimensions are about four times that of standard 35mm, extremely sharp image detail, brighter projection characteristics, and excellent enlargement quality.

Standard 120 roll film cameras produce 12 exposures per standard film roll. However, most of these cameras will accept 220 film which will provide twice the number of exposures of the same size. It is apparent that camera and cost per photograph spiral in proportion to increasing film size compared to the 35mm format. This greater cost is balanced, in the professional's mind, by the fact that the larger negative produces a sharp, relatively grain-free print with considerably less pampering than the smaller formats. If money is no object, there are a number of superb 2¼" x 2¼" cameras for which fine production housings are available. Such photographic systems are capable of producing top quality photographs throughout the entire range of underwater photography. In some cases, available housings can accommodate interchangeable camera backs which can increase capacity up to 70 exposures per roll. And the variety of available films in the 120 format should satisfy the needs of the most discriminating undersea cameraman.

FILM ADVANCE MECHANISMS

In most modern cameras the shutter is cocked and the film advanced in one operation by a rapid-advance lever. On the Nikonos II, a 35mm amphibious camera, the same lever is also used to release the shutter. Advancing the film and cocking the shutter in the same motion insures against accidental double-exposures and permits rapid shooting.

Some 35mm cameras incorporate a spring motor which is quite effective providing fully automatic film advance and shutter cocking as rapidly as the shutter release button can be depressed.

ELECTRIC DRIVE

An even more elaborate arrangement is the electrically-powered film advance mechanism which advances the film and fires the camera automatically, frame by frame or continuously (as many as four exposures per second).

The advantage of the motor drive, in addition to the automatic operation, is the capability of shooting a rapid sequence of photographs capturing fast moving action. As a rule, the action underwater is spontaneous and rapid. The motor drive could eliminate the need for several through-the-housing camera controls although most production housings for motor drive equipped cameras provide conventional camera controls as well.

If there are any disadvantages to the electric drive, one would have to be the slower firing rates required with conventional underwater strobes due to the recycling time required to recharge the strobe capacitor.

Another would be that most electric drive units expand the camera's dimensions and generally involve a bigger underwater housing. For the convenience it provides, it is a trade-off that most subsea photographers make happily.

The neophyte underwater photographer need only stroll through any large camera store to discover the selection of a camera suitable for underwater work means a choice from among an overwhelming number of cameras. To help narrow his selection, a classification of cameras most suitable for underwater work can be made according to the systems of viewing and focusing they use. Basically, the classifications include: viewfinder, range finder, twin-lens reflex, and single lens reflex.

VIEWFINDER CAMERA

Undoubtedly, the majority of cameras currently in use underwater are

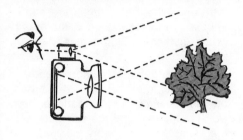

viewfinder cameras . . . most notably the Nikonos II amphibious camera.

In the viewfinder camera, a small optical viewfinder, completely independent of the camera lens, allows the photographer to view the subject approximately as seen by the lens and compose the photograph.

The simple viewfinder has no provision for focusing the lens. When the lens is focused, the photographer must estimate the subject-to-camera distance and adjust the lens focusing ring accordingly. And remember, underwater the camera focuses at the same distance as the eye . . . the apparent distance and *not* the actual distance. If you take a tape-measure underwater and set your camera focus by the measured distance, the picture will be out of focus. You have to use ¾ of the measured distance (for example, the measured distance might be 8

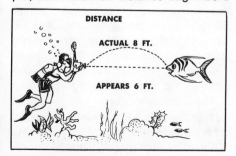

DISTANCE

ACTUAL 8 FT.

APPEARS 6 FT.

feet — your focusing distance would be 6 feet.)

On most viewfinder cameras, including the Nikonos II, the small viewfinder, which is perfectly adequate for surface photography, is totally unuseable underwater. When the camera is inside a housing, and the face encased in a mask, the distance between eye and viewfinder is enough to make the viewfinder impractical. As a result, such camera housing combinations are compelled to use an auxiliary sports finder which works well enough for medium and long shots, but is not without its drawbacks.

SPORTSFINDER

PARALLAX ERROR

The viewfinder cameras are always vulnerable to parallax error — a problem of image displacement which occurs when the subject-to-camera distance is less than three feet, and particularly so when used in conjunction with a sportsfinder-equipped housing.

Parallax is essentially the difference between the image as viewed through the viewfinder and the actual image recorded by the lens, when the camera is focused on a close-up subject. The problem occurs because viewfinder and lens are separated but have parallel optical paths which means that at long or medium range the effects of parallax are negligible since viewfinder and camera lens are seeing basically the same image. At distances of three feet or less, however, what is seen through the viewfinder will be out of the angle of view of the camera lens. As a result, any picture made without correcting for this parallax error will cut off part of the subject as it is composed in the viewfinder.

Even the Nikonos II instruction manual advises the *surface* photographer that parallax is evident at camera-to-subject distances of less than three feet and instructs him to correct by framing the subject in the "parallax indicator lines" of the viewfinder. Using these "lines" brings the image below and to the right of the normal viewfinder frame, thereby correcting the error.

RANGEFINDER CAMERA

The rangefinder camera is a sophisticated, viewfinder camera which has the added facility of focus. The viewing system consists basically of two mirrors, one fixed, the other free to rotate. The photographer looks through the finder and observes two

Picture seen in viewfinder

Picture to appear on film

images. The rangefinder focus control is adjusted until the two images "fuse" into one. At this point the two mirrors are parallel and superimpose the images seen from each by the photographer's eye, which is located behind the fixed mirror. When the two images are superimposed, the focus is pin-sharp. The rangefinder is mechanically coupled to the lens focusing ring. When the images are superimposed in the rangefinder, the appropriate distance is automatically set on the lens.

Some rangefinder cameras show a split image in which case the procedure is the same. The rangefinder control is adjusted until the two halves of the image are perfectly aligned and again, the lens is automatically set for the correct distance. Parallax is still a problem with the rangefinder camera at close range and they are best used at camera-to-subject distances greater than three feet.

Contrary to popular belief, rangefinder cameras are being manufactured today. There are currently about fifty different models on the market ranging from the exceptional M5 Leica to the new Pocket Instamatic.

Its wide popularity in past undersea photographic efforts notwithstanding, the Leica with its excellent lenses has given way to the generation of reflex cameras.

TWIN LENS REFLEX (TLR) CAMERA

The important advantage of the reflex camera over the camera types already discussed is that the photographer, in a sense, sees his photograph before he ever trips the shutter release. Consequently, he composes his picture perfectly, filling the ground-glass viewing screen to the edges of the format. It is exactly as it will appear in the finished photograph.

The twin lens reflex, appropriately, has two lenses — a viewing lens and a taking lens positioned one above the other. The photographic image is projected by the viewing lens onto a mirror which is positioned at an angle 45° to the optical axis of the viewing lens. From the mirror the photographic image is reflected onto the viewfinder's

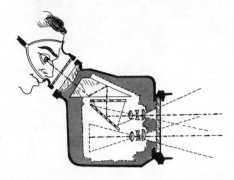

ground-glass screen.

The distance setting for the viewing lens is linked mechanically to that of the camera lens and by bringing the image into sharp focus on the ground glass the photographer automatically sets the focus for the taking lens.

The viewing lens is so arranged that the total distance the light must travel — lens to mirror to ground glass — is exactly the same distance the light must travel from the taking lens to the film plane. Since both lenses are of the same focal length the image formed on the ground-glass screen is identical in size to the image formed on the film.

Although most twin-lens reflex cameras are designed primarily for the 2¼ in. x 2¼ in. film format, at least one, the Rollei, can be adapted to take 12, 16, or 24 exposures per roll of 120 film. If you prefer the 35mm format, it can be adapted to accept the standard 20 or 36 exposure cassettes.

DISADVANTAGES OF THE TWIN LENS REFLEX

Outstanding fish portraits have been made with the twin lens reflex camera by a number of undersea photographers — most notably, Doug Faulkner and Jack McKenney.

But because of the difference in the optical axis of the two lenses, the twin lens reflex does suffer parallax error in close-up photography. At least one camera-housing combination, the Rollei with its Rolleimarin housing, provides a set of close-up lenses which are *corrected* for parallax error. These close-up lenses are hinged in front of the camera lenses allowing the undersea photographer to switch back and forth as the photographic opportunities present themselves.

One major shortcoming of the TLR camera is that the lenses are generally not interchangeable. Since the shutter mechanism is an integral part of the lens and not the camera body, substituting lenses could become most expensive.

It is unquestionably a great advantage to be able to keep your subject in view as you frame, focus, and trigger the shutter, but the ground-glass is useless when the action is fast. The photographic image is reversed on the ground-glass screen, left to right. This factor is somewhat confusing causing the uninitiated to tend to swing the camera in the wrong direction. In fairness, you do become accustomed to it in short order.

Though the classic Rollei in its Rolleimarin housing has set a standard of excellence in underwater photographic equipment design, and will remain such for years to come, the greater movement currently is toward the single lens reflex camera.

SINGLE LENS REFLEX (SLR) CAMERA

With the single lens reflex camera, the photographer views, composes, frames, and focuses the subject through one lens . . . the taking lens.

The light reflected by the subject is projected (like the twin lens reflex) through the lens onto a mirror which is set at a 45° angle between lens and film plane. The photographic image is reflected from the mirror to a prism viewfinder or a ground glass screen.

The difference is that in the SLR camera, the mirror is hinged!

When the shutter release is tripped, the mirror automatically swings up out of the way and the reflected light passes through the lens to form an image on the film plane. Cocking the film advance lever, lowers the mirror to its normal viewing position. The SLR, when equipped with the proper lens, is particularly well suited for close-up photography because of the absence of parallax error and the ability to capture on film exactly what is seen through the lens.

picture area — right side up and unreversed — even when held two and one half inches from the eye) the single lens reflex is a hard camera to beat for underwater photography.

The ability to view the entire subject, compose the picture precisely, bring all detail into crisp focus and make the photograph, all through the same lens, and without the handicap of parallax error, is a tremendous advantage over the other viewing systems.

DISADVANTAGES

If there is any disadvantage to the new wave of SLR cameras, it is probably that composition and focusing become increasingly difficult as the ambient light levels drop. This is particularly important in the rather dim light of the underwater world, particularly on deep dives or early and late in the day. Many photographers solve the problem by attaching an underwater flashlight to the housing approximately in line with the optical axis of the lens. And finally, there are some who object to the noise generated by the mirror snapping up when the shutter is tripped. To the best of my knowledge, I have never lost a shot because a fish was frightened off by that sound.

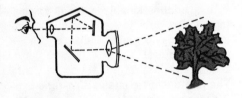

Another great advantage of the SLR camera is the fact that most accommodate interchangeable lenses which are widely varied and extend the camera's versatility immeasurably. And many first-rate production housings are designed to also accommodate a number of different lenses.

Unlike the twin lens reflex, in the single lens reflex viewfinder the image is corrected. In other words, the view of the subject and its movements as seen through the camera viewfinder is as the eye itself would perceive it . . . as it really is and not inverted. As a result the photographer can easily follow in the same direction as the subject's movement. The camera may be swung around to make vertical or horizontal photographs without the confusion of reversed image.

Coupled with a prism reflex sportsfinder (which has an oversized eyepiece capable of showing the entire

INTEGRAL CAMERAS

An integral camera integrates a water and pressure resistant camera body with a lens which may be used in direct contact with the water. Integral cameras range from the inexpensive

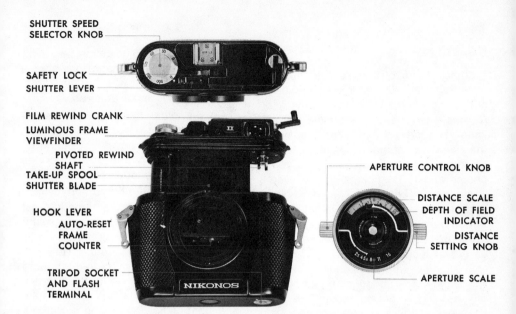

SHUTTER SPEED
SELECTOR KNOB

SAFETY LOCK
SHUTTER LEVER

FILM REWIND CRANK
LUMINOUS FRAME
VIEWFINDER
PIVOTED REWIND
SHAFT
TAKE-UP SPOOL
SHUTTER BLADE

HOOK LEVER
AUTO-RESET
FRAME
COUNTER

TRIPOD SOCKET
AND FLASH
TERMINAL

APERTURE CONTROL KNOB

DISTANCE SCALE
DEPTH OF FIELD
INDICATOR
DISTANCE
SETTING KNOB

APERTURE SCALE

"Mako" designed by Jordan Klein (a molded plastic camera body which used the "Brownie" film transport and shutter mechanism) to the remote-controlled deep-water cameras whose costs range in the tens of thousands.

Somewhere in between lie a generation of compact 35mm cameras which are themselves both pressure-resistant and water-proof. The world's first integral (amphibious) camera was designed in the late fifties by Jean de Wouters, a Belgian optical engineer. His camera, the Calypso-Phot, spawned an almost identical product from the Nikon family — the Nikonos. To say that the de Wouters design contributed to the development and popularity of underwater photography would be a monumental understatement.

The Nikonos II and its predecessors, the Nikonos and the Calypso-Phot, when equipped with the standard 35mm lens, provide the beginning diver-photographer with a super-compact camera which is equally at home in air or underwater.

An incredible number of interchangeable accessories are available to extend the capability of these cameras. Optically corrected wide-angle lenses, close-up lenses, macro-tubes, strobe units, filters, flash heads, optically-corrected viewfinders, thumb-

Thumb-controlled shutter lever

controlled shutter levers, and interchangeable lenses are but a few.

The 35mm amphibious camera is a versatile photographic tool combining all the qualities of a good 35mm *viewfinder* camera free of any awkward and bulky underwater housings. That the integral Nikonos II camera comes close to matching the versatility of any 35mm camera is indisputable. It is not the ultimate underwater camera, however.

DISADVANTAGES

Some of the obvious shortcomings stem from the fact that to date all integral cameras are viewfinder cameras. As explained earlier, a simple viewfinder has no provision for focusing the lens so subject-to-camera distances must be estimated. If the diver-photographer is compelled to use large lens openings because of dim light conditions, the depth of field will be quite short. If the apparent distance is misjudged, the pictures will be out of focus!

Even with the Nikonos special sportsfinder for underwater photography, parallax errors do occur. The optical axis of the sportsfinder is above and to the left of the optical axis of the lens, which is particularly important at close-up subject-to-camera distances. There is always the danger with any frame-type sportsfinder that the diver will, because of the mask he wears, look obliquely through the sportsfinder and see parts of the subject that will not appear on film. This is merely a camera handling problem, which only requires that the diver-photographer hold the sportsfinder squarely against his faceplate.

And the ultimate disadvantage is evidenced by the stern warning printed in red type in the Nikonos instruction manual:

> *"CAUTION:* NEVER UNLOAD THE CAMERA *UNDERWATER."*

THE CHOICE IS YOURS

The final decision in the selection of a camera for underwater work usually leads to some sort of compromise between the system the photographer would like to own — and the system he can afford . . . or really needs.

For those divers who wish only to take an occasional snapshot on that once-a-year diving vacation, an inexpensive Kodak Instamatic in a simple Plexiglas housing will probably suit their purposes most admirably.

On the other hand, several motorized Nikons or Hasselblads in machined aluminum housings and thousands of dollars worth of accessories may be barely enough for the professional underwater photographer.

For someone with a serious interest in underwater photography and a limited budget the following features may indicate a sensible direction to take. While you can always trade-up to more sophisticated equipment, you'll learn a great deal more about photography and controlling light if you work with an adjustable camera rather than with the fixed aperture-fixed focus type box camera.

The camera you select should have variable shutter speeds and accommodate interchangeable lenses. If you are serious about underwater photography, you will find eventually that you need more than one lens. A good beginning point would be a fast lens (preferably not slower than f2.8) to take advantage of the available light. That first lens, ideally, should have a short focal length (wide angle). A wide angle lens (about 35mm) will provide a wider angle of view and good depth of field.

For the serious student of photography, the 35mm format offers the widest choice of films in black and white and color, and a wide selection of cameras which are well suited for underwater use.

In general, the camera should be compact and rugged. All controls must be accessible if it is to be put into an underwater housing and they should operate easily. It should have provisions for synchronizing with flash bulbs and electronic strobe, and it should be easy to reload.

Chapter V.

THE CAMERA HOUSING

Unless the neophyte underwater photographer has selected one of the few cameras which is specially designed and constructed for underwater use, he is confronted with a new problem after selecting the right camera: housing the camera. The valuable camera must be enclosed in a housing which is not only water-tight and pressure-resistant, but must also offer a host of other considerations. The choice of a housing involves almost as many compromises and decisions as the selection of the camera.

BUILD OR BUY?

In its infancy, the art of underwater photography evolved its housings through a generation of hairy improvisation. Pressure cookers, for example, were routinely enlisted in the never-ending struggle to keep the camera dry and reasonably usable underwater.

And the fact of the matter was, if it kept the camera reasonably dry and if it didn't implode if you took it too deep, it was considered a monumental success. Most weren't, of course, but a few were exceptionally good and soon a number of designers were building custom-made housings for virtually any kind of camera. But it was a very expensive way to go.

Since production housings were virtually unheard of during those earliest days, it is a gallant testimony to those technological pioneers that the art and science of underwater photography survived at all.

BUILDING

A number of divers still build their own housings and it can be a most rewarding experience if the end result is a serviceable, well-designed housing which will keep the camera dry and allow full use of the camera controls. But several factors ought to be given careful consideration before you begin.

With respect to cost, for example, while a simple Plexiglas "box" type housing can be managed by most people with a working knowledge of hand tools, there are certain operations which are more precisely accomplished with power equipment. (Cutting a recessed groove for a continuous "0" ring seal is an excellent example.) And if machining costs must be paid, obviously the housing cost increases substantially.

Another point to consider is that a well-built housing for any adjustable camera should have provisions for the manipulation of all camera controls: setting the diaphragm aperture, focusing the lens, adjusting the shutter speed, advancing the film, cocking the shutter and tripping the shutter. Generally speaking, external control shafts, "0" ring glands, control knobs, and end devices will add about $5 to the cost of the housing for each complete control. In other words, if your housing requires five controls, you can automatically tack on another $25 to the cost estimate.

It is undeniably true the talented do-it-yourselfer can save money building his own housing. It is equally true, however, that even home-built housings cost money . . . in some cases as much or more than a production housing would have cost.

If you place high value on your time and talent, the build-it-yourself housing will certainly be more expensive. In that case, you are better off by far buying a production housing. But commercial housings are by no means available for *all* cameras.

If you happen to own a camera for which no production housing is available, if your funds are somewhat limited, or if you simply wish to build your own; you will find great satisfaction in designing and building your own camera housing.

The plexiglas housing illustrated was built many years ago for the 8mm Bolex and was a real eye-popper . . . a result of many hours of tender, loving care. Unfortunately, not all of my housings turned out as well.

If you have the talent (and that means not only the mechanical ability but also the imagination and ability to visualize and design a compact housing) and patience for this project, do yourself a favor and send for a copy of Mort Toggweiler's excellent booklet, HOW TO BUILD YOUR OWN UNDERWATER CAMERA HOUSING. This booklet is available from Hydrotech Co., Box 14444 Long Beach, California 90814.

BUYING

If you're not mechanically inclined and have difficulty using simple hand tools without busting your knuckles or smashing your thumb . . . you needn't despair.

Never before in the history of underwater photography has there been a greater variety of well-designed, production housings available for so many popular cameras.

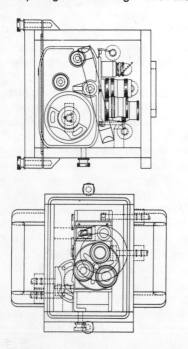

If you own a popular camera, the chances are somebody makes a housing for it. And the quality and reliability of most of the newly available underwater photographic equipment, with few exceptions, is superb. And most of the equipment manufacturers stand confidently behind their products.

Occasionally, the very best quality control programs notwithstanding, equipment will be defective and fail. The measure of the firm to a large degree is their willingness to back a product.

Notable among manufacturers are Jordan Klein of Underwater, Inc., Ike Brigham of Ikelite, Inc. and Joe Flynn of Sub Sea, Inc. When their organizations say absolute guarantee, they really mean it!

Needless to say, there is no such thing as a good, inexpensive housing, but most do provide excellent dollar value.

Precisely which housing-camera combination will best suit your needs is a very individual matter. Final judgement ought to be based on a number of factors. The balance of this chapter reviews the characteristics of a wide cross-section of underwater housings.

DESIGN

Presuming the camera he has selected is suitable for enclosing in a watertight housing (not all of them are) the diver-photographer now must examine a number of special considerations in choosing the housing.

If he is willing to limit his operating depth to 15 feet, almost anything will do . . . even a well-sealed plastic bag! It is obvious that as depth increases, the pressure correspondingly increases on every square inch of surface of the underwater housing. Consequently anything deeper requires some forethought to the most suitable shape for pressure resistance.

SHAPE

It is axiomatic with underwater photographic equipment that the danger of leakage is increased as the water pressure increases. It is further generally conceded — all other things being equal — rectangular housings are the least pressure-resistant shape. On the other hand, a poorly designed or constructed housing is a definite liability regardless of shape. Generally speaking, watertight housings are either rectangular, cylindrical, spherical, or irregular.

RECTANGULAR HOUSINGS

The majority of housings, commercial or home-built, are rectangular in shape for a number of good reasons. Most cameras are rectangular and fit compactly into rectangular housings with a minimum of wasted space.

Rectangular housings are also quite popular with home builders since they are relatively simple to construct. Because all surfaces are flat, the installation of camera controls is a comparatively easy task.

And while it is the least desireable shape from the standpoint of pressure resistance, if properly designed and well-constructed of rigid materials, the rectangular housing should be able to safely withstand the pressure of 200 feet of water.

DISADVANTAGES

Although it is far and away the most popular shape in watertight housings, the rectangular shape has some serious shortcomings that should be given due consideration.

As pressures build with increasing depth, the large flat surfaces inherent in rectangular design tend to deflect inwardly putting great stresses on the

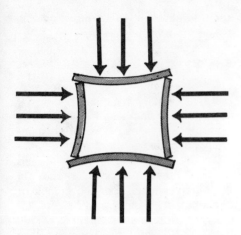

Rectangular housings are the least pressure-resistant shape. Flat surfaces deflect under pressure causing corners to break

edge seams of a rectangular housing. In point of fact, the only housings I have known to implode underwater were of rectangular design. The more welded or cemented seams the housing has, the greater the possibility of leakage. To an appreciable degree, the pressure resistance of the rectangle can be increased by adding reinforcing stiffeners to the large, flat surfaces.

Another shortcoming of the rectangular shape is the sharp edges and corners — particularly in housings fabricated of Plexiglas. If a radial surface — as on a cylinder or sphere — is bumped against a hard surface, little or no harm is done. If the same thing occurs to a corner or edge of a rectangular housing, shattered plastic or a leaky seam is the result.

Still another disadvantage of the rectangular housing is the high degree of resistance caused by the large flat surfaces it offers to the water. Earlier in the book, were described the effects of water's resistance. Pushing a large, flat surface through the water can be a real drag. And the bigger the surface, the more exhausting the experience.

SPHERICAL HOUSINGS

The sphere is the ideal form from the standpoints of 1) hydrodynamic drag and 2) pressure-resistance. Since it is a stream-lined shape with no flat surfaces, it permits the diver-photographer to maneuver easily in the water without the exhausting effects of water's resistance to a large flat surface.

Equally important, water pressure reacts equally and uniformly upon the entire surface of the sphere. As a consequence, since there are no stress points (like corners and edge joints) there is none of the shearing or bending distortion that we might see with pressure-loaded, rectangular housings.

Excluding an excellent housing for the Robot camera of years past, there are spherically shaped housings on the diving market currently. The one that comes immediately to mind is the Movie Marine, manufactured by Sea Research and Development of Bartow,

Movie Marine Spherical Housing

Florida for the Bolex 16mm movie camera.

DISADVANTAGES

While the Movie Marine housing does make efficient use of the space available inside the housing, the sphere is generally an impractical shape for a housing since cameras are usually rectangular. Spherical housings tend to be too big and too bulky for the camera they protect.

From the amateur home-builder's standpoint, the spherical housing is by far the most difficult to build and seal.

CYLINDRICAL HOUSINGS

The cylindrical housing, for a number of good reasons, is becoming increasingly more popular with the advanced do-it-yourselfer as well as commercial enterprises.

Hasseacor housing for the El Hasselblad

Aluminum and Plexiglas tubing are popular building materials which have in common great inherent strength and require only that the ends be closed to become pressure-resistant, water-proof containers.

Closing the ends simply means a welded or cemented joint at one end and a continuous "O" ring seal at the other.

The cylindrical housing offers much greater resistance to external pressure than the rectangular shape although somewhat less than the spherical. A further advantage, it provides little resistance in water and tends to be better balanced than the rectangular shape.

DISADVANTAGES

It is clear that the most compact housings are those which most closely approximate the shape of the camera they are intended to house. Since most cameras are rectangular, it is obvious then that the most compact shape would also be rectangular.

Cylindrical housings, unfortunately, tend to be somewhat wasteful of space and their curved surfaces make the installation of controls much more difficult than on the flat surfaces of a rectangular housing.

Another side effect of the wasted space frequently found in cylindrical and spherical housings is excessive positive buoyancy . . . a condition which can be corrected through judicious attachment of ballasting lead.

SIZE

As we have learned, compactness is a most desirable feature in housing design and good designers go to great lengths to minimize wasted space inside the housing. A well-designed housing will be as small as possible consistent with allowing enough room for the camera control linkages.

Generally speaking, the more com-

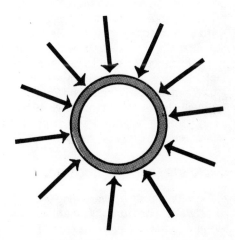

Water pressure exerts a uniform force on a cylindrical surface

pact and streamlined the housing, the easier it is to handle and the less vulnerable to pressure and drag.

Conversely, the larger the housing, the greater the ballasting required, the greater its vulnerability to the stresses of pressure, and the greater its resistance or drag in the water.

WEIGHT

Depending on the camera and your selection of material for the housing, the camera-housing combination will probably tend to be a bit heavy at the surface. But if it is well-designed, it should be very close to neutral buoyancy when underwater.

Though the subsea photographer's prime concern is its weight underwater, a camera housing which is excessively heavy in air can also be a liability . . . particularly when trying to climb into a boat with it during a heavy sea.

The camera and housing should be slightly negative underwater, a preference evidenced by most undersea photographers. Just a few ounces of negative buoyancy give the camera a natural "heft" when held in the hands. A positively buoyant camera, on the other hand, tends to exert a constant upward pull, placing considerable fatiguing stress on the wrists which must force the camera down toward the subject. Even a neutrally-buoyant housing, if not properly ballasted fore and aft, will have this tendency. Obviously, proper balance is an important characteristic of good design.

NECK STRAPS AND BUOYANCY

As with virtually everything else in underwater photography, there are divergent points of view regarding the need for neck straps to support the camera housing. Some underwater photographers find them indispensable, using them routinely not only to support the camera and free the hands, but also to steady the camera. Others argue with equal fervor that the neckstrap is at best a nuisance which frequently becomes entangled with breathing apparatus and can be downright dangerous when the housing is bulky and heavy.

If a diver is carrying two cameras underwater he is compelled to use the neck strap. If you need a neck strap, I favor using nylon cord over which is passed soft rubber tubing which will prevent knotting and tangling.

Depending on the equipment, I generally opt for the convenience of a neck strap. When used with a slightly negative housing, it permits the camera to hang down comfortably from the photographer's neck.

Don't use a neck strap if the equipment is positively buoyant. It will not only float annoyingly around your head or in front of the face mask, but could even become dangerously entangled with the regulator.

And finally, don't attach a neck strap to an excessively heavy or bulky camera. The heavier and bulkier the camera housing, the more energy which will be required to muscle it around underwater.

Occasionally, it would be very desirable to place the housing on the bottom while you attend to something else. Obviously, this could only be done with a negatively buoyant housing.

Indeed, equipment with even the slightest positive buoyancy could get away from the diver and float to the surface. Anyone who has tried to locate a small piece of equipment lost on the surface knows how much fun that can be, particularly when the surface is ruffled by wind and wave action.

MATERIALS

As mentioned earlier in this text, camera housings have been constructed from virtually every conceivable material. Down through the years, due in a large degree to the advancement of space-age technology, the materials most frequently used in the construction of underwater housings appears to have been distilled into two categories: 1) plastics; 2) metals.

RUGGEDNESS

Regardless of the material chosen, the underwater housing must be sufficiently rugged to withstand the inevitable hard treatment and knocking around it is certain to get in transportation, on the boat, while entering or exiting the water, or while underwater.

Recently on a Caribbean dive, for example, I watched a diver smash a new Plexiglas housing to pieces and ruin a fine camera trying to fend himself off a shallow coral head during a sudden squall which had blown up while we were exiting the water. And once, untrusting of baggage handlers, after holding a 16mm camera and Plexiglas housing on my lap for a hot three-hour flight, I stepped down onto the runway and felt the housing handle give way. The housing landed on a corner and shattered three sides of the heavy Plexiglas housing. I had seen aluminum housings fall farther and land harder without a scratch.

On the other hand, Ike Brigham of Ikelite routinely startles visitors to his Indianapolis plant by lobbing one of his molded Lexan[2] housings 20 feet into the air and grinning with smug satisfaction while it bounces off the concrete floor without as much as a chip.

PLASTICS

Plastic camera housings are available in fiberglas, Lucite[3], Plexiglas, and injection molded polycarbonates like *LEXAN.* Plastic housings offer a number of important advantages and a few disadvantages as well. As a rule, housings made of Plexiglas are the most popular since this material is relatively inexpensive, easy to work, holds up well and is impervious to the corrosive effects of salt water.

Much is made of the fact the material (ideally grade "G", clear, unshrunk Plexiglas) is transparent and optically equivalent to the finest glass. It thereby permits the diver full view of the camera and calibrations. This characteristic would seem a definite asset should a leak develop since any water accumulating in the housing would be readily apparent.

More than once, however, I have seen the neophyte diver-photographer swimming around underwater in ignorant bliss holding a Plexiglas housing half flooded with water. A flooded plastic case underwater somehow looks different than the same flooded case in air.

The transparency of the clear plastic housings can be a disadvantage in still another way. Since light rays are free to penetrate the entire housing,

Ikelite SLR housing

[2] Lexan® is a registered trademark of General Electric Co.
[3] Lucite® is a registered trademark of DuPont.

internal reflections may produce "ghost images" and flare.

Recently, a student in my underwater photography class made several nice photographs of a diver silhouetted against the surface which were marred by the unmistakable name NIKON appearing subliminably across the scene. The problem of ghost image can be minimized considerably by using a lens sunshade — housing permitting — or by cementing a sunshade of black Plexiglas to the front plate of the housing.

Still another disadvantage of the plastic housings is the fact that the front plate (lens port) can be easily scratched and care must be exercised to prevent any scratching which could mar the photographs.

Scratches on the external surface of the lens port tend to fill with water which has approximately the same optical characteristics as Plexiglas and produce no serious blemish on the finished photograph. Wide scratches which do distort the optical properties of the Plexiglas can be polished out with moist cotton balls covered with a thin film of abrasive and changed frequently.

Automobile rubbing compounds and common tooth pastes work quite well. Scratches on the inside of the lens port will definitely show up on photographs and must be polished out.

The danger of the housing breaking under impact is particularly likely with a rectangular shape if a flat surface is rapped solidly against a hard object. However, plastic housings are quite durable and sensible treatment will insure many years of dependable service. Over the years, I've used a number of Plexiglas housings several of which are still providing excellent service.

All other things being equal, plastic housings are less rugged than housings made of metal. Those who manufacture plastic housings make a good point when they argue that the camera housing should be treated sensibly and not tossed about carelessly. Severe shocks which may not damage the housing can be transmitted to the camera inside, damaging the camera or throwing the lens out of calibration.

It is only fair to mention that while fiberglas is rather difficult to work for the do-it-yourselfer, it is a rugged, highly desireable construction material for underwater housings. The Sampson-Hall line of housings is a good example of reliability in fiberglas housings.

Surfer-filmmaker, George Greenough builds his own fiberglas housings for the cameras he uses to film his surfing movies. One can hardly imagine a more rugged test of a material's ability to withstand a constant heavy pounding and yet the fiberglas housings stand up quite well.

METAL

Speaking in terms of all-around ruggedness and impact resistance, the metal housing is rather hard to beat. It offers inherent high strength and relatively low density. As a result, it is rugged enough to withstand heavy impact and still provide good water displacement-to-weight ratio.

Aluminum housings, for example, are obviously heavier in air than plastic housings. Yet their buoyancy characteristics in water are generally excellent and the better ones are quite easy to handle . . . a most important feature of any housing.

Since flash or strobe must often be hand held a considerable distance from the lens, a good housing must be sufficiently well-balanced to allow the diver-photographer to steady the housing and release the shuttter with only one hand. In the current wave of well-designed underwater housings, aluminum appears to be the number one choice of the equipment designers . . . and for good reason. If you can afford the added expense, and a good aluminum housing will probably cost twice as much as a plastic housing, you'll be hard pressed to find a material as well suited for underwater applications as aluminum. Another advantage is that aluminum housings can be cast from a mold designed to make the most efficient use of space by following the camera's contours and form. The result is a compact package at no loss in strength integrity.

The problem of internal reflection that can ruin photographs in a transparent housing is virtually non-existent in metal housings since the only light which can pass into the housing must enter through the lens port.

DISADVANTAGES

For obvious reasons, commercial *metal* housings tend to be considerably more expensive than those constructed of less expensive, easier-to-work materials. With respect to do-it-yourself projects, I have seen a few extraordinary home-built housings constructed of welded and cast aluminum. It should be obvious, however, that this type of construction is beyond the ability of the diver of average mechanical talent.

And while the problem of internal reflection does not trouble the metal housing, neither does the diver-photograher have the advantage of complete visibility of the camera inside . . . with the exception of aluminum housings with large dome ports like Bates Littlehale's OCEANEYE. This makes checking on potential leaks vastly more difficult.

Probably, the single greatest drawback of the metal housing is its poor resistance to the corrosive effects of sea water. To a degree, all metals react corrosively in seawater and unprotected aluminum is particularly vulnerable. Corrosion in sea water oc-

curs through electrolysis caused generally by dissimilar metals being in contact. Aluminum housings with stainless steel quick-release fasteners would be a good example.

The corrosion problem is easily controlled, fortunately. Serious corrosion can occur with surprising quickness if the metal is unprotected and neglected. The better aluminum housings are anodized and coated with a good quality epoxy and are rarely underwater long enough to undergo noticeable electrolysis.

On the other hand, pockets of salt water can be trapped on the surface of the housing when it is removed from the sea. The pocket areas will begin to corrode rapidly if the housing is not carefully rinsed in fresh water immediately. Particularly vulnerable subjects are the tiny set screws which secure the housing knobs and triggers to their control shafts.

CONTROLS

While we are on the subject of controls, consideration should be given to

Oceaneye Housing

a few general rules when building or buying a housing. In order for any

49

control to operate effectively, the camera must be securely anchored inside the housing. Nothing is more frustrating than to set up a perfect photograph, press the shutter release only to feel the camera rock inside the housing . . . or worse, feel it slide forward or backward, unmeshing the controls.

A good housing provides enough external controls to utilize the camera's versatility. The controls should be comfortably and conveniently arranged. For example, the diver-photographer should be able to grip the housing handle and trip the shutter release with the same hand.

My biggest objection to many production housings are the small control knobs that are almost impossible to grip when the diver is wearing gloves. Another pet peeve is that frequently they are so inconveniently located that a tweezer is almost required to turn them.

Controls should be: 1) conveniently located, 2) large enough to grip comfortably . . . even when wearing gloves, 3) easily activated with smooth action, 4) sufficiently rugged to withstand the inevitable knock occasionally, 5) if a calibrated dial is utilized with an indicator on the knob the markings should be large and legible enough to be read in the dim light conditions we find underwater, 6) the control shafts should be easily removable for periodic inspection and replacement of "0" ring seals.

A few words of caution. Piston or plunger-action controls, though simplest to construct and install, are undesirable for underwater housings since increasing water pressure tends to force them into the housing. My first housing had a plunger-action shutter release. Invariably, when I dove to 35 or 40 feet, several things happened in rapid succession. First, the water pressure jammed the plunger down, automatically taking the first photograph. The plunger, despite my most strenuous efforts, flatly refused to return to its upward position. I was therefore compelled to ascend about 20 feet to relieve the pressure on it at which depth it behaved most admirably.

It is also well to remember that excessive pressures can be transmitted through the control linkages to the camera controls. Be careful never to force a control when resistance is felt. Otherwise the camera may be overwound or its controls jammed. And finally, it should be obvious the more controls, the more through-the-hull openings required. The more openings, the greater the potential for a leak developing.

SEALS

At the risk of emphasizing the obvious, the principal function of the housing is to keep the camera dry. I have a most vivid recollection of stepping off a diving platform one bright Caribbean morning with a 75 pound helmet on my sholders and my favorite camera in a Plexiglas housing in my hands. As I fell inexorably to the sea floor 50 feet below, I watched helplessly as a stream of water flooded relentlessly into the housing bathing my favorite camera in highly corrosive salt water.

One experience like that leaves forever an indelible impression in the undersea photographer's mind . . . and a staunch dedication to a careful check-out of the housing seals before entering the water.

In the old days, most housings were equipped with pressurizing valves. The idea was that several pounds of air pressure pumped inside the housing would signal a leak when submerged by trickling a stream of air bubbles into the water.

One cautious photographer told me that he intended to play it extra safe with the beautiful Plexiglas housing he had painstakingly crafted. He stopped to pressurize the housing at a service station on the way to a dive. While the rectangular housing undoubtedly could have withstood an external pressure equivalent to a depth of 150 feet of water, it exploded under an *internal pressure* of only 25 p.s.i. hurling chunks of Plexiglas and camera for really impressive distances.

More sophisticated undersea cameras of days gone by, were equipped with their own automatic pressurizing systems which were very much like open circuit scuba, utilizing cylinders of high pressure air, automatic demand regulators and exhaust systems. These elaborate systems theoretically eliminated the possibility of leaks by balancing the pressure inside the housing with the water pressure.

The pressurizing concept is a thing of the past made obsolete in part by today's space-technology metals which are sufficiently light and strong to resist the pressure of the deepest ocean without complicated pressurizing systems. But even without space-age metal, pressurizing would still have been replaced by the vastly more practical self-sealing concept.

In self-sealing, a continuous rubber "0" ring is lubricated with silicone grease and placed in a continuous machined groove. Then a lid is positioned over the "0" ring and snapped securely in place by quick-release fasteners. As the cover is snapped on, the "0" ring is somewhat flattened into a seal.

As the external pressure on the housing builds with increasing depth, the cover is pressed down tighter onto the "0" ring further deforming it and forcing it to fill the gap as illustrated. The housing is consequently sealed even tighter against the increasing pressure.

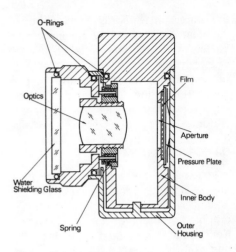

The Nikonos employs a pressure-resistant aluminum body and 18 "0" rings to make the camera completely watertight

CAUTION

The "0" ring seals do require attention and it is imperative they be lubricated frequently with silicone grease. Lubricating the "0" rings each time the film is changed would not be too often. The "0" ring and its groove should be carefully checked as frequently for cuts, nicks or grains of sand which could compromise the housing's watertight integrity. Almost every case of leakage is a result of carelessness.

TESTING

If you have any misgivings about

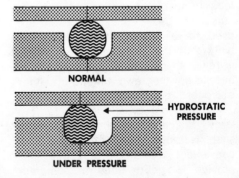

the watertight integrity of your housing, test it! The *empty* housing may be lowered on a line or taken underwater by the diver. Ideally it should be tested to a depth pressure 25 per cent greater than its intended maximum operating depth for a safety factor.

CAMERA REMOVAL

Imagine the perfect diving day! Picture yourself anchored over a beautiful reef with clear water, great photographic opportunities and plenty of air. Could you imagine being satisfied with one roll of exposed film? Yet I've seen some underwater photographers do that very thing rather than face the ordeal of removing 32 wingnuts and spending thirty angry minutes removing the camera from the housing.

There must be a better way . . . and there is. Ideally, the housing cover or back plate should be easily and quickly removable and provide direct access to the camera back for rapid unloading and reloading of film.

A really well-planned design permits this without necessitating the removal of the camera from the housing or even disengagement of control linkages. On some housings the camera is secured to the housing backplate and slides free of the controls as the backplate is removed from the housing . . . also a good system.

Above all, the closure system must be quick, foolproof, and positive locking. If special tools or small wingnuts and tripod socket screws are used, there is a mighty strong possibility that the first time the camera is removed on rough water, wingnuts or hold-down screws will end up either overboard or in the bilge.

My personal preference is for the large stainless steel quick-release snap fasteners which are not only convenient and foolproof, but also provide a good uniform compression of the sealing "0" ring. It is hard to find fault with these fasteners. However, I do object to the very small ones some manufacturers insist on using. They invariably must be pried up with fingernails and because of very sharp edges, like the sharp corners on some rectangular housings, can puncture the diver, his exposure suit or his inflatable vest. And, although I've never known it to happen, there is the possibility that a snap could hang up on something and inadvertently release itself underwater.

CARRYING CASE

It never fails to amaze me that some divers will spend a great deal of money for an elaborate camera-housing, then pack it all in a canvas bag, drop it on the deck of a dive boat and forget about it until they're ready to enter the water.

I've sat on a rolling boat and winced as $1,000 worth of camera and strobe slid back and forth across a deck while its owner sat talking, completely unconcerned.

Any photographic equipment worth using should be protected in a rugged carrying case. There are a number of excellent, heavy-duty aluminum cases (Halliburton, for example) that are designed specifically for photographic equipment. On the other hand, a good carrying case can easily and

inexpensively be made from plywood. Ideally, it should be padded with one of the synthetic foam materials which are quite inexpensive and can easily be tailored with a razor blade to accommodate the camera, housing and accessory shapes. Once snugly fitted, the equipment is reasonably shock-resistant and well protected.

I no longer bother building my own carrying cases. Instead, I use super-rugged fiberglas cases which have stainless-steel snap fasteners and are "0" ring sealed. These surplus typewriter cases are inexpensive and available through surplus outlets like Leonard Joseph's of St. Louis, Missouri. Even when loaded with gear, I find them to be positively buoyant and, because of the continuous "0" ring, virtually unsinkable.

SPORTSFINDER

Almost all camera housings are equipped with some sort of sighting

device to help the photographer frame his composition. While all sportsfinders are adequate for medium and long distance photographs, most begin to suffer parallax problems as subject-to-camera distances are shortened.

The most notable of the underwater photographic systems which suffer from close-up parallax error is the Nikonos. The Nikonos sportsfinder is not only in a different horizontal line-of-sight than the lens, but also in a different vertical line-of-sight. If this parallax error is not corrected, the neophyte underwater photographer will find much of his photographic work being consigned to the waste basket.

The only solution is to learn the parallax error of your sportsfinder underwater by shooting several practice rolls at different short camera-to-subject distances. After you have learned to correct for parallax error, aiming and framing with the sportsfinder becomes second nature.

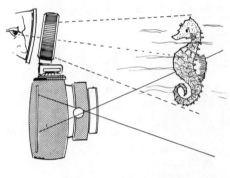

SUBJECT AS SEEN
THROUGH VIEWFINDER

SUBJECT AS SEEN
THROUGH LENS

When building or buying a sportsfinder, keep in mind that it must be rugged and should have a positive locking device to prevent its twisting which can also result in ruined photographs because of parallax. It should be apparent that the ideal underwater photographic system is one which permits the diver-photographer to frame, compose and focus through the taking lens. Only in this way is parallax, the inherent problem of the sportsfinder, eliminated. Even so, most reflex camera housings also provide a sportsfinder for action shots which may occur so fast that time does not allow through-the-lens composition.

LENS PORT

One of the most — if not *the* most — important features of a camera housing is the lens port . . . the window through which the picture is taken.

Interchangeable lens ports for Ikelite SLR housing

Earlier we discussed the phenomenon of magnification underwater not only causing objects to appear larger and closer than their actual size and distance, but also causing an apparent one-third increase in the focal length of the camera's lens along with a corresponding narrowing of the lens' field of view.

As a result of this telescopic effect, the underwater photographer is compelled to increase the subject-to-camera distance in order to entirely frame his subject. Even in the clearest water, because of scattering and light absorption, any increase in subject-to-camera distance tends to degrade picture quality.

The culprit in this case is the conventional *flat* port used in most underwater housings. It is unable to correct for the distortion produced by the differences between the indexes of refraction of light in air and water.

CONCENTRIC DOME PORT

It is possible, however, for a lens to have the same full angle of coverage underwater as it has in air. Such a lens is said to be *water-corrected* for magnification distortion.

Actually, the camera lens isn't changed at all! The flat port of the camera housing is replaced by a concentric dome, glass or acrylic, which is water-corrected.

When the optical axis of the camera lens is precisely aligned with that of the concentric dome port, the lens will intercept the image projected by the refractive combination of water and air. In this manner is the same full angle of coverage of the lens restored or "corrected" to its in-air perspectives. An excellent example of a 180° concentric dome is the Oceaneye 100 designed for the 35mm Nikon F by Bates Littlehales and Gomer McNeil.

MAINTENANCE

Let's face it. Cameras, housings, strobes — or for that matter any device used in photography — are expensive, rather delicate instruments designed to reward the owner with precise and accurate results. It is certain that as your photographic skills develop your appreciation for your camera equipment will also grow. It is equally certain that if you don't learn to perform routine preventative maintenance on the equipment, you can look forward to having — at the very least — a diving holiday ruined because of equipment malfunction.

And I'm not for a moment suggesting you get out the old tool box and try to repair that sticking shutter. Most modern cameras are far too complex in design and construction for anyone,

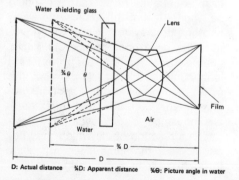

Water shielding glass

Lens

¾θ θ

Film

Air

Water

¾ D

D

D: Actual distance   ¾D: Apparent distance   ¾Θ: Picture angle in water short of trained camera technicians, to attempt repairs.

The answer is obvious. The key to your camera's continued reliability and accuracy is the same good treatment you would give any expensive and delicate instrument. That means, above all, keeping it clean and insuring good working order by having it checked out annually by a qualified camera repair shop.

It is hard to overemphasize the importance of immediately rinsing underwater photographic gear in fresh water after use. Underwater flash reflectors, for example, if somewhat oxidized produce only 70 per cent of the reflectance of a clean reflector.

GIVE IT A BATH

Few underwater photographers are really aware of the incredible swiftness with which sea water corrosion can attack camera equipment after an ocean dive. The following is a routine which, if followed religiously, will reward the underwater photographer with years of trouble-free service from his equipment.

Immediately after the dive:

1) Fill a tub with fresh water and immerse the camera housing, strobe and light meter. Allow it to rinse away any salt water residue for approximately 15 minutes. Be sure to flush any pockets where salt water might accumulate. Blot the equipment dry using a soft towel. Be particularly careful not to scratch the housing's lens port.

2) When the equipment has been carefully dried, remove all cable connectors and disassemble the housing and strobe. When removing the cable connectors, they should be carefully wiped clean and sprayed lightly with silicone. (Caution: Silicone spray has a destructive effect on some plastics. Consequently, it should never be sprayed in close proximity to plas-

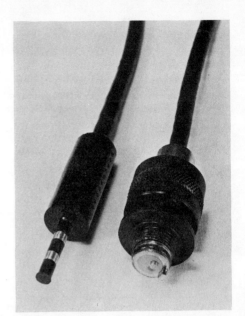

E.O. male termination (left) and Nikonos connector

tic housings, etc.)

E. O.-type connectors (female end) can be cleaned occasionally with a 22 caliber bore brush. The E. O. male termination can be cleaned easily with a small wire brush.

3) Check for moisture due to condensation or possible leakage. Condensation can be a significant problem, particularly with metal housings. Since the problem is caused by the condensation of the relatively warm air inside the housing by the relatively cold water on the outside, the logical prevention is to keep the temperature of the air inside the housing cool . . . or at least don't let it get too hot. In other words, don't load the camera in a hot cabin or allow it to stand in the direct sunlight. And by all means, tape a packet of moisture absorbing silica gel inside the housing. Be sure to *tape* it in place. Otherwise it will probably turn up in front of your lens, just when you are about to take an important shot.

4) Remove and check all "0" rings.

If the "0" rings are worn, scratched or cut, they should be immediately replaced. Check that the "0" ring groove is clean and free of any particles of dirt or sand that might prevent proper sealing. While the "0" rings are out, rinse them care-

fully and dry. Dab a bit of silicone grease on the ball of your thumb. By pulling the "0" ring between the thumb and forefinger it will be evenly lubricated. The excess should be wiped away and the "0" ring refitted in its groove.

5) Remove all batteries from their units, and examine the terminals for any sign of corrosion. It is fundamental to the successful firing of the strobe that all electrical contacts be clean. If corrosion is evident, gently sand the terminals with emery cloth until completely clean. Spray the cleaned contacts with silicone spray to retard subsequent corrosion. Fresh batteries are equally important to the successful firing of the strobe. Never, never, under any circumstances, *store* any battery-powered photographic device with the batteries

inside. I made that mistake once and actually had to drill and grind the batteries out. While in the camera, the batteries had leaked and virtually welded themselves in. As soon as the batteries begin to lose their charge, replace them. Batteries for flashbulb units have a life expectancy of approximately six months, depending on the usage. The 510 volt dry cell batteries used in some of the more powerful, underwater strobes should be replaced about twice as frequently. If the unit is being used extensively, it is a good idea to have two batteries, alternating them from day to day. When allowed to revitalize thusly, the battery life is extended considerably. Since the shelf life of such batteries is rather short, they should be stored in a refrigerator, between assignments, to gain a longer useful life.

6) One of the kinkiest trouble-spots, from a maintenance point of view, is the flashbulb socket. In its dark inner recesses saltwater can accumulate and corrode vulnerable contacts. This area should be rinsed extensively and examined carefully for any evidence of corrosion. All corrosion must be removed from the hard-to-get-at contacts inside the socket if misfires are to be avoided. Spraying the dry socket with silicone spray will help retard corrosion.

7) To prevent flash or strobe misfiring, particular care must be given any electrical wiring which is exposed to the water. The principal cause is salt water which is forced by water pressure under the rubber jacket insulating the copper wire. In a short while, this unseen salt water can corrode the strands of copper wire, causing them to weaken and finally break. The result, total failure of the unit.

CAMERA FIRST AID KIT

Most all photographers carry an accessory bag loaded with paraphernalia, much of it vital to every day picture taking . . . most of it complex gadgetry that always seems to be too much trouble to assemble to the camera. The following items, however, are important and should be included in every underwater photographer's camera case:

"0" rings — at least one spare for every "0" ring in your equipment (camera housing, strobe housing, etc.)

Ear syringe — to blow dust from lenses, etc.,

Folded paper towels

Spray can WD-40

Small wire brush

Silicone grease

22 caliber bore brush

Camel hair brush, retractable, with cover

Chemically pure alcohol; plastic bottle

Desiccant, small packets of silica gel

Cotton swabs (Q-tips)

Photographic grade lens tissue

Emery cloth (fine grit)

Set of small screwdrivers

Allen wrenches as required

Small crescent wrench

Tooth brush

Silicone Spray (e.g. DIL-Divelube)

LENS CARE

The best advice concerning photographic lenses is to keep them as clean as possible. And don't be one of those ding-dongs whose idea of cleaning a lens is to exhale on it, then rub the condensate off with a shirt tail or cuff. And please, keep your fingers off the lens elements. Fingerprints contain body acids or perspiration salts which permanently etch glass. Remove fingerprint smudges as soon as you notice them. First, use an ear syringe to blow off any lint or dust particles which may cover the lens. Hold the camera with the lens pointing down and blow the air upwards. In this way, the particles will fall away from the lens as they are blown off. Then, try breathing on the lens to moisten it. Now use a cotton swab gently to dust off the condensate from your breath and hopefully any traces of the fingerprint.

If the fingerprint is still there, you can try a clean cotton swab, barely dampened with alcohol or lens cleaner. Wipe gently! Do not rub hard! Do not rub in the same direction too long! Use an *easy, circular,* brushing motion.

Speaking about brushing, be very careful about using brushes to clean lenses. If used carelessly, they tend to attract grease and grit and could even scratch the lens if they are not discarded soon enough.

Also, eye glass tissue is for spectacles and toilet tissue is for . . . ., and both are marvelously well suited to their intended functions. They are *not,* however, to be used to clean the sensitive glass of photographic lenses.

Even the so-called photographic lens tissue can damage the delicate lens coating if applied with excessive gusto. You can save yourself a lot of trouble by using a lens dust cap to cover your lens when not in use. The dust cap keeps the lens free of grime or dust. And it's an excellent idea to keep a protective cover of some sort over the housing port, as well.

Before we leave the subject of lenses, remember to keep all threaded or fastening surfaces clean. To avoid damage to lens threads or bayonet mounts caused by the abrasive wearing of grit, you need only brush them clean occasionally with a toothbrush and use an ear syringe to blow off the grit.

HEAT AND BRIGHT SUNLIGHT

Camera equipment is particularly vulnerable to heat and correspondingly to bright sunlight. Neither cameras nor film should ever be stored on deck or in automobile trunks or glove compartments. Nor should they be allowed to sit on the beach exposed to the direct sunlight. Excessive heat will ruin camera equipment. After the dive, at home, your photographic equipment should be stored in a cool, but dry room.

THE CAMERA

A soft brush can be used to dust lint or film fragments from inside the camera. Cotton swabs are also useful in removing small pockets of grit. If you're using a reflex camera, check the mirror for lint or dust and use the ear syringe to blow it clear.

CHECKING SHUTTER SYNCHRONIZATION

Making a habit of checking your camera's synchronization will greatly reduce the risk of failure and disappointment stemming from equipment breakdown.

The technique is simple. Remove the lens. Open the camera back and insert a business card sized scrap of white paper under the film pressure plate. Do not replace the lens! Set the shutter speed to the recommended speed for electronic flash, connect and switch on the strobe. Now, by squeezing the shutter, you will see the entire card exposed at once as the shutter opens and closes.

Changing the shutter speed to any other will throw the shutter out of synchronization and your eye will see a shutter pattern. In other words, assuming the strobe is firing, only part of the card will be seen while the shutter is open. This test is only for cameras which have focal plane shutters. If you are shooting with a Hasselblad or Rollei or any other front

shutter, for that matter, the wide open diaphragm will cause a large, bright hole to appear as the shutter is triggered.

FLOODED HOUSINGS

There is probably no sensation in the imagination of man that can produce that awful twisting, deep in your stomach, when you finally realize that your favorite camera is sitting in a housing filled with sea water.

Over the years, I've seen a few camera housings flood. Usually the photographer was in too big a hurry to check the "0" ring, but occasionally, because of an actual equipment failure. The following is a procedure you should follow in the unhappy event that your equipment should ever flood:

1) *Immediately*, remove the camera or strobe from its housing and drain all the water completely. At the same time, remove any film or batteries.

2) Place the camera or strobe in a fresh water bath and flush the camera carefully, activating all control mechanisms to remove any small pockets of sea water which might be trapped inside. Do the same with the housing.

3) Remove the camera from the fresh water bath and rinse thoroughly with a solution of 50 per cent fresh water and 50 per cent alcohol.

4) Remove from the alcohol rinse and dry thoroughly. A very gentle stream of cylinder air pressure will help. Activate the camera controls frequently to eliminate any pockets of rinse solution.

5) When the unit is thoroughly dried, insert a packet or two of silica gel desiccant to help drying and take the camera to your nearest certified camera repairman as soon as possible.

". . . through this photographic eye you will be able to look out on a new light-world, a world for the most part uncharted and unexplored, a world that lies waiting to be discovered and revealed."

Edward Weston

Chapter VI.

THE PHOTOGRAPHIC EYE

It is not the purpose of this chapter to explore the application of intricate mathematical formulae in the design and construction of sophisticated lens systems. Rather, it is treated in a more practical manner, providing the student-photographer with a working knowledge of photographic optics. And armed with some knowledge of the basic principles and construction of lenses, he will no longer be intimidated by the photographer's vocabulary. Instead, he will understand them as common terms which distinguish different lenses from one another.

This knowledge, in turn, enables the diver-photographer to understand the potentials, as well as the limitations, of a particular lens helping him to select the right lens for a given photographic situation.

In short, the purpose of this chapter — indeed, this book — is to help the reader learn to control light. And a working knowledge of the lens will go a long way toward enabling the diver-photographer to consistently achieve higher quality negatives.

LENS FUNCTION

Try another experiment!
Hold a positive lens of medium fo-

cal length over a lamp and the light bulb trademark will be projected on your ceiling. The point is the function of any lens is to form an image . . . a sharp, undistorted image. But what of the pinhole camera? It apparently can form an image *without* a lens.

True enough. It can, indeed. As we have learned, virtually everything seen by our eyes is a result of reflected light. Light beamed on an object is reflected *uncontrolled* from each point of that object in the form of minute points of light. From each of the thousands of points which make up an object, corresponding thousands of rays of light are reflected.

Earlier, a lens was defined as "an optically shaped glass which gathers light rays reflected from a subject, bends, and projects them in the form of a sharp image on the film . . ."

The function of a lens, then, is to gather and refract *all* points of light reflected from an object — regardless where they strike the lens — and converge and reproduce each to its respective image position on the film plane. Photographs taken by the pinhole camera require exceptionally long exposure times due to the small diameter of the hole.

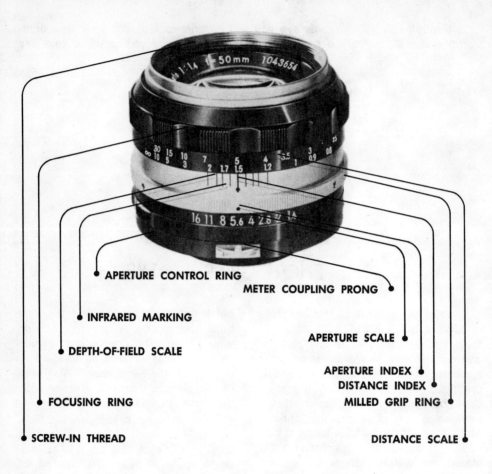

APERTURE CONTROL RING

METER COUPLING PRONG

INFRARED MARKING

APERTURE SCALE

DEPTH-OF-FIELD SCALE

APERTURE INDEX

DISTANCE INDEX

FOCUSING RING

MILLED GRIP RING

SCREW-IN THREAD

DISTANCE SCALE

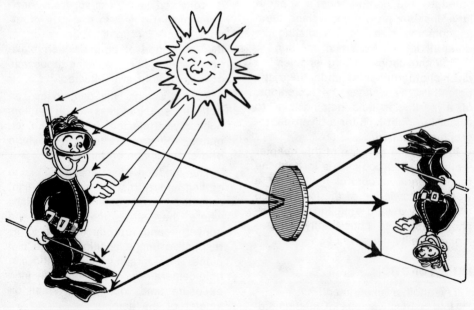

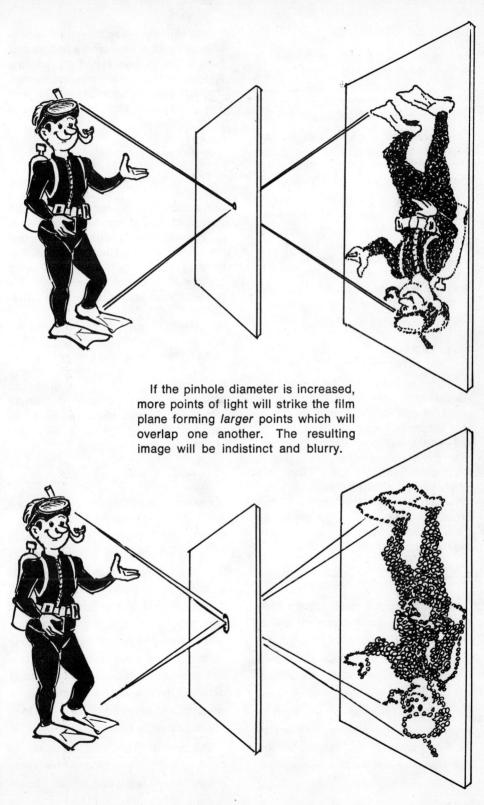

If the pinhole diameter is increased, more points of light will strike the film plane forming *larger* points which will overlap one another. The resulting image will be indistinct and blurry.

CIRCLE OF CONFUSION

In order to achieve an image of perfect detail and focus, the minute points of reflected light would have to be of *immeasurable* diameter . . . obviously an impossible goal.

However, it is true the sharpest and most distinct photographs are made when the diameter of the points of reflected light are *as small as possible.*

By measuring the "circle of confusion", the diameter of the circle to which the image-forming point of reflected light will spread, the degree of accuracy with which any particular lens will form and focus an image can be determined. Consequently, one of the factors which determines the quality of a lens is its ability to resolve the circles of confusion to their smallest possible size consistent with the sharpest possible image.

Summarizing, the sharpest, most detailed photographs are made when the circle of confusion is *smallest.* Pinhole cameras using small apertures and extremely long exposure times can make acceptable photographs when conditions are ideal. But only with a lens, which gathers all stray light rays through the aperture, can larger apertures and correspondingly short exposure times be used to produce sharp photographs.

INVERTED IMAGES

The photographic image reconstructed by these points of light is backwards and up-side-down. If a photograph of a man was made through a pinhole, his image would be inverted.

If straight lines are plotted from any point on the diver in the illustration, through the pinhole, and on to the film plane . . . the reason for the inversion of photographic images will be seen immediately.

Interestingly, the inverted image phenomenon of the camera occurs similarly in the human eye. Light passing through the cornea forms an upside-down image on the retina of the eye. The human eye and the camera have other similarities.

THE HUMAN EYE

The eye is rather like a camera. The lens of the eye functions much like a camera lens. Light entering the curved cornea is focused by the lens as a clear image on the light-sensitive retina. This light stimulates the retina, sending impulses through the optic nerves to the sight centers in the brain, where the impulses are interpreted.

While the *pupil* serves only as an opening through which light is admitted, the *iris* is a diaphragm which opens or closes in response to the brightness of light. The amount of light which can reach the retina is thereby regulated. This action corresponds to the functions of the lens and diaphragm of the camera.

PRINCIPLE OF THE LENS

Earlier we discussed refraction, a principle of light's behavior. It was defined: "light travels in a straight path as it travels through a substance of the same density or as it passes into a second substance of a different density, provided it enters the second substance at a right angle to its surface." However, when light rays pass obliquely from a substance of one density into a substance of a different density, they undergo a change in velocity and *direction.* That is, they are refracted or bent.

The pencil illustrated appears to bend in the water and it is this same phenomenon, *refraction,* which causes

light to change direction as it passes
through a prism.

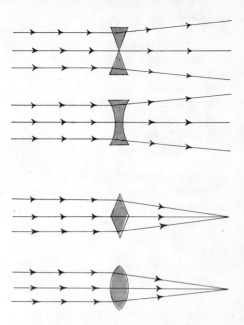

THE SIMPLE LENS

A ray of light passing through a
prism will change directions twice,
both directional changes will be made
toward the base of the prism. The first
directional change will occur because
light entering a dense substance
(prism) from a less dense substance
(air) will be bent *toward* the perpendicular. The s e c o n d directional
change will occur because light entering one substance (air) from a denser
substance (prism) will be bent *away*
from the perpendicular.

If two prisms are cemented base-to-
base (the basis of a simple convex
lens), and parallel rays of light beamed
on them, the rays will converge. In a
simple (positive) lens, the rays of light
which pass through the lens will converge at some point behind the lens
to form an image. The point at which
a sharp and distinct image is formed
is called the *focus*.

A divergent lens can be made by
connecting the two prisms at their
apex. Parallel light rays diverge as
they pass through the negative (divergent) lens.

Generally, lenses are categorized by
their geometric shape and fall into
two basic classes:
1) Positive (convergent) lenses
   which have at least one convex
   surface and;
2) Negative (divergent) lenses
   which have at least one concave
   surface.

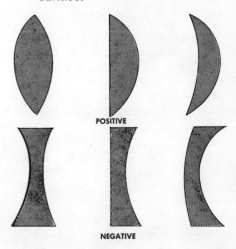

POSITIVE

NEGATIVE

THE COMPOUND LENS

Even the most inexpensive of box cameras uses a combination of at least two lenses or more specifically two lens *elements*. A sophisticated lens like the 50 to 300mm Auto-Nikkor Zoom may incorporate as many as 20 lens elements.

Aberrations are optical defects which are present in the best of simple lenses. In order to correct the effect of these aberrations, the compound lens combines a variety of simple, positive and negative lenses which tend to cancel out each other's optical defects.

The lens elements illustrated repre-

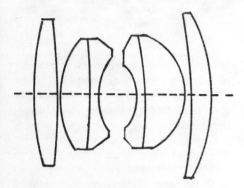

sent the most widely used lens in underwater photography currently, the 35mm f/2.5 W-Nikkor for the Nikonos II camera.

THE COLOR CORRECTED LENS

White light, as we have seen, is dispersed into seven colors as it passes through a prism. Since a convergent lens is — in effect — two prisms cemented base-to-base, it is apparent that wave lengths of the different col-

ors will be refracted differently and not converge at the same point behind the lens.

The result, in color or black and white photography, is that each color will come into sharp focus at different points causing a general blurry or soft focus effect. This optical defect is termed chromatic aberration.

A color-corrected lens incorporates a combination of lens elements, each having a different refractive index. By cancelling out each other's chromatic aberration, all color wavelengths converge at almost exactly the same point on the film plane.

FOCAL LENGTH

The point behind the lens where the refracted rays of light converge

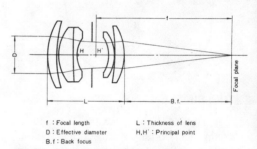

f : Focal length   L : Thickness of lens
D : Effective diameter   H,H´ : Principal point
B.f : Back focus

to form a photographic image is termed the *focal plane*. It is precisely at this point the film is held. The *focal length* of a lens is the distance of the optical center of the lens from the focal plane of the camera when the lens is focused at infinity. The focal length of a lens is almost always expressed in millimeters and in point of fact, the focal length of a lens can usually be found engraved on the lens barrel.

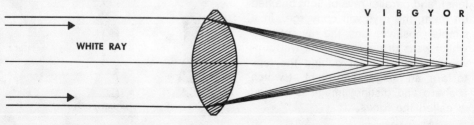

WHITE RAY

V I B G Y O R

MILLIMETERS

INCHES

1 inch = 25.4 millimeters

When the lens is focused at *infinity*, light reflected by the photographic subject is so distant from the camera that it passes through the lens as parallel rays and comes into focus at the film plane. As the distance between photographic subject and lens decreases, however, the distance between focal plane and the optical center of the lens must be increased to keep the subject sharply focused. This is because rays of light reflected from any point of the nearer photographic object no longer enter the lens as parallel rays but instead diverge slightly.

As a rule, divergent light rays passing through a lens will form a sharp image further behind the lens than would parallel rays.

Note: Since the focal length of a lens is determined when it is focused at *infinity*, changing the lens-to-film plane distance does not change the focal length.

IMAGE SIZE

The size of the photographic image formed on the film plane is directly proportional to the focal length of the camera's lens.

Let's say we photograph the same subject with three different lenses:
1) short focal length (wide angle lens)
2) standard focal length (so called "normal" lens)
3) long focal length (telephoto lens)

Assuming that all three photographs are made at the same camera-to-subject distance, equally well defined images will be obtained. The *image size* of each, however, will be quite different in relation to the film size.

Assemble a 50mm (standard) lens to a 35mm reflex camera. Position the camera at a subject-to-camera distance at which the subject forms an image precisely one-half (½) inch high on the ground glass screen. Now — without altering the subject-to-camera distance — change lenses. Substitute a lens with a focal length of 100mm. The image on the screen will now be exactly one inch high. And if a lens of 25mm focal length is interchanged, an image one quarter (¼) inch high will appear on the screen.

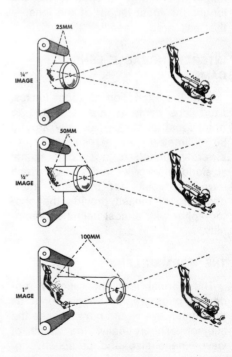

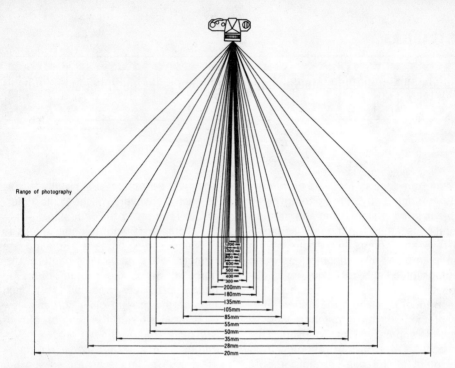

Range of photography

200mm
1000mm
800mm
600mm
500mm
400mm
300mm
200mm
180mm
135mm
105mm
85mm
55mm
50mm
35mm
28mm
20mm

ANGLE OF VIEW

The amount of area "seen" by the lens is termed its *angle of view* and it is inversely proportional to the focal length of the lens. In other words, the longer the focal length of the lens — the less area "seen."

INTERCHANGEABLE LENS CAMERAS

With the exception of zoom lenses, fixed lens cameras are restricted to a set focal length . . . usually around 50 millimeters. As a result, they are severely limited to a specific image size and angle of view. Cameras which have the facility for the rapid interchanging of lenses provide the photographer with almost unlimited versatility.

THE NORMAL LENS

The normal lens theoretically renders a photographic image about as the human eye would normally see the subject. Theoretically, the angle of view, image size and perspective of

the photographic subject appear identical as seen by either the human eye or the normal lens. The so-called "normal" lens has been arbitrarily set by most lens manufacturers at a focal length of 50 millimeters for the 35mm (film size) camera.

A basic rule for a normal lens is that its focal length is roughly equal to the film format diagonal — regard-

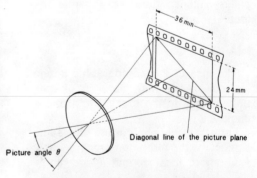

36 min.

24 mm

Diagonal line of the picture plane

Picture angle θ

less of film size. In other words, the diagonal of the 35mm film format is 43 millimeters, the distance measured diagonally across the 24mm x 36mm film.

While it appears that a 43mm lens

would render an image closer to "normal" than a 50mm lens, the choice is really the photographer's. And many professional photographers consider a *35mm focal length* lens as their "normal" lens. That it is *film size* which determines the focal length of a normal lens is worth repeating.

While the 50mm lens is considered normal for the 35mm format, the diagonal of the 2¼ x 2¼ film format is 85 millimeters. As a result, a normal lens for that film format would have a corresponding focal length of *85mm*!

THE NORMAL LENS UNDERWATER

Due to the magnification caused by refraction underwater, any lens used behind a flat lens port of a housing suffers a substantial loss in its angle of view — in effect, extending its focal length.

The standard 35mm, f/2.5 lens used with the Nikonos II camera has an angle of view of 62° on land; coverage which falls well within the definition of a wide angle lens. Underwater, however, the angle of view is reduced to 46.5°. As a result, the wide angle lens is — in effect — changed to a normal lens.

Since this "telescopic" effect applies to *any* lens used behind a flat port, it follows that a normal lens will suffer a corresponding reduction in angle of view becoming, in effect, a slightly *telephoto* lens! Unfortunately, some misguided, beginning underwater photographers shun the normal lens entirely in preference to the shortest focal length, wide angle lens they can afford. As a result, the novice too often exhibits beautifully exposed and crisply focused photographs in which the subject — usually a small reef fish — is represented by a tiny image *lost* in the center of an overwhelming background of blue water. The desired effect is lost and the reason is abundantly clear. Wide angle lenses do

not permit the short subject-to-camera distances required for large image sizes. The normal lens is ideal for small subjects at subject-to-camera distances of three feet or less. The narrow angle of view of such a lens renders a relatively large image size of a fish.

TELEPHOTO LENS

The telephoto lens has a long focal length and like a telescope, produces a correspondingly large image size of a distant subject with little or no distortion.

Contrary to popular belief, the telephoto lens can be used effectively underwater. It can be a particularly useful tool for the fish portrait specialist because its telescopic effect permits the shooting of fish "close-ups" without the photographer getting close enough to spook the fish.

THE WIDE ANGLE LENS

Due to the refraction of light as it passes from the water through the flat housing port into the air space between the camera lens and the port, the effective focal length of the lens is substantially lengthened. Photographic subjects therefore appear larger by one third.

To retrieve the same image size underwater as the lens rendered in air the photographer is forced to increase the camera-to-subject distance. Even in the clearest of water, the greater the distance light must travel . . . the greater the loss of its intensity. Consequently, the further the camera must be moved from the subject, the greater the loss of contrast and degradation of the photograph.

For relatively large subjects at medium (3 to 6 feet) and long (6 to 10 feet) subject-to-camera distances underwater, the wide angle lens is ideal. Wide angle lenses have short focal lengths and the shorter the lens focal length, the more area "seen" by the lens. This can be a most important advantage underwater, when photographing large subjects or under conditions of poor visibility, since the wide angle lens permits short camera-to-subject distances. There is much less water between lens and subject to scatter and diffuse the light rays. Photographs, therefore, suffer little loss of contrast or picture quality. And because of the short focal length of the wide angle lens, more area in front and behind the subject will be in acceptable focus . . . a decided advantage over normal and telephoto lenses.

However, the wide angle lens must be used carefully if the photographer is to avoid the pitfall of losing the subject in a confusing welter of blue water or distracting background material.

DISADVANTAGES

As the angle of view of the wide angle lens increases beyond 60°, certain distortions begin to appear and become progressively more extreme with shorter focal lengths.

Vignetting, for example, produces a sharp image of the center of the subject on the film plane, however, an increasingly distinct loss of sharpness occurs toward the edges of the film format.

Also, subjects which are shot close-up with wide angle lenses are distorted and appear exaggeratedly elephantine in relation to subjects more distant from the lens.

With the more extreme wide angle lenses, fish-eyes or semi fish-eyes which may produce an angle of view up to an incredible 180°, distortions become even more obvious. Most common is barrel distortion in which the subject appears as a circular image while the edges of the film format away from the circular image are black.

These problems result because light reflected from the subject enters the

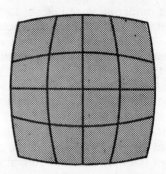

center of the lens as parallel rays and come sharply into focus on the film. Light reflected from points distant from the center of the subject, on the other hand, may be partially blocked or miss the lens entirely.

Another type of optical problem characteristic of the extreme wide-

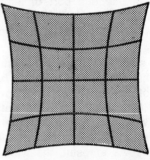

angle lens is *pillow distortion*. It causes straight lines in the photograph to appear to curve toward the center of the film format. The further the line from the optical center of the lens, the greater its apparent curving.

CONCENTRIC DOME PORT

Originally designed for aerial reconaissance photography and later, viewports for submersibles and periscope systems — the principles of the concentric dome have been successfully applied to underwater photographic systems.

The two people most responsible for the successful application of the concentric dome principle to underwater photography are Greg Morris, Vice-President of Seacor, Inc. and Gomer

McNeil, President of the Photogrammetry Division of the Data Corporation. Greg has designed and manufactured water corrected lens systems using the concentric dome principle for a number of underwater housings including Harold Edgerton's 70mm deep sea camera, Bolex, Niko-Mar, the Hasseacor for the super-wide Has-

Seacor 21mm Sea-Eye

selblad, as well as the 21mm Sea-Eye underwater lens.

The revolutionary 21mm f/3.3 corrected lens and Nikon's even more exciting 15mm f/2.8 corrected lens

UW Nikkor 15mm f/2.8

eliminate many of the problems inherent in wide angle lenses used behind a flat port. The concentric dome cancels the effect of the water's refraction by reducing the subject's size and proportionally foreshortening the camera to subject distance. The lens behind the dome port becomes, in effect, a close-up lens.

Gomer McNeil and National Geographic photographer, Bates Littlehales have developed a housing for the 35mm Nikon F which incorporates a large concentric dome. The 180° dome port permits rapid interchanging of a wide variety of lenses (from the 7.5 Nikkor fish-eye to the 135mm Nikkor). Another advantage of this type of housing is its use of the single lens reflex camera and prism reflex sportsfinder. With these, the diver-photographer can achieve nearly perfect focus and composition through the ground glass screen. It is a fact that a well-designed, concentric dome can restore the same full coverage angle the lens produces in air, a significant advantage underwater.

PRINCIPLE OF THE CONCENTRIC DOME

Thus far, we have discussed only the image formed on the film plane as light rays reflected from the subject converge at the point of principal focus *behind* the lens. This image is optically termed the *real image.*

In order to fully comprehend the principle of the concentric dome, it is necessary to understand another type of image . . . the *virtual image.* Hold a negative lens up to your eye! As you look through the lens, an image of the subject appears to form in *front* of the lens. This image is not a real image at all, but an apparent, or virtual image. The virtual image makes the subject appear much nearer and smaller than it actually is. This happens because the negative lens bends and deflects incoming light rays outward forming the apparent image in front

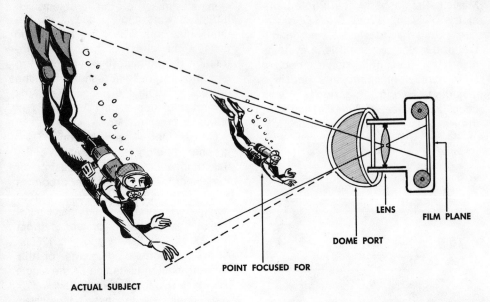

LENS

FILM PLANE

DOME PORT

POINT FOCUSED FOR

ACTUAL SUBJECT

of the lens where the light rays converge. To the eye, however, it appears that the light rays have traveled straight through the lens.

The concentric dome functions in water just like a negative lens, "seeing" an apparent or virtual image. And the virtual image is always formed on the water side of the concentric dome.

Light rays reflected from the photographic subject are refracted first at the water-dome interface and again at the dome-air interface. Upon entering the air space between dome and lens, the rays diverge. Were the photographer to look through the dome, in the path of the diverging rays, toward the subject, it would now appear much smaller and much closer to the dome. The point is, the virtual image forms because the reflected light passes from water — through the dome — and into the air. It is important to note that this phenomenon is a result of the concentric dome and would occur even if there were no camera or lens behind the dome.

Consequently, the lens is focused not on the actual subject, but on the virtual image which, depending on the dome radius, will probably be less than

12 inches from the dome. This water distance of virtual image-to-dome is treated as though it were an actual in-air subject-to-camera distance. And as the camera to actual subject distance is reduced, the camera to virtual image distance is correspondingly reduced.

It is obvious that the lens must be capable of focusing at these short distances. If it is not, the effect photographically is like the person who is unable to focus on close objects. But wearing eyeglasses, which are in effect converging lenses, will enable that person to focus on close-up subjects. The same is true of the lens. If it is unable to focus at the short distances required, extension rings or special close-up lenses commonly called *diopters* (diopter being an expression of measurement of the magnifying power of the lens) must be added. Diopters are commonly used in close-up photography and can be either positive or negative. In this application, positive (converging) diopters would be required.

Finally, to avoid any optical aberrations the optical center of the lens must be precisely aligned with that of the concentric dome.

In summary, only with the corrected port can proper perspective be regained underwater. Not only is refractive distortion eliminated, but there is no significant distortion in the corners of the format or vignetting or reduction in resolution.

THE WET LENS CAMERA

An entirely new generation of undersea cameras designed specifically for scientific work may become the "last word" in lens design for underwater applications. These are the so-called "wet lens" cameras which cancel out the refraction of the water-glass interface described earlier since the concentric front lens element is in direct contact with the sea. Such lenses produce sharp and distinct images to the very borders of the film format.

One "wet lens" mounted in the Aqua Scan camera used by the Naval Photographic Center consistently makes underwater photographs of incredibly fine detail over a 50° x 120° field.

DEPTH OF FIELD

As indicated by the number of beginning photographers who have trouble getting consistently well focused results, it appears there is general lack of understanding of depth of field. It's really quite simple.

Every photographic subject has depth. That is to say, certain components of the photographic subject are closer to the lens than are others. For example, let's say you wished to photograph an approaching train head-on. The engine would obviously be closer to the lens than the caboose. Ideally, you would like to have both engine and caboose — as well as all the cars between — in crisp and distinct focus. In order to do this, the lens must be capable of focusing with reasonable sharpness throughout the subject depth. Depth of field, therefore, refers to the distance between the points nearest to and farthest from the lens at which the images are in acceptably sharp focus.

The sharpest, most detailed photographs are made when the circle of confusion is smallest. Picture "sharpness" therefore, is a measure-

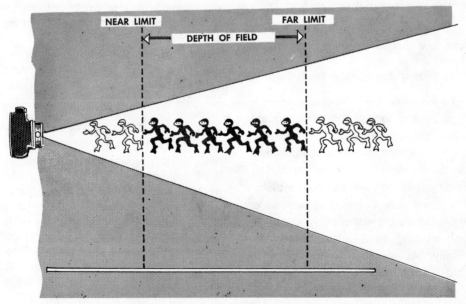

ment of a circle of confusion, which can be from 1/150th to 1/1000th of an inch in top quality lenses.

The human eye, however, cannot distinguish such critical sharpness. The eye actually sees a "zone of focus", that distance before and behind the subject in acceptably sharp focus. The points where this zone of focus begins to lose its sharpness are the boundaries of the depth of field. This obvious loss of sharpness occurs as the circles of confusion grow large enough to overlap one another, causing the blurry focus.

Depth of field, to a large extent, is determined by the effective aperture of the lens and on the distance 'at which the lens is focused. More about that later.

At this moment, the important point is that the focal length of a lens — to a great degree — determines its depth of field. The *shorter* the focal length of the lens, the *greater* its depth of field. For example, because of their extremely short focal lengths, fish-eye lenses provide such fantastic depth of field that focusing is unnecessary. Underwater, the depth of field of a fish eye lens in a Seacor domed adapter ranges from five inches to infinity. Certainly this range of depth of field is a great advantage in underwater photography.

To minimize the hassle of constantly adjusting focus, the wise underwater photographer will use a wide angle lens with the greatest possible depth of field whenever practical. Finding one should be no problem. There are any number of fine wide angle lenses providing sharp depth of field ranging from a few inches to infinity. As we shall learn, depth of field is also determined by: a) lens focal length; b) lens aperture c) subject-to-camera distance.

LENS FOCAL LENGTH

There is an important relationship between the subject-to-lens distance and the lens-to-focal plane distance. The shorter the focal length of a lens, the greater its depth of field and conversely, the longer the focal length, the shorter the depth of field. For example, the 7.5mm fisheye lens provides a depth of field range from *a few inches to infinity.*

On the other hand, by extending the focal length of the W-Nikkor 35mm lens with a 1:1 extension tube, depth of field is reduced to only ¼ of an inch. It is also notable that while the standard Nikonos lens (the W-Nikkor 35mm) has a near focus limit of 2.75 feet, the wider 15mm UW-Nikkor can be focused down to 12 inches.

LENS APERTURE

The loss of image sharpness noticed at the limits of depth of field can be reduced by stopping down the lens diaphragm. By reducing the lens aperture, the points of light reflected by the subject entering the lens are effectively limited. In this manner, the overlapping of the circles of confusion and subsequent image blurring are prevented.

The smaller the lens aperture (f/22), the greater the depth of field. And conversely, the larger the aperature, the shorter the depth of field.

Focus on a subject at a distance of six feet. If the lens is opened up to its largest aperture (f/2.5), the depth of field will be reduced to approximately 12 inches. This can be particularly helpful when foreground or background are dull, disinteresting or distracting. Keep in mind that with such limited depth of field, focus must be quite accurate. The closest part of the subject must be no closer than the near limit of the depth of field since it is usually this part which is most noticeable to the eye.

Nikonos lenses are equipped with depth of field indicators which demonstrate this relationship clearly.

Stop down to the smallest lens opening (f/22) on the 35mm lens, for example, and you find the depth of field — if you had focused on a subject six feet from the lens — would range from 3 feet to 30 feet. In other words, anything within that zone of focus (3 to 30 feet) would be in acceptably sharp focus.

Of course, exposure is also determined by f/stop. The smaller the f-stop, the less light entering the lens. Controlling depth of field by varying the f-stop only works when there is adequate light to insure proper exposure.

Since larger lens openings mean less depth of field, the subsea photographer can emphasize his main subject by throwing foreground and background out of focus.

SUBJECT-TO-CAMERA DISTANCE

It doesn't take long for the beginner to notice that depth of field always seems to be greater beyond the subject of principal focus rather than in front of it. This is simply because at longer subject-to-camera distances, the subject and background appear to the eye to be on the same plane. As the subject-to-camera distance increases, circles of confusion formed by light reflected from both the main subject and background converge almost equally on the film plane. If the principal subject were focused on at a short camera-to-subject distance, only the subject would be sharply focused. Foreground and background would form large circles of confusion because they would converge to form an image in front of the film plane. These larger circles of confusion would appear as a blurred image. Remember, the camera lens focuses precisely on only one camera-to-subject dis-

tance at a time. Therefore, the greater the subject-to-camera distance — the greater the depth of field. And the shorter the subject-to-camera distance, the shorter the depth of field.

Hopefully, it is now apparent that an inter-relationship exists between lens focal length, aperture, camera-to-subject distance and depth of field. All lenses of the same speed and same focal length will produce the same depth of field.

FLARE

Occasionally, the photographer may find his pictures are turning out with poor contrast or faded and washed-out or fogged images or even "hot" spots (extreme cases where a large portion of negative is greatly overexposed). The culprit is almost certainly *flare*. When excessive lighting conditions are present, light may enter the camera and lens not as image-forming reflected rays — but as extraneous light. This light may be reflected around the camera body, bouncing off any bright screw heads or mirrors (as in reflex cameras) before finally reaching the film plane and degrading the film image.

For years, everyone pointed a finger at the lens and surmised, perhaps with some justification, that as light rays passed through the lens elements — part of each ray was reflected back and forth between the lens elements. But lens manufacturers have substantially reduced the flare problem by covering lens elements with multicoatings designed specifically to reduce flare. Recent tests by Modern Photography magazine provide substantial evidence that while the lens may contribute, the culprit is really the camera body. Always use a lens hood, housing permitting, to shield the lens from extraneous light.

APERTURE

Earlier, aperture was described as an adjustable hole which controls the precise amount of light reaching the film when the shutter is opened. The pupil performs essentially the same function for the eye as the aperture does for the camera. And as the amount of light admitted to the eye is controlled by the contraction or ex-

f/22   f/11   f/5.6   f/2.8

pansion of the *iris,* the "iris diaphragm" of the camera — in the same manner — controls the size of the aperture. It lies between the lens elements and is made of thin metal leaves arranged circularly about the aperture. These leaves overlap and can open up or close down the diameter of the aperture.

THE "f-STOP" MYSTIQUE

Any good lens will provide a range of apertures or f-stops, for example: f/22, f/16, f/11, f/8, f/5.6, f/4, f/2.8, f/2, and f/1.4. Lovely, but what does f/22, f/16, etc. etc. mean? There is no real mystery about it. First of all, "f" is a symbol for the word *fraction* and denotes a mathematical relationship.

Don't panic!

The relationship is simply a ratio or fraction between the *focal length* of a lens and the *diameter* of the lens aperture. Perhaps a better way to express it would be that an "f-stop" is a measurement of the lens opening . . . or more accurately, the effective aperture. As a result, a lens with a focal length of 50 millimeters and an aperture diameter (always based on the maximum lens opening) of 25 millimeters would have a maximum "f-stop" of f/2. Or you might say, to de-

termine the diameter of the aperture of any f-stop, simply divide the focal length of the lens by the f-stop number.

For example: 50 ÷ 2 = 25

Simple, isn't it?

Remember, the largest diameter of the aperture corresponds with the lowest f-number. So while f/22 would, in this case, be the smallest aperture diameter — f/2 would be the largest. The f/2 would be engraved on the lens denoting its largest lens opening and correspondingly, its light passing ability or "speed".

THE SPEED OF A LENS

Ordinarily in surface photography, a fast lens is something of a luxury. It adds to the lens cost and the average in-air photographer rarely finds himself in the low-lighting situations which might require a super fast lens. The underwater photographer, however, is a different case. He really does utilize the "fast" lens because of the constantly changing lighting conditions underwater. The "speed" of a lens is a measurement of the intensity of light that reaches the film. The greater the intensity of light, the "faster" the lens.

An excellent indicator of lens "speed" would be: the larger the aperture diameter in proportion to the lens focal length, the greater the speed of the lens.

Summarizing, lens speed is determined by the diameter of the effective aperture — optically termed the "entrance pupil" — and the focal length of the lens.

APERTURE — LENS SPEED RELATIONSHIP

It is logical that the larger the aperture, the greater the amount of light that will pass through it. It would also seem logical, since f/11 is twice the diameter of f/22, that f/11 would pass twice the amount of light passed by f/22. *However, it does not!*

The amount of light passed through an aperture *does not* double with the doubling of the aperture diameter. The fact of the matter is, f/11 will pass four times the amount of light as f/22. A glance at the illustration will

help in understanding why. The areas of the two circles are in proportion to the areas of the two squares. Since the area of the large square is four times the area of the small square, it follows that the area of the large circle is four times that of the small circle. The diameter of the large circle is only twice that of the small circle. As a result, f/11 will pass not twice the amount of light as f/22, but four times the amount.

The amount of light passed through different f/stops would correspond in this manner:

FOCAL LENGTH — LENS SPEED RELATIONSHIP

Lens speed is determined by the effective aperture and the focal length of a lens. Focal length prescribes the distance light must travel to reach the film plane. The longer the focal length, the farther light must travel.

It is no secret, the farther away from a light you are, the greater will be its loss of brightness. Correspondingly, the closer you are to the light, the greater its intensity.

Essentially the same thing happens to the lens. The intensity of light falls off rapidly with the distance it must travel inside the lens. More precisely, the brightness of the photographic image is inversely proportional to the square of the focal length.

Let's apply that to a lens! Say that a photographic image registers a given intensity on a film plane after it passes through a lens with a focal length of 10 millimeters. Substituting a lens with a focal length of 100 millimeters would reduce the image brightness to one-one hundredth (1/100) of the 10mm lens. Conversely, a focal length of 10 millimeters provides 100 times the image brightness of a focal length of 100 millimeters — presuming the aperture diameter is the same.

The phenomenon described is the Inverse Square Law of light intensity and is more fully described in Chapter IX — Electronic Sunshine.

f/1.4	passes twice the amount of light as does . . .		f/2	and passes four times the amount of light as does . . .		f/2.8
f/2	"	"	f/2.8	"	"	f/4
f/2.8	"	"	f/4	"	"	f/5.6
f/4	"	"	f/5.6	"	"	f/8
f/5.6	"	"	f/8	"	"	f/11
f/8	"	"	f/11	"	"	f/16
f/11	"	"	f/16	"	"	f/22
f/16	"	"	f/22			

SUMMARY

The speed of a lens is directly proportional to the square of the diameter (d) of the effective aperture and inversely proportional to the square of the focal length (f). This ratio is expressed as d^2/f^2; or even more simply, d/f.

Therefore, a lens having an effective aperture diameter of 25 millimeters and a focal length of 50 millimeters would be:

$$d/f = 25mm/50mm = ½ = f/2$$

THE SHUTTER

Earlier the shutter was defined as a spring-driven mechanism which controls the precise time that the film is exposed to light admitted by the aperture. And the basic purpose of aperture and shutter is simply to provide the photographer with the means to control light.

To appreciate the tremendous strides in photographic technology, one need only consider this. In the not too distant past, when his camera and subject were ready, the photographer exposed his film plate by removing a light-tight cap from the lens. Then he carefully observed his pocket watch and when he judged sufficient time had elapsed, he simply replaced the cap.

Compare that technique with the modern adjustable camera! Today's camera utilizes a mechanical shutter — or perhaps electronic timing circuitry — which operates in time spans so brief they are measured in units of milliseconds! One millisecond, by the way, is equal to one one-thousandth (1/1000) of a second!

There are basically two types of shutters which satisfy the enormous requirements of today's high speed films and lenses. They are the front (leaf) shutter and the focal plane shutter. Though their principles of design and mechanics are radically different, their purpose is the same.

Each, in its own way, controls the exact time and, therefore, the precise amount of light that strikes the film plane.

THE FRONT SHUTTER

Call it compur shutter, leaf shutter, iris shutter, iris diaphragm shutter, between-the-lens shutter or simply, front shutter. Whichever name you use, the shutter remains the same. And in appearance, it closely resembles an iris-diaphragm.

That is, like the iris-diaphragm it lies between the lens elements. And it is made of five overlapping leaves.

 ALMOST CLOSED

 OPENING

 FULLY OPEN

 CLOSING

These thin metal leaves are arranged in a circle, like the spokes of a wheel, and open or close at the center.

The power drive for the shutter action is generally derived from a spring-loaded mechanism.

When the shutter release is triggered, each blade must swing open, stop for a predetermined time forming a star-shaped aperture, then snap closed again. Interestingly, the shutter speed set on the camera is *not* the actual time the shutter is open. The shutter spring on most modern cameras is coupled with the film advance mechanism and automatically cocked as the film is advanced.

Contrary to popular belief, the speed of a front shutter is not determined by total open time, but by the interval between the half-open and half-closed position of the blades. Actually, it is this interval which exposes the major part of the film. The opening and closing times contribute little to the exposure. For example, a good front shutter set at 1/500 of a second (2 milliseconds) will actually be open 3 milliseconds. The shutter blades will need one millisecond to open fully, another millisecond to completely close, and the shutter will probably be held open for one full millisecond.

Since the blades require ½ millisecond each to reach the half-open and half-closed position, the effective exposure time is 2 milliseconds (1/500th of a second).

Unfortunately, most cameras which use the front shutter do not accommodate interchangeable lenses. However, a few of the more expensive front shutter cameras feature interchangeable lenses which have built-in shutters.

Perhaps the greatest advantages of the front shutter are: 1) its ability to expose the total picture area (angle of view) at the same time, and 2) the ability to synchronize with flash at any speed. Both advantages are particularly important in flash photography.

DISADVANTAGES

If there is any disadvantage to the front shutter — *aside from the lack of lens interchangeability* — it is that most front shutters are limited to a top speed of 1/500 of a second (2 milliseconds).

That does not appear to compare favorably with the focal plane shutter of the Nikon F2 camera, for example, which has a top speed of 1/2,000 of a second (½ millisecond). However, this so-called disadvantage is of little consequence in underwater photography. It would be most difficult to conceive of a situation underwater requiring a shutter speed of 1/2000th.

SHUTTER SPEED

The speed at which a shutter is set determines how long it will be held open and, how much light reaches the film. Shutter speeds are measured in fractions of a second and graduated on the camera so each consecutive shutter speed is either one half (½) or twice (2) as fast as the shutter speed on either side. The following table shows that relationship.

	Fractional Shutter Speed	Commonly Expressed	Twice as Fast As a Shutter Speed of:	Will Pass Twice the Light of:
	1/1	1	—	2
	1/2	2	1	4
	1/4	4	2	8
Slower ↑	1/8	8	4	15
	1/15	15	8	30
	1/30	30	15	60
	1/60	60	30	125
Faster ↓	1/125	125	60	250
	1/250	250	125	500
	1/500	500	250	1000
	1/1000	1000	500	2000
	1/2000	2000	1000	—

Note: It is apparent from the table that the slower the shutter speed, the more light that will reach the film. Assuming the same lens aperture a shutter speed of 1/60th will pass twice as much light as 1/125th, but only half as much as 1/30th.

SHUTTER SPEED RANGE

It is obvious from the table that good shutters offer a range of shutter speeds. The Nikonos II camera, for example, offers settings of 30, 60, 125, 250, 500, and "B". The B (bulb) setting holds the shutter open until the shutter trigger is released.

Additionally, many cameras also have a "T" (time) setting. This setting is for time exposures which require that the shutter be held open for longer intervals. It usually has a locking device so that the shutter can be held open without finger pressure on the shutter release.

THE FOCAL PLANE SHUTTER

The focal plane shutter is used in most 35mm and a growing number of 2¼ x 2¼ single lens reflex cameras. The focal plane shutter consists of

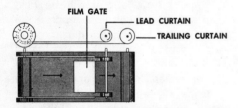

FILM GATE

LEAD CURTAIN

TRAILING CURTAIN

Focal-plane shutter

two (2) parallel, light-tight curtains which travel across the film plane, one a measured time and distance ahead of the other, to form an adjustable slit. The width of the slit (light opening) and its speed across the film plane determines the precise amount of light that will reach the film. The curtains may be all metal like the titanium foil of the Nikon F2 or rubberized cloth like the Pentax Spotmatic. They may travel vertically across the film plane like the Nikonos or horizontally like the Nikon F2.

Each curtain is wound on rollers which are under spring tension. This tension determines the rate of travel of the curtains and varies with the shutter speed selected. The shutter is cocked (spring tensed) by advancing the film advance lever. When the shutter release is triggered, the lead curtain is released first and after a measured time, trips the trailing curtain. The film is exposed to the light passing through the slit, in successive stages, as the overlapping curtains travel across the film plane. Only a narrow strip of the photographic image is rendered on the film at each stage of shutter travel. Since the slit exposes the film in strips, each strip could be considered a separate exposure.

With focal plane shutters, shutter speed is determined by the time each strip is exposed, and *not* by the time required for the shutter to travel across the entire film plane. At a shutter speed of 1/250th, for example, each strip of film will be exposed to light for precisely 1/250th, but the slit may take 1/50th to travel across the entire film plane.

Exposure depends on the size of the slit and the spring tension. The spring tension determines the curtains' rate of travel, the size of the slit and the intensity of light which strikes the film.

Short exposures are provided by narrow slits. The longer the exposure required, the wider the slit must be.

ADVANTAGES

Since the focal plane shutter is inside the camera body and very close to the film plane (instead of between the lens elements as in the front shutter), the camera body uses the same focal plane shutter while accommodating a wide variety of interchangeable lenses.

Through-the-lens focusing is possible, thereby eliminating the close-up parallax problem inherent in twin lens reflex cameras which use the front shutter. And finally, faster shutter speeds are possible since the movement of the focal plane is one directional compared to the front shutter which must swing open, expose, then swing closed again.

DISADVANTAGES

Some photographers object to the curtain movement of focal plane shutters, feeling that the sound is noisy and tends to distract or frighten "skittish" subjects.

The only real disadvantage of the focal plane shutter is that it can only synchronize with electronic strobe at the slowest shutter speeds. This occurs because unlike the front shutter — which exposes the whole angle of view simultaneously — the focal plane shutter does not expose the entire film plane to light at one time.

"STOP ACTION"

The undersea world is a photographic panorama of beauty-in-motion.

Fish glide by. Sea fans and gorgonia wave in a current breeze. Lobster

scuttle quickly across the ocean floor. The barracuda cruises by slowly, eye-balling everything through a jaundiced eye. Like it or not, a large part of the "beauty" divers see underwater must be ascribed to the existence of this state of unending movement. Much of the challenge of underwater photography lies with the photographer's ability to capture these subjects-in-motion on film. A great deal more than mechanical skills is involved. The really good subsea photographer also develops the ability to convey in his photographs a sense of movement and life. Make no mistake! Even the lowly "box" camera with its fixed shutter speed and fixed aperture can make exciting action shots when skillfully handled.

TIMING

Needless to say, one of the magical ingredients for a successful action picture is to be "where the action is".

Being in the right place at the right time is nice, of course. But there is a great deal more to consistently good action photography. The number one rule, in my judgement, is to be absolutely intimate with your camera system. When a once-in-a-lifetime grab shot happens suddenly by, this is certainly not the time to be fumbling with the equipment.

And a lot of very good photographers have blown priceless shots just for that reason. It's hard to forgive yourself, after you've blown a great shot, when you discover that the Nikonos shutter isn't really jammed. You simply forgot to retract the shutter lever safety lock.

Frequently, dramatic photographic opportunities appear suddenly, are there for a fleeting second, and gone. The undersea photographer must develop quick reflexes to capture those moments. He must be constantly alert for possible subjects.

"PEAK" ACTION

There is a precise moment during almost any motion when all movement stops, like the motion-stoppage of a stingray's wings when they are at the very top of their movement . . . just before they begin their downward thrust. In stop-action photography, this moment is called "peak action". It lends dramatic punch to the photograph. But capturing the instant of peak action requires patience and practice. The undersea photographer must learn to anticipate that instant. It's sort of like trap shooting. If you shoot where it is, you'll hit where it was! Your reflexes must be conditioned to be quick. You say you already have lightning quick reflexes? Prove it!

Have someone fold a dollar bill in half (the long way) and hold it half way down between your extended thumb and forefinger (about a 1" separation will do nicely) and release it. If you catch it, you're right. You do have good reflexes. If you missed, better practice.

NOTE: By the way, since your brain already knows the moment of release — releasing it for yourself is no test of your reflexes.

As an event develops before you, the most dramatic moment in that unfolding is also the peak action.

Selecting the correct shutter speed to stop motion is determined by: 1) the direction in which the subject is moving, relative to the camera position, and 2) the effect you wish to achieve.

"FREEZING" MOTION

The time the shutter is open determines not only the exposure, but also to what degree the subject's movement can be frozen. The faster the shutter speed, the faster the movement that can be "stopped." Correspondingly, the slower the shutter speed, the more blurring that will result.

Electronic strobes have flash durations lasting from 1/500 to 1/15,000 of a second and are perfect for capturing stop action. Natural light photography underwater, on the other hand, generally requires large lens openings and slow shutter speeds making motion "stopping" vastly more difficult. It's a good idea never to shoot at a shutter speed slower than 1/60th, but there may come a time when you must. Then it becomes critically important to hold the camera as steady as possible to prevent blurring. One way to gain a little advantage is to use high speed films which give greater shutter speed latitude. A shutter speed of 1/125th is fast enough to capture the exhaust bubbling from a diver's regulator and will freeze most slow swimming subjects.

Fast swimming subjects may be somewhat blurred which can be corrected by adjusting to a higher shutter speed. But blurring is not necessarily an undesirable effect.

BLURRED MOTION

While "frozen" motion has its place, it leaves many people with the impression a dead fish has been posed for the photograph. A more realistic method of stopping action, one which has life and seems to the viewer more as it would really look underwater, is to shoot at a somewhat slower shutter speed to cause some blurring. To create an illusion of motion, the subject must be photographed in a position which conveys the impression that it is moving.

A diver photographed without exhaust bubbles, for example, appears lifeless. Shoot the same picture at a shutter speed of 1/30th and wait till the diver exhales. The diver will register in good detail, but the bubbles will be extremely blurred. Now, shift to a shutter speed of 1/60th. The result is recognizable bubbles, but somewhat blurred conveying an attractive impression of movement.

CONTROLLING BLUR

The direction of the subject's movement relative to the camera position is also of importance as is the subject's rate of travel across the film plane. If the subject is moving directly toward or away from the camera, there is no movement across the film and consequently little if any blur. On the other hand, if the subject is moving at an oblique angle to the film plane, there is image movement which will be recorded on the film as blurring. The most image blurring results when the image travels across the film plane . . . in other words, when the subject path is parallel to the film plane.

PANNING

There is yet another method to stop motion. "Panning" simply means carefully aiming your camera at a moving subject and following its path with the camera, exactly matching its rate of travel. As the subject moves past you, the shutter is triggered, effectively stopping the motion against a blurred background. The resulting photograph will give the impression of movement, and hopefully, the subject detail will be in crisp focus.

TARGET FOCUS

Trying to focus on a fast moving subject is difficult at the surface and nearly impossible in dimly lit waters. So we employ a delightfully simple technique, target focus. For example, a subsea photographer establishes the camera position and instructs his model to drive a diver propulsion vehicle over a designated spot. He simply prefocuses on that spot so when the model is exactly over the spot, he need only frame the subject and squeeze the shutter.

Presto!

Instant focus.

ZONE FOCUS

While target focus provides a more exact point of focus, zone focusing makes use of the depth of field of a lens. The idea is to pre-set the focus for a rather wide zone of focus. Remember, the smaller the aperture — the greater the depth of field. Now, all the subsea photographer need do is sit back and wait until his intended subject is within that zone of focus. Then, he simply triggers the shutter release.

"... it cannot be too strongly emphasized that reflected light is the photographer's subject matter. Whether you photograph shoes, ships, or sealing wax, it is the light reflected from your subject that forms your image."

Edward Weston

Chapter VII.

AVOIDING INDECENT EXPOSURE

To the beginning undersea photographer nothing can be quite as frustrating as discovering an entire roll of film has been ruined because of under or over-exposure. And apparently nothing is more mysterious than the art of determining the optimum exposure for a given set of underwater lighting conditions.

Though the novice may argue the point, the fact is that there really is no mystery to it at all. And after he has been shooting pictures for but a short while, he will find that a substantial percentage of his best photographs have been made at identical exposure settings.

Now, the only problem is how to determine which settings to use to control the exact amount of light passing through the lens and reaching the light-sensitive film.

FILM SPEED

Before we even consider the interrelationship between the different light-controlling devices, we must select a film or, more importantly, a film speed. Although there are other standards of film speed rating, the most widely recognized and used is ASA. This film rating is issued by all film manufacturers and is based on test standards prescribed by the American National Standards Institute. ASA, by the way, is a contraction of the American Standards Association, forerunner of the American National Standards Institute.

The speed of a film indicates its degree of sensitivity to light. In effect, it assigns a numerical value to a film which corresponds with the amount of light required to produce an optimum exposure. Films having low ASA numbers (so called "slow films") require lots of light, while those with high ASA ratings ("fast films") require much less light to produce optimum exposure. The lower ASA numbered films, generally speaking, produce beautifully detailed photographs with extremely fine grain when light is ample. On the other hand, the higher ASA numbered films are used extensively with low light levels or to "stop" moving subjects.

THE APERTURE-SHUTTER SPEED RELATIONSHIP

We have seen how the lens aperture and the shutter, each in their way, controls the light passing into the

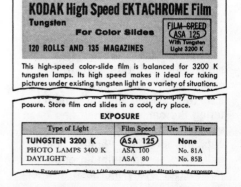

lens. Though their principles of light control are quite different, each must be used in harmony with the other to achieve optimum exposure for a delicate balance of photographic effects depends on their successful inter-relationship.

In the simplest terms, the lens aperture is only an opening through which light flows. The larger the lens opening, the more light that will flow into the lens in a given time. The shutter is really just that . . . a shutter. It shuts off the light from the film. But the shutter is also opened to allow a measured amount of light to pass the lens in a measured time. If there is an abundance of natural light, a small lens aperture can be used with a fast shutter speed. If the light level is low, a proportionally larger aperture is necessary as is a slower shutter speed. But optimum exposure is not our sole interest. We are also concerned with depth of field, stopping action, etc. And so we have adjustable lens apertures and shutter speeds which can be used in various combinations to suit our photographic requirements.

The following are combinations of shutter speeds and lens apertures which would produce equal exposure assuming all other conditions equal:

Shutter Speed		Lens Aperture
1/30th	of a second	f/22
1/60th	" " "	f/16
1/125th	" " "	f/11
1/250th	" " "	f/8
1/500th	" " "	f/5.6
1/1000th	" " "	f/4
1/2000th	" " "	f/2.8

Note: As can be seen from the chart, each consecutive higher f/ stop reduces the amount of light entering the camera by half and each successive higher shutter speed cuts the shutter's "open" time by half. In order to maintain equal exposure, for every increase in aperture there must be a corresponding increase in shutter speed.

LONGER FOCAL LENGTH — LONGER EXPOSURE?

Having learned light's intensity falls off quickly as the distance it travels from its source increases, beginning photographers may become a little confused over the f-stop — exposure relationship. It is true, presuming lenses of equal quality, that a lens with a long focal length requires a proportionally larger aperture to pass the same amount of light as would a lens of shorter focal length. Since f-stops are proportionate to the focal length of the lens, however, exposures are consistent. If a light meter indicates, for example, optimum exposure is f/11 at 1/125th of a second on your normal lens, you can also use f/11 at 1/125th on your wide angle or tele-photo or any other lens of equal quality.

GETTING IT TOGETHER

It may seem at this point that determining optimum exposure is an updated form of alchemy, but don't be misled. After you've settled into the routine of establishing the best exposure — transposing the existing light conditions to just the right lens aperture and shutter speed settings becomes second nature. And it doesn't take too many rolls of film to get to that point.

To a degree, the conditions in which you will be shooting set the ASA range of film types you can use. After that, it is largely a matter of personal preference.

The light meter, when properly used, will provide a range of shutter speed and lens aperture combinations from which can be selected one that will give the desired photographic results. If you are shooting a sweeping panorama of coral reef, for example, you will want great depth of field and, consequently, must shoot at a small lens aperture and probably a slower shutter speed.

When shooting people pictures, on the other hand, you may not be interested in depth of field and consequently can use a large lens aperture and a fast shutter speed. In the final analysis, everything hinges on the photographer's ability to interpret the lighting conditions and transpose this data into optimum exposure. And that really means, among other things, buying a light meter and learning how to use it.

IDEAL EXPOSURE

The light meter, it is true, can tell the photographer how much light is available but it cannot tell him what the "ideal exposure" is. Ideal exposure means different things to different people. Quite honestly, ideal exposure is judged by the appearance of the photograph and even expert judges often disagree, as much as two stops, over whether a photograph has ideal exposure. Generally speaking, light must first be photometrically measured and later — with judgement gained from experience — adjusted to suit the photographer's view of the "ideal" exposure. The distinction being that photometric measurement, while it is probably technically correct, does not necessarily have the appearance that will appeal to an audience.

Don't get the idea I'm putting down the light meter. Quite to the contrary, I never take a camera underwater without one. But, I have also seen enough lifeless photographs to know that the best light meter is only as good as the photographer's knowledge of its capabilities under all lighting conditions. The so-called "automatic exposure" cameras notwithstanding, no light meter can analyze the effects you want to achieve photographically. And if you expect it to, you're going to be badly disappointed.

THE LIGHT METER

To accurately measure the level of light available underwater, the subsea photographer needs a light meter. And, within the limits of your budget, the more sensitive the meter — the more accurate the measurement.

With a housing, most any light meter can be used underwater. And there are a number of relatively inexpensive production housings available for some of the more popular meters. There are other meters, like Sekonic's Marine

Meter, which are designed specifically for underwater photography. They are self-contained, needing no special housing.

Whichever you choose, there are certain desirable characteristics to look for. Among these are accuracy and sensitivity to low light conditions. But it should also be: rugged enough to take an occasional pounding, direct reading so that no fumbling with controls is necessary, and large, easy-to-read calibrations (large enough to be read even at very low light levels.) Light meters, depending on their design, measure either reflected light or incident light. Either type is suitable for underwater photography.

INCIDENT LIGHT METER

Incident-light meters measure the light which illuminates (falls onto) a subject as opposed to a reflected light meter, which measures the amount of light reflected by the photographic subject. Normally, the incident-light meter is held close to the photographic subject and pointed back toward the camera's position. In this manner, the precise amount of light falling on the subject and illuminating it is measured.

REFLECTED LIGHT METER

As its name implies, the reflected light meter is normally held at the camera position and pointed toward the subject. In this way, it measures the intensity of the light *reflected* by the subject. Reflected light meters seem to be more popular with underwater photographers than the incident-light meters.

METER MECHANICS

Most exposure meters use a photo-electric cell to convert the light reflected by the subject into a weak electric current. The strength of this current correlates with the intensity of light on the subject. It is measured by the movement of a pointer across a scale calibrated to give f/stop and shutter speed combinations. The film ASA determines the combinations which correspond to the proper exposure for the lighting conditions measured. And the stronger the intensity of the light measured, the greater the current generated and the wider will be the pointer swing across the meter scale.

Because of the poor lighting conditions underwater, a meter which is sensitive to low light levels is highly desirable. There are some meters, like the Sekonic Marine Meter, which do not use photo-electric cells. Instead, they measure light intensity by setting up a resistance to the incoming light. The current for such meters is supplied by a small mercury battery.

When the meter is switched on, the current from the mercury battery is too weak to measure light because of the electrical resistance. As the light intensity increases, however, the resistance decreases and the current swings the pointer across the scale. Since the meter has its own power supply and is not dependent upon the light intensity for power, much more accurate measurements can be made in extremely weak light.

When shooting natural light photographs, regardless of the type of meter used, the intensity of light to a major degree determines the exposure. And the intensity of light underwater, as we know, is quite variable. To a lesser degree, another determining factor is the reflectivity of the photographic subject. Dark objects absorb light reflecting little and conversely, light objects are highly reflective. These factors, the intensity of light and reflectivity of subjects, are quite important in determining exposure.

The wide range of varying brightness of underwater subjects notwithstanding, it is reasonably fair to categorize them in three classes:

1) bright subjects
2) average bright subjects
3) dark subjects

TECHNIQUES

To make things perfectly clear at the outset, determining underwater exposure with a light meter is far from an automatic procedure. Most light meters are somewhat imperfect devices in that they measure the average brightness of a scene. For example, when a reflected light meter is pointed at the subject, its coverage may be considerably wider than the intended subject. If the overall scene is of average brightness, the exposure indicated by the meter will probably be correct. If the principal subject in the scene is substantially brighter or darker than the background, however, the resulting photograph will be disappointing.

The meter provides exposure settings based on the most influential lighting condition which, in this case, is the overall average brightness of the scene. As a result, the principal subject, which is brighter or darker, will be over or under-exposed. The light meter is also affected by the behavior of light in water. Since the fall-off of light intensity increases as subject-to-camera distance is increased, exposures determined by incident-light meters held at the subject position are only reliable for relatively short subject-to-camera distances. Reflected-light meters, on the other hand, are influenced by the rather even, overall illumination that we find underwater. Consequently, determining ideal exposure underwater is not quite as easy as it is in air and experience with different lighting conditions is as important as using a good meter.

BEING PREPARED

Many factors determine the intensity of light underwater, and the good photographer makes it a practice to continually check the overall illumination with his meter. Subtle factors, like the sun being obscured by clouds, can lower the light level underwater without the photographer even noticing. And should the wind pick up, the surface water may develop enough of a chop to reduce light intensity underwater. And since the diver's eyes adjust automatically to these gradual changes, he may not be aware of them. Even the same photographic subject may give different exposures when the light is measured from different positions.

Invariably, when you enter the water and start down, if you don't immediately take a general light meter reading and adjust your camera accordingly, you'll bump into a lonesome manta ray or some other equally great shot. And by the time you take a light meter reading and set your camera, the subject is long gone.

AVERAGE BRIGHTNESS

When measuring underwater scenes of average brightness with a reflected light meter, the photographer need only aim the meter directly at the subject to get his exposure. What constitutes average brightness? If the picture area is uniformly illuminated, and there are no important areas which vary widely in brightness, the scene is of average brightness.

Unfortunately, in many situations underwater, the intended subjects also include large and small patches of brightness and darkness. The exposure is determined not so much by average brightness, but by the area of greatest importance. If a dark area is more important, like a dark stingray against a bright sand bottom, take your meter reading at close range on the dark area and overexpose the bright area. If both the dark and the bright areas are equally important, take separate meter readings on each area and select an exposure midway between the two.

AIMING THE METER

Always aim the meter carefully, particularly in shallow water where, incidentally, the most colorful natural light photographs are made. Never point the meter toward the surface. Tip the meter slightly downward to avoid picking up false readings caused by extraneous sunlight at the surface. Similarly, white sandy bottoms can cause abnormally high meter readings resulting in underexposure by as many as 2 or 3 full stops. There are several possible remedies for the situation. If

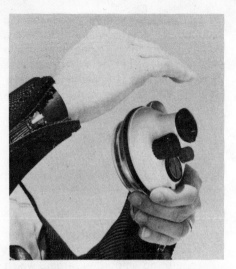

the subject is close enough, you can try shielding the light meter with one hand, thereby reducing its coverage and blocking extraneous light which might otherwise cause a false reading. Or you could take an obviously high reading and arbitrarily open up the lens a stop or two.

SPOT METERING

Most reflected-light meters cover a rather wide field of acceptance. There are reflected-light meters, however, that measure the intensity of light in a rather small area or "spot", without being influenced by the brightness of the surrounding area. On the other hand, most any reflected-light meter can measure the light intensity of a small area if only it is moved close enough to the subject.

CLOSE-UP LIGHT MEASUREMENT

To measure the light intensity of a small area, move the meter in as close as possible to the subject to reduce its angle of acceptance and block the light reflected by the surrounding area. Hold the meter at least within a foot or two of the subject being certain not to cast a shadow over the area being measured.

Close-up light measurement is quite

accurate if you are shooting at short camera-to-subject distances. Due to the scattering and absorption of light underwater, however, the greater this distance, the greater the fall off of light reflected from the subject that actually reaches the film. Therefore, close-up measurements made for long subject-to-camera distances usually indicate higher settings than necessary. The result? Under-exposed photographs.

SUBSTITUTE SUBJECT TECHNIQUE

There are times when you cannot get near enough to the subject to take a close-up reading. In this situation, find a substitute subject of approximately the same brightness. For example, you wish to photograph a diver shaded by a coral outcropping. You can closely approximate the ideal exposure by measuring the light falling on your own hand held in the shade.

Or you may wish to photograph a large moray eel peering from a shaded crevice in a white coral reef . . . but you're not too crazy about holding a meter six inches from his toothy grin. Find a nearby subject of about the same apparent brightness and take your reading. In attempting a long distance meter reading on the moray, which is really the principal subject, the meter would be deceived by the light reflected from the white coral. The meter would, therefore, indicate less exposure than necessary to properly expose the moray.

ADJUSTING WITH JUDGEMENT

Presuming that your meter is accurate, it can effectively measure all sorts of lighting conditions underwater. Its limitations are really only those imposed by the photographer's skill.

In many underwater scenes, the photographer is going to have to take' more than one meter reading.

If the subsea cameraman casually points his meter in the general direction of a subject and takes a reading, the meter will recognize no areas of different brightness. It will, instead, average all the light and indicate an exposure in which all areas, foreground — principal subject — and background, are recorded at essentially the same density. The result, as you might surmise, would be a rather "blah" picture.

If the scene contains equally important subjects of varying brightness, take readings of the darkest and brightest areas. The f/stop midway between those indicated by the meter readings will produce the most acceptable exposure.

As you gain experience and become more and more familiar with the exposures required for different lighting conditions, you will find yourself second-guessing the meter. If the meter should indicate excessively high or low, the readings probably should be rejected and your best guess used instead. Then, check the accuracy of your meter.

CHECKING THE LIGHT METER

Since it is a delicate instrument, sensitive to extreme heat, cold temperature, and rough handling, it's accuracy should be checked regularly.

There are any number of excellent tests which will check out the accuracy of a light meter. Unfortunately, all of them require large, expensive testing instruments. There is, however, one easy field test which can be quickly run on your meter. If you've already checked the suspect meter against another in good working order and found the results wanting, you might try the "f/16 rule."

"f/16 RULE"

The rule basically states that a reasonably accurate light meter should — when aimed at an average subject, on a clear, bright day — yield an exposure equal to the reciprocal of the ASA speed of the film used when the aperture is set at f/16.

In other words, if the meter is set for Kodachrome II film (daylight), ASA 25 — the meter should indicate an exposure of 1/25th at f/16. The reciprocal of 25 being 1/25.

Or, using Tri-X Pan at ASA 400 — the meter should indicate an exposure of 1/400th at f/16. The reciprocal of 400 being 1/400.

If your meter is within plus or minus ($\pm$) one-half f/stop, it is reasonably accurate. If it isn't close, take it to a reputable repair shop.

CHANGING FILM SPEED

Occasionally, despite his best efforts, an undersea photographer may find his photographs are consistently over-exposed or under-exposed. The fault is probably caused by a combination of factors. For example, the ASA values published by film manufacturers are determined in a laboratory using finely calibrated photometric instruments. And these values are not designed specifically for any particular camera or exposure meter. Consequently, the exposure meter may be slightly in error and the shutter, a bit off. And the film emulsion itself may very well be off a little. Ordinarily, such multiple error has minimal effect on the exposures since the errors are just as likely to offset one another and because the film itself offers some latitude. But occasionally, if the errors happen to be in the same direction, they are compounded and a consistent exposure error occurs. The solution? Simple. Just change the film speed for better exposures.

If, when using Ektachrome X (ASA 64) for example, your pictures are *consistently* too light, decrease the exposure by plugging a higher ASA speed into your exposure meter. Set it at 100 ASA (approximately equal to one half f/stop less exposure) or 125 ASA (approximately one full f/stop). Conversely, if the pictures consistently appear underexposed (too dark) try setting the meter at a lower speed (ASA 50 would be approximately ½ f/stop of additional exposure or ASA 32, about one full f/stop).

EXPOSURE BRACKETING

Despite everything you have learned thus far, there is no absolute assurance that you are going to consistently get ideal exposures. Most undersea photographers consider the practice of "bracketing" exposures a sensible and inexpensive method of insuring a photograph.

"Bracketing" simply means taking additional photographs of the same subject at f/stops above and below the f/stop indicated by the exposure meter. Everything else — shutter speed, ASA value, camera-to-subject distance — remains the same. Coupled with the film's built-in exposure latitude (approximately a full f/stop for black and white films and ½ f/stop for color films) bracketing is about the cheapest insurance you can get for a good photograph. Some professional photographers bracket with at least four additional photographs; two at smaller apertures and two at larger lens openings. It really isn't very expensive when you balance the cost of four film exposures against the total costs of getting out on the dive site with a camera in your hands. And it's a lot better than kicking yourself later because the *only* picture you took of that once-in-a-lifetime subject was returned from the processor over-exposed.

BRACKETING SHUTTER SPEEDS

Recalling the relationship between f/stops and shutter speeds, it is clear exposures can also be bracketed by varying shutter speeds. If the exposure meter indicates that the proper settings are — for example — f/8 at a shutter speed of 1/125th of a second, by shooting an additional photograph at a shutter speed of 1/60th the exposure time is *increased* the equivalent of one full f/stop. And by shooting another picture at 1/250th, the exposure time is *decreased* by one full f/stop.

MOUNTING THE LIGHTMETER

If you're the type who doesn't mind things hanging around the neck or dangling from the wrist, banging into coral or dragging through sand, then you will undoubtedly be perfectly content carrying your light meter this way. On the other hand, if you like things uncluttered and safe, you might prefer to mount your lightmeter to the camera-housing.

There are any number of fine, commercially-produced meter holders that can be clamped to most any housing and several designed specifically for the Nikonos amphibious camera. If no commercial holder is available for your meter, one of those adjustable hose clamps used on automobile radiator hoses can be used to secure the meter to the housing or flash arm. By the way, be sure that the clamp is made of stainless steel.

If you're building a clear Plexiglas housing, you might consider mounting the meter inside.

COUPLED THRU-THE-LENS METERING

There are a number of excellent cameras offering coupled through-the-lens metering. Most of these, unfortunately, are unusable underwater. For one thing, too many extra controls would be required. And, to use the meter underwater, the photographer must be able to frame the subject through the small viewfinder prism which would be almost impossible because of the space between his eye and the prism created by the camera housing and face mask.

Built-in meters are just like any other reflected light meter providing exposures which frequently must be adjusted and compensated like any hand-held meter.

AUTOMATIC EXPOSURE CONTROL

There are a growing number of cameras featuring automatic exposure control and, within reason, they can be used successfully underwater. Basically, it is simply a camera with an integrated light meter which, not only measures the incoming light but, automatically adjusts the lens aperture. Many experienced photographers, with some justification, tend to put down such cameras because the automatic function does not allow for manual operation. Since the meter in the automatic control is influenced by the same confusing light conditions the handheld meter encounters, particularly underwater, the chances of less than ideal exposure is probably more likely with the automatic camera.

On the other hand, for average lighting conditions, the automatic camera will probably produce a higher percentage of well-exposed pictures for the beginning underwater

photographer than he would get measuring light intensity himself. And if the automatic control can be over-ridden, the photographer has the added advantage of being able to take multiple readings and adjusting for the preferred exposure.

Viewed in the proper perspective, the automatic camera can be a valuable piece of equipment. It is not presently, however, a sure-fire method of insuring ideal exposures in underwater photography.

METERLESS EXPOSURE SETTINGS

Reluctant as I am to do this, I include a simple method of "guesstimating" underwater exposures only to be used in the event that your light meter should fail and another is not available.

If you are using an adjustable camera and your exposure meter does leak, or if you don't have time to take a light reading when a great "grab shot" comes swimming by, estimate your exposures! The value of the ability to estimate exposures becomes quite obvious should your light meter take a bath and threaten to spoil a dive trip. Of course, if your diving buddy has a meter, you can simply peek over his shoulder. But even if he doesn't, you can still get well-exposed pictures. It's not impossible . . . only a little more difficult.

The instruction sheet packaged with your film has a daylight exposure table which provides the proper shutter

DAYLIGHT EXPOSURE TABLE FOR PANATOMIC-X FILM				
For average subjects, use f-number below appropriate lighting condition.				
Shutter Speed 1/125 Second			Shutter Speed 1/60 Second	
Bright or Hazy Sun on Light Sand or Snow	Bright or Hazy Sun (Distinct Shadows)	Cloudy Bright (No Shadows)	Heavy Overcast	Open Shade†
f/11	f/8*	f/4	f/4	f/4

*f/4 at 1/125 second for backlighted close-up subjects.
†Subject shaded from the sun but lighted by a large area of sky.

For handy reference, slip this table into your camera case.

speed and f/stop combinations for a range of in-air lighting conditions. You need only determine the setting for your surface lighting conditions and increase the exposure one full f/stop for each additional 15 feet of depth. For example, if your camera is loaded with Ektachrome X and the surface lighting conditions are bright and sunny, the film data sheet would recommend a shutter speed of 1/60th at f/16. At a depth of 15 feet, presuming relatively clear water, you would open up to f/11. At 30 feet, f/8 and f/5.6 at 45 feet.

By bracketing your exposures and adjusting with judgement, giving dark subjects more exposure and bright subjects less, you've got a reasonably successful method of "guess-timating" exposures.

This method is by no stretching of the imagination a substitute for a light meter. It is instead an emergency technique which could rescue an otherwise ruined dive trip. Remember, exposures are rarely exactly the same for any two underwater scenes. Any exposure table made for underwater use is, at best, the photographer's best guess of what the exposure should be in a rather rigid set of conditions. All the properties of the water in which you're diving influence the final exposure. And finally, there is no substitute for an accurate light meter and the experience to use it well.

KEEP A PHOTOGRAPHIC NOTEBOOK

One of the best ways the beginning photographer can quickly develop his skills and avoid costly mistakes is by keeping a record of pertinent photographic data. By judicious use of this data, the photographer will become vastly more familiar with the equipment's capabilities and learn the steps to take to improve the quality of his work.

When the beginner has settled on a film that suits his taste, he should make a series of test exposures. Shoot a roll at different f/stops, different shutter speeds, and various combinations of the two. Shoot another at different strobe intensities and different flash-to-subject distances.

Take a slate underwater with you and jot down all the pertinent data about each shot. The data ideally would include: film speed (ASA), lens, filter, shutter speed, lens aperture, subject-to-camera distance, and subject reflectivity (dark or bright). And if you are shooting natural light photographs, the data should also include light conditions. If you are using strobe or flashbulbs, the power setting or type of bulb should be included. Note the details after the shot or have your model hold a slate with appropriate data noted thereon for the shot. In this way, since the data is already recorded on the photograph, there can be no question about what shutter speed or aperture setting was used. Later, after the film has been processed, in all likelihood a few of the pictures will be perfectly exposed. Most will not be, however. You are now ready to analyze the photographs and find the most successful exposure combination. If you have kept faithful record of these shots, you'll be able to quickly determine which settings provided the perfect exposure. This data should then be transferred to your notebook for a permanent record.

Using this information on your next roll of film should produce a majority of well-exposed photographs. If you have kept no records, there is no reason to expect your next photographic attempt will meet with any more success than the first, and it won't!

". . . I take to my darkroom out of affection for others. There I make friends with the world again. There I learn to look away, to focus on infinity. There I play God with film, paper, chemicals, and lenses. There, in the dark, I begin to see."

Aaron Sussman
"The Amateur Photographers Handbook"

Chapter VIII.

FILM AND FILTERS FOR THE TWILIGHT WORLD

Today's underwater photographer has a seemingly limitless variety of excellent films from which to choose. Modern film is of such high quality and so fool-proof, it would probably evoke waves of cynical laughter from Louis Boutan were he to revisit the world today.

In his day, Boutan was compelled to make his own film! His photographic plates (actually glass plates) were carefully coated with light-sensitive chemicals, a job which was not only unforgiving of the slightest error, but also incredibly tedious. Due to the nature of the chemicals, the plates had to be exposed while the chemicals were still wet. I sometimes wonder how many of us would still be interested in underwater photography were we to face the same obstacles which confronted Boutan.

UNDERSTANDING FILM

By now, everyone understands how the lens forms a photographic image at the camera's film plane. The question is . . . how is the photographic image recorded and, equally important, . . . preserved? The answer is *photochemically.*

Film is nothing more than light-sensitive chemicals which undergo a physical change when exposed to light. This concept isn't very hard to grasp if you recall pale-skinned acquaintances who have been tanned or burned at the beach. In a sense, film is like the skin. Both are light-sensitive and will undergo changes when exposed to the sun long enough.

WHAT IS IT?

Most all photography begins with the same basic ingredients: a light-sensitive substance called the emulsion and a transparent material called the film base. The function of the film emulsion is to photographically record visual images.

The film base is a thin plastic material which supports the emulsion. It is strong enough to resist tearing and has excellent optical properties. It is extremely flexible and although 35mm roll film normally has a base thickness of 5.25 mils, the new super-strong polyester film base is only 2.5 mils or less than half. Since the emulsion is only a fraction of the thickness of the film base, it is mostly base you handle when loading film.

The emulsion is a glue-like gelatin in which is dissolved millions of microscopic grains of light-sensitive silver bromide. The emulsion itself has no strength; hence the need for the base.

Film sensitivity depends, to a great degree, on the size of the silver bromide crystals. As a rule, the faster the film — the larger the grains and the greater the loss of sharpness. Con-

95

versely, the slower films produce the greatest sharpness but require much more light.

THE WAY IT WORKS

Everything described thus far applies equally to film for still photography or movies and for black and white or color. For now, however, let's concentrate on black and white film.

When the shutter release is triggered, light floods through the lens aperture and strikes the grains of light-sensitive silver bromide. The film is no longer the same. The light-struck crystals have been altered and rearranged. When the film is developed, the crystals which have been light-struck will be darkened and produce a so-called "latent" image. Only after the film has been "developed" will an image actually be seen.

DEVELOPING THE FILM

After the film has been exposed, it must be processed through a series of important steps. First, the film must be immersed in a bath of "developer" solution. In this step the silver bromide crystals which have been light-struck are split into either image-forming grains of silver or bromide which is poured off with the developer.

After the developer has been poured off and the film washed, the processing is only partially completed. The silver bromide crystals which were *not* light struck are not affected by the developer bath. To remove these crystals from the emulsion, the film is placed in a "fixing" bath — a solution which dissolves the unexposed silver bromide crystals. It is rinsed once again and dried. The film is now "developed."

THE NEGATIVE

Now the photographic image can actually be seen. Unfortunately, it is in negative form. The developed film is, at this stage, a reversed image of the photographic subject. Consequently, the blackest areas of the negative (the most dense accumulations of silver) correspond to the brightest areas of the original subject which reflected the most light back to the film. Conversely, the brightest areas of the negative correspond to the darkest areas of the original subject which reflected little, if any, light. On a black and white negative, therefore, the black or gray areas are actually particles of silver suspended in gelatin.

THE PRINT

A print is a *positive* reproduction of the original photographic subject. Unlike the negative which shows the subject's light areas as black and dark areas as light, the print puts the black and white areas exactly as they were in the original subject. "Printing" is just as much a photographic process as making the original picture and developing the negative.

In a *darkroom,* a measured amount of light is passed through the negative onto a special photographic paper coated with a light-sensitive compound, much like film. As the light passes through the negative, the areas of the positive paper immediately under the darkened areas of the negative will not get much light. Consequently, these areas will appear unexposed or white on the "print". Conversely, the areas under the transparent areas of the negative will be greatly exposed and appear black on the final print.

Once again, like film, the paper must be bathed in developer solution, washed, placed in a fix bath, washed, and dried.

HOW IS COLOR REPRODUCED ON FILM?

Light is color and can be split into all colors of the spectrum. Yet any

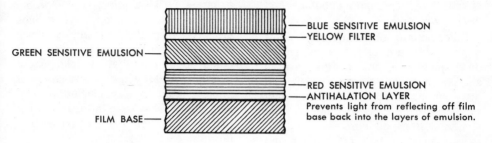

GREEN SENSITIVE EMULSION——

——BLUE SENSITIVE EMULSION
——YELLOW FILTER

——RED SENSITIVE EMULSION
——ANTIHALATION LAYER
Prevents light from reflecting off film
base back into the layers of emulsion.

FILM BASE——

color in the visible spectrum can be reproduced when only three colors — red, green and blue — are used in combination with one another. And this is the basis of color photography.

Most any photographic subject can be reduced to these three primary colors which are registered on film in proportion to their density in the subject. To accomplish this, color films use three separate emulsions superimposed on one film base and each is sensitive to a different color. In addition, a yellow filter separates the top (blue-sensitive) emulsion from the other two emulsions thereby preventing blue light from reaching the lower emulsions. The others are the green-recording middle layer and red-recording bottom layer.

When a color negative film is exposed, chemicals in the emulsions form dye images and silver images in each layer. During film processing, the silver is removed and the dyes formed in each emulsion combine to produce a color negative. When used with color photographic paper with matching emulsions, the result is a color print whose colors accurately reproduce those of the original scene.

The dye colors displayed in the negative are complimentary and opposite to those of the original photographic subject. For example, areas of the subject which are blue will render corresponding areas on the film negative yellow. Likewise, a red area will produce a greenish-blue dye and green will produce a purple dye. This fact

is not immediately obvious, however, since these negative films (Kodacolor or Ektacolor, for example) are coated with an orange-tinted masking dye which masks any imperfections in the emulsion dyes.

In color reversal films the procedure is somewhat different. After the film has been exposed, it is first developed to yield a negative image in each emulsion. Then by chemical processing for some films (E-4 process) or by exposure to strong white light for others, a positive image is produced by dye-forming chemicals as the silver image is bleached out. The resulting transparency, when strong white light is passed through it, projects an image which reproduces the precise colors of the original subject.

It is really difficult to fully appreciate the marvel of modern color film. An incredibly high standard of technological advancement is built into each and every roll of the most frequently used film types chosen by underwater photographers: color negative film and color reversal film.

COLOR NEGATIVE FILM

As is true of black and white negative film, color negative film also produces a negative from which positive prints are made. While certain color negative films can be used underwater to produce beautiful color prints, the photographer is rather limited in his choice of color negative films. He is particularly limited in terms of film speed, ASA 100 being about as fast as he will find.

Color prints obtained from color negative film are, as a rule, expensive and generally lacking the overall sharpness offered by reversal film. It also suffers from all the attendant problems of prints, e.g. finger print smudges from careless handling. It is true, however, both color prints and black and white prints can be made from the color negative. Any film that carries the suffix "color" indicates a color negative film, e.g., Ekta*color,* Koda*color.*

COLOR REVERSAL FILM

The film most widely used by underwater photographers is color reversal film and . . . for a number of good reasons.

Color reversal film, once processed, becomes the final photograph — a transparency which shows a positive image. And it is unlikely to be damaged by careless hands since, unlike prints which must be passed from hand to hand for viewing, a transparency is projected. The final film — be it movie, slide or other form of transparency — is still the original film. Processed, to be sure, but still one and the same. And immediately upon processing, the film can be projected. Also, color or black and white prints can be made from color reversal film.

One of the most significant advantages of color reversal over color negative film is the variety and speeds available. For exceptionally fine detail in macrophotography, the undersea photographer might choose Kodachrome 25 (ASA 25). At the other end of the spectrum, when shooting natural light pictures under low light levels, the photographer could select GAF 500 — a color reversal film with an ASA of 500.

Generally, color reversal films are identified by the suffix "chrome". For example: Ekta*chrome,* Dyna*chrome* and Agfa*chrome.* Even if your films are processed commercially, you will find the processing for reversal film costs about half that of color negative film. And if you aspire to see your photographic work published — and who doesn't? — keep in mind that the picture editors of most magazines prefer transparencies.

Another point worth considering is that reversal film yields *one* transparency per exposure. Negative film, on the other hand, provides *any number* of prints from the same negative. And finally, color reversal films don't provide nearly the exposure latitude that black and white negative films or color negative films offer. Exposure calculations, as a result, must be right-on in accuracy.

COLOR BALANCE (TEMPERATURE)

As his skills and photographic knowledge increase, the serious student of underwater photography soon learns to appreciate the importance of color temperature in getting consistently high quality color photographs. The relationship between the color film and the light source the photographer selects for his subject is most critical. Light is composed of many colors whose intensities can be measured in temperature and expressed in degrees, Kelvin. As can be seen from the following chart, for example, the standard incandescent light bulb is rated at 2600° Kelvin (K) while daylight registers 5500° K. In order to achieve correct color balance, the film *temperature* must be "balanced" with that of the light source.

If film and light are mismatched, an obvious color imbalance results. If the Kelvin temperature of the light source is greater than that of the film, the resulting photograph will have an overall blue cast. As an example, if a tungsten color emulsion is used in day-

COLOR TEMPERATURE SCALE

Kelvin Degree Scale	Color	Light Source	Film
0° K	Black		
1,000° K			
1,800° K	Red		
2,600° K		Electric Light Bulb	
2,760° K		Tungsten Lamp 40 watts	
2,790° K		Tungsten Lamp 60 watts	
2,860° K		Tungsten Lamp 100 watts	
2,950° K		Tungsten Lamp 500 watts	
3,000° K		Tungsten Lamp 1000 watts	
3,200° K	Yellow	Studio lamps	Tungsten Emulsion
3,380° K		Photo-flood	
3,400° K			Photo-flood Emulsion
3,800° K		Clear flash bulb	
4,200° K		Cool white flourescent	
4,800° K		Blue photo-flood (115-120v)	
5,400° K		Blue flash bulb	
5,500° K	White	Daylight	
5,600° K			Daylight Emulsion
6,000° K		Strobe Light	
6,500° K		"Daylight" flourescent lamp Heavily overcast sky	
7,500° K		Lightly-overcast sky	
8,000° K	Blue		
9,000° K		Hazy, lightly overcast sky	
25,000° K		Clear Blue Sky	

light, the picture will be cold and blue. On the other hand, if the Kelvin temperature of the light is less than that of the film, the resulting photograph will have an overall red cast. It is obvious, then, that film and light must be matched and not mixed.

No discussion of underwater color photography is complete without notice given the opposing schools of art and documentary underwater photography. Underwater artists argue that fantastic colors exist underwater and only await the photographer's strobe light to bring them into brilliant reality. Purists contend the world underwater — with the exception only of the shallowest reefs — is a monochromatic world where only green exists. The truth for me lies somewhere between. The gauge of a photograph's success is whether or not it appeals . . . whether or not someone finds it attractive!

LATITUDE

In photography, the term *latitude* refers to the range of exposures (under-exposure to over-exposure) which will yield photographs of *reasonably* high quality. Certain films — some black and white negative films — for example, permit a range of latitude as wide as four full f-stops. While others — color reversal film, for example — yield as little exposure latitude as one-half f-stop.

For the beginning photographer this means to be reasonably assured of acceptably exposed photographs, learn with a wide latitude black and white negative film before moving up to color reversal film.

DEFINITION

The term "definition" describes the clear, crisp, *measurable* sharpness of detail of a photograph. Frequently, in discussions with other photographers and occasionally, in print, the terms definition and sharpness are used in-terchangeably. They are apparently meant to mean the same thing. They do not!

Definition describes over-all image appearance as determined by three rather important factors: sharpness, graininess, and resolving power.

SHARPNESS

Sharpness is a visual impression made by a photograph on the mind of the person studying that photograph. Hence, it is a term used, most frequently, to describe a subjective rather than measurable quality. But it can be and is measurable. Kodak measures the sharpness of all their films and categorizes them as:

LOW: Kodak High-Speed Infrared
MODERATELY LOW: Kodak Royal-X
MEDIUM: Kodak High-Speed
  Ektachrome
HIGH: Kodachrome 25
VERY HIGH: Kodak Plus-X
EXTREMELY HIGH: Kodak Panatom-
  ic X

The *sharpness* of a photograph, then, refers to the crispness of the edges of different detail in the picture.

GRAININESS

This film characteristic describes the detail-destroying and sharpness-dulling action of a photograph caused by the clustering of silver bromide grains during development. Graininess is not particularly detracting in small photographs but it can become devastating as the image is enlarged. The films with the ability to reproduce fine detail are those which have the smallest (finest) silver crystals in their emulsions. In other words, film graininess increases with the coarseness of the silver crystals. Since the most sensitive emulsions (the fastest films) are those with the largest and most rapidly clustering grains, it is logical to assume the faster the film — the greater its graininess. Conversely, the slower the film — the finer its detail. Underwater photographers primarily interested in fine detail will choose slow-speed films. It is important to note that graininess is not limited to certain films. To a degree, it can also be increased or decreased in any film during development.

RESOLVING POWER

A film's resolving power is its ability to distinguish and register fine detail. "Fine detail" refers to the quantity of distinct objects, regardless of size, contained in the subject which can be recorded on film. Certain factors tend to increase resolving power. A film's graininess is a primary factor determining resolving power. Coarse grain films significantly *decrease* resolving power while fine grain *increases* it. Resolving power can be easily measured with a standard test chart. The resolving power test chart is composed of a series of parallel

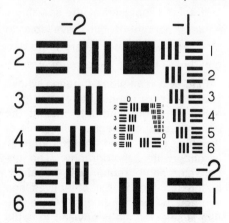

Standard test target of the U.S. Air Force test laboratories

lines of varying length, width and spacing. The objective is to photograph the chart and examine the resulting photographic image under a microscope. At a given magnification, a certain number of separate lines can be counted in a measured millimeter. The

greatest number of individual lines which can be counted in one millimeter determines the resolving power. The human eye, on the average, has a resolving power of approximately 10 lines per millimeter. Film, however, since it is usually greatly enlarged in projection or printing must have substantially greater resolving power. For example, the resolving power of Panatomic-X — a film of extremely fine grain — has been measured as high as 500 lines per millimeter.

CONTRAST

The term "contrast" refers to the diversity of tone in a photograph. In any photograph, color or black and white, each different color in a scene is registered on film as a different *tone.* And these tones are determined by the densities of the silvers and dyes produced on the film. In black and white photography we can get some idea of contrast by comparing the density of the silver clusters on a negative with the transparent areas. The blacker the area, the greater the density of the silver on the negative. Therefore, less light will pass through that area of the negative onto the printing paper. The matching area on the print, as a result, will be *light.* Reversing the process, the more light passed by the negative — the darker the tone of the corresponding area on the print. A vast range of such tones exists between the lightest and the darkest colors of any scene. Ordinarily, in surface photography, a photographer strives for normal contrast. Underwater, however, photography frequently has rules of its own.

Because of the diffused nature of light underwater, contrast tends to be quite low. The more pure blacks and whites in a photograph, the greater its contrast. In black and white photography underwater, however, the loss of contrast gives everything an overall gray appearance. The photographer's eye may be able to clearly distinguish dark shadows and bright highlights. Most film, unfortunately, is unable to detect or capture the diversity of tone that the more perfect human eye is capable of recording.

Degraded contrast is by no means unique to black and white photography. In underwater color photography, the effects can be just as disastrous. Loss of contrast in color photographs transposes into lifeless, dull colors or even worse . . . photographs in which everything appears a uniformly scrubbed-out blue.

To insure good contrast in underwater scenes where shadow and highlight detail is degraded by the diffused lighting, the undersea photographer can:

1) limit his natural light photography to shallow depths (33 feet or less),
2) use strobe lighting,
3) work with high contrast films,
4) use wide-angle lenses to reduce subject-to-camera distance, and
5) employ filters judiciously.

ASA RATINGS

Earlier, ASA exposure index was described as the most widely recognized and used film speed rating system. The "speed" of film begins with an arbitrary value of ASA 1 and ranges to over ASA 8,000. We have already learned how the ASA numerical value grows larger in proportion to the film's sensitivity. As an example, Kodachrome 25 has an exposure index rating of ASA 25. This rather slow film is highly desirable where there is plenty of light and lots of detail to be recorded. On the other hand, a film such as GAF 500 offers a reversal film which can be "pushed" to a film speed of ASA 1,000! Such a film can be most useful when natural lighting conditions are poor. The advan-

tage is, of course, that the underwater photographer can shoot at faster shutter speeds and smaller lens apertures. Consequently, a faster film should provide greater depth of field and sharper image resolution. However, it is at best a compromise since "fast" films appear excessively grainy and lack the sharpness of the fine grain "slow" films. On the other hand, anytime a film with an ASA rating twice that of another film is used, the aperture is stopped down one full f/stop. For example, Panatomic-X film is rated at ASA 32. Ektachrome X has an ASA rating of 64, twice that of Panatomic X. Since it is twice as fast, it needs only half the light. So when the ASA rating is doubled, optimum exposure requires one less f/stop.

SELECTING A FILM

It is not surprising that the beginning underwater photographer is, at first, totally confused by the seemingly endless parade of films available to him. And worse luck, there is no single "best" film for underwater use.

Film is a marvelous creation whose characteristics cannot be learned over night. The following will aquaint the underwater photographer with some of the film types used most frequently in underwater photography. The underwater photographer will, hopefully, match the film to his objectives and average water conditions. Once the film is selected, he is advised to settle down to serious picture-taking and experimentation. Only in this way, by learning one film and learning it well, can the beginning underwater photographer really fathom the limits of a film's capabilities as well as that of his camera. Hop-scotching from one film to the next will not increase his storehouse of photographic knowledge. It will only serve to confuse him.

WHAT ARE THE REQUIREMENTS?

Let's begin with the most obvious. Are you going to shoot in black and white or color? Frankly, I like the idea of black and white for beginners for a number of reasons:

1) There is a full range of ASA film speed ratings from which to choose;
2) Black and white film, as well as processing costs, is substantially less than that of color;
3) Black and white films are relatively easy for the beginner to process at home;
4) Black and white films generally offer greater latitude and are consequently more forgiving of inexact exposure settings than color films.

On the other hand, black and white photographs have their limits. There is the obvious advantage of capturing the fantastic coloring of the underwater world when shooting color film. Also, color slides can be shown to large audiences.

Other factors the underwater photographer should consider are the average visibility of his diving waters, the average depth at which he routinely operates, and the average light intensity. All these factors tend to reduce the amount of natural light underwater and the deeper, darker and dirtier the water, the faster the film you will need.

At least in the beginning, the novice underwater photographer should work with natural light photography, developing his skills and acquiring the "feel" of his camera. Afterwards, he can and should move up to strobe photography. Strobe photography is really the only way colors can be recorded in deep, dark water where natural light photography can only produce pictures which are overwhelmingly blue or green. If you're going to operate in relatively shallow water (a good place

to be if you're going to shoot fish portraiture), use a relatively slow film and take advantage of the bright light penetration to produce finely detailed photographs. Where the operating depth is deep and natural light penetration minimal, the photographer will do well to select a film with high inherent contrast, high ASA film speed, and, if color film is used, high color saturation.

Summarizing, beginners are encouraged to start with black and white photography for the reasons given and it is well that they do. But don't get the impression it is any easier to make good black and white photographs than it is color photographs. Under certain circumstances, it can be considerably more difficult.

For example, the underwater photographer must always be extremely careful when composing black and white pictures to avoid placing his principal subject against backgrounds with the same basic colors. As a result of such poor composition, black and white film will record the subject color and background color in essentially the same tones with little or no contrast between them. The advantage of beginning with black and white film is this. The underwater photographer starts his career with an immediate concern for good composition. And this is a trait which, once developed, will pay handsome dividends throughout his photographic career.

BLACK AND WHITE FILMS

PANATOMIC-X (ASA 32)

Of all the black and white films, I favor this very slow, exceptionally fine grain film. It yields extremely sharp negatives capable of an exceptionally high degree of enlargement. Natural light pictures, however, must be limited to the shallowest and clearest waters. Panatomic-X is an excellent close-up film for registering fine detail with either natural or flash lighting.

PLUS-X PAN (ASA 125)

Plus-X is a highly favored general purpose film. It is a fine grain film capable of a high degree of enlargement. Its medium speed (ASA 125) permits natural light photography within the safe depth range of sport diving and will still produce very sharp pictures in clear water. Plus-X offers greater contrast and greater latitude than does Panatomic-X. Generally, it is a good overall film for underwater work in natural lighting or with strobe.

TRI-X PAN (ASA 400)

This film has been the black and white film standard for years for deep, dark or dirty waters where its high speed produced photographs where slower films could not. Tri-X can be "pushed" (photographer's vernacular for over-development) to obtain film speeds as high as ASA 2400, although with a very noticeable increase in graininess. Tri-X is a relatively fine grained film which is best used under extremely low natural light levels or where high shutter speeds and good depth of field are required. It offers excellent latitude and works as well for flash as for natural light conditions.

ROYAL-X PAN (ASA 1250)

Royal-X Pan is only available in 120 film size. This extremely high speed film has been used successfully to produce photographs deep underwater under incredibly low natural lighting conditions. It is, understandably, a grainy film with poor enlargement characteristics. It is a special purpose film which should be used only where lighting conditions are inadequate for finer grained films.

HIGH SPEED RECORDING FILM TYPE 2485 (ASA 8000)

Type 2485 is an extremely fast, panchromatic film which is particularly red sensitive. This film is coarse grained and tolerates practically no degree of enlargement. But if grain is unimportant, here is a film that can literally "take the picture, if the photographer can *see* the subject." There is no question that Type 2485 can produce speed and reasonably low contrast. However, it is grainy and lacks definition and detail. Interestingly, processing can be matched to a variety of effective speeds: e.g. *8,000; 6,500; 5,000; 3,200;* or *800.*

Naturally, the lower the speed, the better the film characteristics. For example, definition, tone and latitude are all improved and there is less graininess. To shoot and process Type 2485 at ASA 8,000, the photographer must use Kodak's #857 developer at 95° for 3½ minutes. Other developers may be used for the slower film speeds.

COLOR REVERSAL FILMS

KODACHROME 25 (ASA 25)

This inherently slow film provides, far and away, the best detail of all the color reversal films. It also offers virtually no grain, excellent color balance, relatively low contrast, and high resolving power. Kodachrome 25 produces incredibly sharp images even when enlarged and, because of this extreme sharpness, it is a favorite film for close-up work and particularly macrophotography. It is a daylight film color balanced to 5500° K. Consequently, it can be used with either strobe or blue flashbulbs. It has good latitude, in the range of plus or minus one f-stop. The color saturation of Kodachrome 25 renders excellent skin tones, firey reds and oranges, natural greens and yellows and also provides sharp detail between shadows and highlights. Its obvious shortcoming is its slow speed which makes it a rather poor choice for natural light shooting underwater at long and medium distances.

KODACHROME II, PROFESSIONAL (ASA 40)

Professional (Type A) is the tungsten light counterpart of Kodachrome 25 daylight. While it is designed to be used with photoflood lamps (3400° K), it can also be used in daylight by shooting through a #85 filter at an ASA of 25.

AGFACHROME 64 (ASA 64)

Agfachrome 64 is a medium speed, moderately fine-grained film which produces deep color saturation, excellent warm colors and sharp detail. It is a lively film which favors slightly "warm" colors and tends to give skin tones a magenta cast. It provides a latitude of at least plus or minus one stop. It is a good film for natural light photography and since it is balanced for 5500° K, it can be used with strobe or blue flashbulbs as well. For additional data on AGFA-CHROME 64, contact:

AGFA — GEVAERT
275 North Street
Teterboro, New Jersey 07608

DYNACHROME 64 (ASA 64)

Dynachrome 64 provides extremely soft color saturation. Reds and oranges are rendered well and excellent greens and blues brighten this gentle film. It is balanced for 6000° K (approximately daylight) and provides about plus or minus one stop of latitude. It is only a fairly sharp film due to its moderate grain. But if your preference goes toward soft and quiet color saturation, Dynachrome 64 is certainly worth a try. For additional data on Dynachrome 64, contact:

3 M Corporation
2501 Hudson Road
St. Paul, Minnesota 55101

EKTACHROME-X (ASA 64)

Probably the most widely used film underwater, Ektachrome X is an extremely fine grain film which produces a sharpness second only to the Kodachromes. As a result, it is a versatile underwater performer producing excellent artificially-lighted close-ups of fish or panoramas of divers and reefs. Ektachrome X provides high color saturation. The colors of Ektachrome X photographs appear more genuine, more like those actually found underwater than any other color film can produce. Brilliantly warm reds and oranges, bright greens, true yellows all help to give available light underwater pictures a little extra punch. Ektachrome X is balanced for 5500° K and offers a latitude of plus or minus one f-stop. For additional data on any Kodak film contact:

Eastman Kodak Company
Customer Service Division
343 State Street
Rochester, New York 14650

GAF 64 (ASA 64)

GAF 64 is a sharp and most forgiving film which offers the photographer rich color saturation and an exposure latitude of approximately plus or minus 2 f-stops. This low contrast, medium-fine grain film yields rich reds and oranges, rich and deep blues, soft greens and excellent pastel colors as well. It is color balanced for about 6000° K. For additional data on any GAF film contact:

GAF Corporation
140 West 51st Street
New York, New York 10020

KODACHROME 64 (ASA 64)

Kodachrome 64 was the first color reversal film to be packaged for the pocket instamatic film size 110. It is also available in standard instamatic 126 and 35mm formats. Kodachrome 64 is an extremely fine grain film offering a high degree of sharpness and deep color saturation. Reds and oranges are extremely warm and greens are excellent. Kodachrome 64 has overcome the tendency of its predecessor, Kodachrome X, toward muted and slightly violet blues which gave underwater photographs a subdued color quality. The new film provides brilliant color rendition and reduced contrast. It is balanced for 5500° K and offers an exposure latitude of plus or minus one f-stop.

FUJICHROME R 100 (ASA 100)

Fujichrome R 100 is a medium-fine grain film that offers good sharpness, and interesting color saturation. Reds are brilliant, blues and oranges are rich, skin tones are excellent and greens are natural. Fujichrome R 100 has an exposure latitude of about plus or minus one f-stop. It is balanced for 6000° K (approximately daylight). For additional information on Fujichrome R 100 contact:

FUJI Photo Film USA, Inc.
350 Fifth Avenue
New York, New York 10001

HIGH SPEED EKTACHROME (ASA 160 — DAYLIGHT)

High Speed Ektachrome has been a natural light favorite of underwater photographers for years principally because of high inherent speed and its ability to be pushed to even faster speeds. Small apertures and fast shutter speeds can thereby be used even in the dim natural light as deep as 150 feet in clear water. But there is a penalty you must pay for that speed. The penalty is in the graininess (which precludes close-up work with this film), low contrast, poor resolving power and low color saturation. This film tends toward blues and greens generally favoring the cooler colors. It is balanced for 5500° K and has an exposure latitude of about plus or minus 1½ f-stops. High speed Ektachrome is an ideal film for low natural light levels where a high speed color film is required. But don't expect fine detail and deep color saturation.

GAF 200 (ASA 200)

The color rendition of GAF 200 is almost identical to GAF 64 although somewhat warmer. Reds and oranges are favored by this film and rendition is great. Skin tones are somewhat red and greens are rather brown and dull. GAF 200 is a coarse-grained film yielding medium sharpness. It can be a useful film underwater where small lens openings or high shutter speeds are necessary for low light levels. It is color balanced for 6000° K and has an exposure latitude of approximately one f-stop.

GAF 500 (ASA 500)

GAF 500 is a fast color film which can be made even faster. With special processing the film may be shot at ASA 1000! While GAF 500 does show visible grain, image sharpness is adequate. This film is color balanced for 6000° K (approximately daylight) and offers an exposure latitude of approximately plus or minus one f-stop. GAF 500 provides only fair color rendition. Colors, particularly the reds and oranges, are contrasty and muddled. Skin tones are noticeably reddish. Greens are dull and disinteresting; blues are violet favored and even the whites are slightly magenta.

COLOR NEGATIVE FILMS

KODACOLOR X (ASA 80)

Kodacolor X is a fine-grained, all-around sharp film offering wide exposure latitude for the beginning underwater photographer (as much as plus or minus two full f-stops). It is balanced for daylight and can be used with either strobe or blue flash. Color prints or transparencies can be made from the negative. Although the film has inherently good color balance, it is particularly sensitive to blue, as is true of any color negative film. The color renditions are determined by how the negatives are printed.

EKTACOLOR PROFESSIONAL, TYPE S (ASA 100)

Type S is considered a professional photographer's film requiring professional processing. Like Kodacolor X, it is also balanced for daylight and can be shot without a filter with blue flash or strobe lighting. Ektacolor is the favorite of underwater photographers who need a color negative film. Unlike Kodacolor X which tends to be blue-sensitive. Ektacolor is particularly sensitive to reds . . . a definite advantage in underwater photography. Again, the color characteristics of Ektacolor depend, to the greatest degree, on how the negative is printed.

KODACOLOR II (ASA 80)

This is a relatively new film designed for, and presently available only in, 110 (pocket instamatic) size. Kodacolor II appears to be an ideal snapshot format producing color prints which appear equivalent in every respect to its big brother Kodacolor X. It is balanced for daylight and has good exposure latitude. Color rendition depends on the printing of the negatives. The only shortcoming appears to be the inability of this film to survive any appreciable degree of enlargement due to its coarse grain.

OTHERS

There are a number of other negative films currently available and each has a unique and individual color personality. To find the one that appeals most to you, examine them all. Others you might check out are Fujicolor N-100 (ASA 100), Dynachrome Color Print Film (ASA 64), Agfacolor CNS (ASA 80), and GAF Color Print Film (ASA 80).

EXPERIMENTAL FILMS

Perhaps the most frequently overlooked source of films suitable for underwater use are the films used in aerial reconnaissance. Among the more desirable features of such films are good color saturation, high contrast, fine grain and high speed.

The GAF Corporation has developed an experimental film which has been extensively tested off Andros Island in the Bahamas. The interesting aspect of this color film was that it had no blue-sensitive emulsion! As every underwater photographer knows, blue light is the least absorbed and most scattered light underwater. Hence, the pronounced blue cast to most underwater photographs. Blue light accounts for the "haze" underwater in addition to the distinct loss of contrast suffered by underwater photographs.

Still another factor that causes blue light to impair underwater photography is the fact that in color-corrected optics, image sharpness is somewhat reduced because blue light does not focus at precisely the same point as do red and green light. As a result, GAF's new film minus a blue-recording layer seemed a logical move to optimize underwater photography. The results of the tests were sufficiently successful to indicate that many underwater photographic problems are well on their way to being solved. "Haze" was substantially reduced; contrast improved; and image sharpness in color-corrected lenses restored.

KODAK EKTACHROME INFRA RED AERO (TYPE 8443)

For an unusual underwater effect, try one of the most unusual films available to the underwater photographer: Ektachrome Infrared Aero. Water is rendered in rose tones and green plants or animals take on mind-blowing reds, violets and purples. The film does require special processing which most any custom processing house can easily handle. Or, if you know your way around an E-4 processing kit, you can develop it yourself. Just keep in mind that all infrared film must be processed in *absolute darkness.* That means *no* safelight, too! Type 8443 differs from conventional color film in that its top layer is not blue-sensitive, but infrared-sensitive. Consequently, infrared light is recorded in the upper emulsion. Upon processing, no dyes are formed in the upper or middle layers. The red-recording layer does form a magenta dye which gives the shots their unique coloring. Rate at ASA 100 for underwater use.

KODAK EKTACHROME AERO TYPE 8442 (ASA 160)

Type 8442 is an aerial color film (reversal) which has been successfully used underwater. Significant among noticeable improvements over more common films is the vast improvement of contrast and color saturation. On the other hand, Type 8442 doesn't offer much latitude (a characteristic common to any high contrast film) and exposure calculations must be within ½ stop of optimum exposure. Also, Type 8442 does produce excessive graininess.

KODAK AERIAL COLOR FILM SO-121 (ASA 64)

Although this film is available exclusively on a large quantity basis -(350 rolls minimum), perhaps you know somebody in the aerial mapping business who might sell a roll. It may very well be worth your while for the deep color saturation and excellent contrast it offers. Graininess with SO-121 is no greater than any conventional fine-grain film. Photographs made by strobe lighting produce startling colors because of the high contrast characteristic of the aerial films.

MOVIE FILM

KODACHROME II (ASA 25)

Kodachrome II is an excellent choice of film for underwater movie-making. It is an extremely fine-grained film with excellent resolving power. It offers the same fantastic color saturation as its Kodachrome still film equivalent. It is balanced for approximate daylight and has an exposure latitude of about plus or minus one half (½) stop. It is available both in super 8 and 16mm formats.

EKTACHROME 160 MOVIE FILM (ASA 160)

Kodak's High Speed Ektachrome movie film is fast (it's rated at a full 2 stops faster than most other super 8 color films) a characteristic which is particularly desirable in underwater movie making. When used with one of the new Kodak X-L movie cameras (with the 230° shutter) the film gets 40% more exposure. This compared to more conventional super 8 camera and film combinations means a gain of as much as 4½ f-stops. Ektachrome 160 provides good image sharpness, moderate grain, and excellent color balance. It is currently only available in super 8 format.

EKTACHROME COMMERCIAL 7252 (ASA 16 DAYLIGHT; ASA 25 TUNGSTEN)

Type 7252 is a fine quality film widely used in professional underwater movie making. It is a fine-grain film offering good resolving power and excellent color balance. It is balanced for 3200° K and has an exposure latitude of plus or minus one f-stop. It is a moderate contrast film rated at ASA 25 (tungsten). However, it may also be used for daylight shooting with a 80 filter, which lowers its speed rating to ASA 16.

EKTACHROME EF (7242 TUNGSTEN OR 7241 DAYLIGHT)

Type 7241 Daylight has a speed rating of 160 ASA and Type 7242 Tungsten, ASA 125 (ASA 80 with 85 filter). Type 7242 is color balanced for 3200° K. Color rendition is surprisingly good despite the film's speed. Grain is poor, however, as might be expected. The film's resolving power also leaves something to be desired. On the other hand, the photographer is offered moderate contrast and excellent exposure latitude, in the range of plus or minus one and one half (1½) f-stops.

HOW TO DEVELOP

One of photography's most oft-cited truisms states that "you can't get good prints from lousy processing." And it is certainly true that the very best film is only as good as the processing it receives.

There is much to be said in favor of the photographer who processes his own film. He can't help but learn his film more thoroughly than the photographer who sends his to the corner drug store for processing. And interestingly enough, it's really quite easy. Just a few of the benefits of processing your own film are:

1) *Immediate Results:* Shoot the pictures and process them immediately. There is no waiting for the lab to send them back. This is a terrific asset when you're visiting an unforgettable dive area.

If you should blow a shot, you know it immediately and can go out and retake it. If you must wait until you return home to find out, the opportunity may never again present itself.

2) *Control:* Equally important, the photographer who does his own film processing can insure a consistency to the quality of his work.

All films have some latitude and commercial film labs attempt to strike a median of processing and printing which will be acceptable to the majority of their customers. Unfortunately, you may not necessarily be part of the majority which finds the results acceptable! Therefore, you are compelled to use a custom lab which will process to your exact specifications, if you can find one which is reliable and does quality work. And when you do, you will *pay* handsomely for such service.

As long as you have to go through all this trouble, why not process the film yourself? You can increase contrast, for example, by using a high contrast developer like ACUFINE or simply extending the immersion time in normal developer by about 15%. Still another way to improve contrast is through the use of high contrast photographic paper when printing the negatives.

"FORCED" DEVELOPMENT

Sometimes a film which produces only moderately successful photographs when developed normally, will yield outstanding results when the developing process is "pushed" or forced developed. For example, Ektachrome X which is normally rated at ASA 64 may be up-rated and shot at ASA 600 if "forced" development is used. High Speed Ektachrome normally rated at ASA 160 is routinely rated and shot at ASA 400. Fujichrome R 100 normally rated at ASA 100 can be pushed to ASA 250 and still give good results. As a matter of fact, Kodak even offers special processing mailers for the forced development of Ektachrome X (pushed to ASA 160) or High Speed Ektachrome (pushed to ASA 400). Certain custom processing laboratories also provide the same service and frequently offer even faster "pushed" speeds.

Since Ektachrome X and High Speed Ektachrome enjoy such wide spread popularity, it seems incredible that any underwater photographer who shoots with one or the other would not process them himself. The Kodak E-4 processing kits are extremely easy-to-use (believe it or not) and allow for normal development or "pushed" development of either Ektachrome X or High Speed Ektachrome.

Actually, "pushing" simply means increasing the film's time in the developer over normal development time or, as mentioned earlier, through the use of high-activity developer. For example, to rate Ektachrome X at ASA 600, increase the first developer time by 100%. Normal first developer time is 6 *minutes.* To force process to ASA 600, use a first developer time of 12 *minutes.*

Incidentally, even Fujichrome R 100 can be processed with the same chemicals contained in the E-4 kits. GAF 1000 (Type 2575) normally rated at ASA 1000 is usually immersed for 12 minutes in the first developer. By simply increasing the time to 21 minutes, the film can be exposed at ASA 2000.

DRAWBACKS?

"Pushing" is not without its drawbacks, however. As is true of almost everything else, a gain in one direction usually involves a compromise or "trade-off" in something else. Generally, when a film is "forced developed", contrast increases, graininess increases, exposure latitude de-creases, and a shifting of color occurs. In the Ektachrome films, the color shift is slightly toward the green.

KODAK'S E-4 PROCESS

In days gone by, one need only casually mention that he processed his own color film and he was immediately rewarded with a respect and esteem which was totally out-of-proportion to the skills he possessed. The implication was that anyone — outside of Kodak — who could process color film was in a league with the devil and had mastered the black arts.

The fact of the matter is that Kodak's E-4 process is surprisingly easy to master. The E-4 processing kit (½ gallon size) is comparatively inexpensive (capable of processing approximately 14 rolls of 36 exposures). This breaks down to an average cost of just a penny or two per slide.

The E-4 Process consists of 13 steps:

1. PRE HARDENER
2. NEUTRALIZER
3. FIRST DEVELOPER
4. FIRST STOP
5. WASH
6. COLOR DEVELOPER
7. SECOND STOP
8. WASH
9. BLEACH
10. FIXER
11. WASH
12. STABILIZER
13. DRYING

That may seem like a lot but, this whole process only takes 55 minutes! The only really critical factor in the entire E-4 Process is the temperatures of certain of the processing chemicals. The allowable temperature range of the majority of these is between 83° and 87° F. And a temperature range of 4 degrees is quite easy to maintain.

On the other hand, the prehardener temperature must be maintained within plus or minus one-half a degree of

85° F. Maintaining such a critical temperature would seem to be difficult but, fortunately, it is not. The processing chemicals are simply immersed in water baths to stabilize chemical temperatures. All that is needed is a good photographic thermometer and access to hot and cold water. Once the water is stabilized to a particular temperature it is easy to maintain at that temperature.

TIMING

Since the time for each of the thirteen processing steps is different — and fairly critical — the would-be home processor should have some reasonably accurate method of timing each step. Most do-it-yourself color film processors use standard darkroom timers. I've tumbled onto an idea that is much more convenient and kind of fun.

I use a cassette tape player with a 55 minute tape recording. Instead of the old timer reminding me whenever it is time to change steps, a recorded message does the job.

As the tape begins, for example, the recorded voice begins a check-list of all materials and equipment required for the processing. Once processing begins, the recording keeps precise track of time and warns me accordingly. For example, the voice will announce:

"Once the film is in the prehardener it must remain in that solution for three minutes. Get ready . . . Now!" When the film must be agitated, the tape reminds me to agitate. Near the end of the three-minute period (about 10 seconds before the end), the tape instructs me to begin draining the film so that one processing step is ended in time to begin the next step on schedule. Between instructions, the tape entertains me with whatever musical selection I've programmed into it. For home processing, tape your own timing recording.

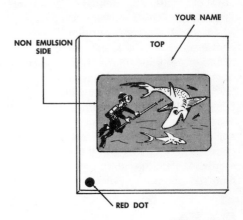

To avoid the usual problems inherent in handling slides, simply mark them with rubber stamps.

FILM CARE

It seems appropriate at this point to mention a few thoughts about the care of film, a point many photographers seem to carelessly overlook. Since its role is one of equal importance, it would seem logical that film deserves the same attention and care that your camera gets. With more and more divers making exotic diving trips to the tropical waters of the South Pacific, Indian Ocean and Caribbean, it is important to appreciate the destruction that can be worked on film by heat and humidity.

KEEP FILM OUT OF THE SUN

If you want to render your film useless, just load your camera and leave it on the car's dashboard — or in the trunk — or glove compartment. If the climate is hot and humid enough, just leaving the film in the camera too long will ruin it.

KEEP IT COOL

As soon as possible after exposing, have film processed. Exposed color films are especially susceptible to high

111

temperatures. Black and white films are not nearly as delicate as color films and will generally keep well when stored for short periods in a dry, cool area. For best results, when possible, store your film — unexposed or exposed — in a refrigerator. Due to the temperature sensitivity of the film emulsions, however, the film should be allowed to warm again to ambient temperature before it is exposed. If not, the rated film speed may not give the cold film sufficient time for optimum exposure.

FILM AGE

All films are marked with an expiration date. If the films are used after that date, it is quite likely the resulting photographs will be disappointing. Beware of out-of-date film even at bargain prices. All fresh film should have an expiration date of at least one year from the date of purchase.

PROTECT FROM MOISTURE

Moisture can damage film. Consider the fact that the silver bromide grains are suspended in *gelatin,* which is not water-resistant, and you can appreciate the need to keep film dry. For short periods of time, package film (exposed and unexposed) in a plastic bag containing several packets of silica gel, an excellent moisture desiccant.

Store your films in a cool dry place. There are two things that are absolutely incompatible, *cameras* and *water.* Handle the camera carelessly when loading or unloading; get a few drops of salt water in the camera and you'll be amazed at the extent of the corrosive damage. If you are wearing a wet suit, be careful that drops of water don't trickle from the sleeves into the camera. Dry yourself carefully to avoid water drops. If possible, change film below decks to avoid the possibility of sea spray damaging the camera. Film is light-sensitive and must be shaded from light to prevent exposure. Always load and unload cameras in shade and never, never in strong, open sunlight. If you must remove your camera from the housing to take pictures in a boat, take this sensible precaution. Place the camera in a plastic bag and rubber-band the bag to the lens barrel thereby exposing only the lens. Protect the front element of the lens with an inexpensive ultra-violet filter.

THE AIRPORT X-RAY THREAT

The airlines are understandably concerned about the danger of skyjackers as well as the threat of bombs planted aboard aircraft. After the initial hysteria calmed down, a highly successful deterrent program was put into effect by the security forces at the airports. The most effective deterrent, from the standpoints of actual discovery of guns and other weaponry and also as a psychological deterrent, is the surveilance equipment used by airport security. These include metal detectors, magnetometers, and to a great degree, X-ray machinery. In fact, the airlines have spent more than $5 million on X-ray machines.

While the various metal detection apparatus has no effect on film, that is — unfortunately — not the case with X-ray machinery. In fact, Kodak has issued a warning to air-travelling photographers to the effect if their films are subjected to examination by X-ray machinery or Fluoroscope which are not *"film-safe"* there is a strong possibility their films will be ruined. Earlier, most airlines denied using X-ray equipment to scan luggage for weapons. And a lot of travellers mistakenly presumed that the gun-type metal detectors used to check-out boarding travellers were X-ray machines. However, metal detectors cannot damage film. But X-rays can. And X-ray equipment is used.

HOW X-RAYS DAMAGE FILM

In the event film is exposed to X-rays, the most characteristic effect of such exposure will be *radiation fogging,* a general overall hazing or obscuring of the film. This can happen to unopened film cassettes as well as exposed film or, for that matter, film in the camera. Generally, the more sensitive (faster) the film, the greater the extent of the fogging. Film in a camera may record images of the camera's internal components while the film may register shadow images of film cassettes or spools or even sprocket holes.

PREVENTION IS THE BEST PROTECTION

The best insurance is to make certain your film is not X-rayed. That transposes simply into carrying your film with you. Anytime your film is in luggage and out of your sight and control, there is a possibility it may be X-rayed. If you must ship your film ahead, buy lots of commercial warning labels and paste them all over the film containers. They should read to the effect:

WARNING

Protect From:
X-Ray
Fluoroscope
Radioactive Material

PHOTOGRAPHIC FILM

The trouble is, no one is legally bound to comply with the orders of these labels. Take the time and trouble to carry the film with you. Advise the passenger agent that you are carrying film and naturally don't want it X-rayed. An ounce of prevention . . . . . .

FILTERS UNDERWATER

It is surprising how many underwater photographers completely overlook the use of filters to improve the quality of their pictures. Some underwater photographers contend that while filters are excellent aids in correcting unbalanced color problems when shooting "in-air" photographs, they tend to produce colors the diver really doesn't see and are, therefore, undesirable for underwater photography. The other school of thought argues that judicious use of filters will aid the underwater photographer enormously by:

1) *Adding contrast to black and white* pictures. In the processing stage especially, filtering can be done like mad. Since there is no lack of light, the film can be exposed as long as desired. When the subsea photographer shoots his film through *a filter,* he can get his desired contrast through normal processing.

2) *Correcting color* degraded due to "scattering" and selective absorption underwater, color photographs made with natural light (in all but the shallowest of waters) tend to be tinted in blue or green. Color correcting filters can be used under such circumstances to improve color rendition.

The fact of the matter is, when properly used, filters can improve your photographs. But the degree of color correction or contrast is, to a large extent, a matter of taste. Invest in a filter (preferably a CC30R if shooting color or a K-2 if shooting black and white.) Don't rush out and buy all kinds of filters. There are hundreds and contrary to what you might have heard, or read, they aren't cheap. Since they are made in various sizes, be sure to get the one that fits your lens. Take the time to shoot a few rolls of film through a filter. In describing the function of filters, all the material presented stands equally true for still photography as well as for movies.

WHAT IS A FILTER?

A filter is basically a disc of dyed glass or gelatin which is slipped over or screwed into the camera lens. The dye used to color the glass or gelatin is determined by the color that is to be *filtered*. Filtering, of course, means the removal of something undesired, by passing through a filter. A photographic filter removes undesired wavelengths (colors) of light by absorbing them. As an example, a yellow filter appears yellow because it is made up of red and green light whose wave lengths are transmitted freely through the yellow filter and are seen by the human eye as yellow. Blue light, however, is absorbed. A red filter absorbs the wavelengths of blue and green and passes that of red. Consequently, the filter appears red.

Picture this! Arrange three slide projectors side by side so that their projected images overlap somewhat. In projector "A", place a red slide and project it on the screen. In projector "B", place a green slide and project. On the screen, where the red and green overlap, we now see *yellow*! Place a blue slide in projector "C". Where the blue overlaps the red and green, *white* is produced! But where the blue overlaps only the green we have a new color, cyan . . . a greenish-blue. And where the blue overlaps only the red, we find magenta . . . a purplish red.

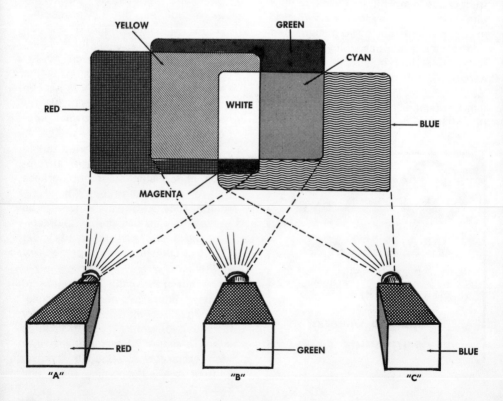

COLOR FILTERS

Since color films are made basically of three color emulsions (cyan, magenta, and yellow) color compensating filters control only red, blue and green light. Incidentally color compensating filters are routinely designated by a coding. For example, a CC30R filter is a favorite among underwater photographers and is used frequently to enrich normal skin tones and overall color rendition in natural or strobe lighting. The "CC" prefix designates a color compensating filter. The number 30 indicates the filter's density. And the "R", of course, the filter's color. It is evident that filters come in varying strengths and different colors.

EXPERIMENT

The point is the underwater photographer must be an innovator and he must be willing to experiment. Inexpensive gelatin filter is available in sheet material which can be cut small enough to cover the rear elements of most any lens. Experiment with filters of varying intensities! The higher the number, the greater the density of the filter. CC filters are also available in yellow (e.g. CC30Y) or magenta (e.g. CC30M).

What color filter should you use? The rule-of-thumb is, if the water you are shooting in is blue or green, use a CCR (red) filter. The idea is to minimize the "blue haze" effect caused by scattering and absorption by filtering out the greens and blues and passing only warmer colors. If the waters appear yellow, use a CCM (magenta) filter. But, this is only a rule-of-thumb. Experiment, Experiment, Experiment!

What determines the density of the filter you should use? When shooting natural light photography, the answer is water clarity and depth. In shallow water, color-compensating filters are really most effective. Since the color spectrum is lost with increasing depth, the filters become increasingly less effective. At some point underwater, depending upon the water clarity, sun angle, and other less important factors, the reds and yellows will have been completely absorbed. At this point, the filter is worthless. It cannot restore a color which, under the illumination of natural light, no longer exists.

FILTERS AND FLASH

The truth is that exciting photographic subjects are to be found at all and any depths. Therefore, the undersea photographer has only one choice if he is to restore some reasonable approximation of normal color balance to his pictures at depth. He must use artificial light.

When the undersea photographer brings the strobe close to his subject, very likely he still could use a color compensating filter. Once he introduces a powerful source of light, the photographer uncovers more red, blue and green light which must be effectively filtered to increase picture contrast or improve color rendition.

FILTERS FOR BLACK AND WHITE FILM

When shooting black and white film underwater, in natural light, contrast can be dramatically increased with the use of filters. Yellow filters, and occasionally red filters, can produce photographs in which the differences between similarly shaded areas is emphasized into distinct shades of gray which might otherwise photograph as disappointingly lacking in detail. The cause of the failure of the film to register detail is the blue "haze" of the underwater world. Yellow filters like the K-2 or red filters (CC30R) can, to some degree, neutralize this blue haze and increase contrast.

All filters, as a general rule, absorb (subtract) light. The greater the density of the filter, the more light it will absorb. As an example, a filter tends to absorb light reflected from the subject if the subject is the same color as the filter. Naturally, the more reflected light absorbed by the filter, the less which strikes the film. Such areas register as light areas on the film negative but quite dark on the print. By the same token, light passed by the filter registers as a dark area on the negative and light on the print.

And the greater the density of the filter, the greater the loss of image-forming, reflected light. This can be a particularly significant problem underwater where, when shooting natural light pictures, the photographer has little enough light as it is. A good choice for black and white photography underwater is the K-2 yellow filter. Although not as strong as the red filters, a K-2 does increase contrast noticeably without subtracting a lot of light. The questions you must ask yourself are:

1) How much contrast does the film require? and
2) How much light is available?

FILTER FACTORS

Filters, by absorbing light, tend to keep some of the light from reaching the film. As a result, there is an increase in exposure required. And the greater the filter density, the greater the loss of light and the greater the increase in exposure necessary to properly expose the film. To determine exactly how much an increase of ex-

posure is required for a particular filter, the photographer must first know how much light the filter absorbs. Manufacturers carefully measure the light-absorbing characteristics of their filters and assign a *filter factor* to each filter. This *filter factor* corresponds to the amount of light absorbed by a particular filter. For example, a K-2 yellow filter has a filter factor of 2 when used with Panatomic-X film. This means a K-2 filter will absorb (subtract) one half the light reflected by a scene. Correspondingly, the filter factor may be said to be the number of times the exposure must be proportionally increased to compensate for the light loss. For a filter factor of 2, the lens aperture must be *opened one full* f-stop *or* the shutter speed must be reduced by half.

Still another method is to divide the films speed (ASA) by the filter factor. For example, Panatomic-X has an ASA of 32. If a photographer were using a K-2 yellow filter to improve contrast, (32 divided by 2 = 16) his new ASA rating would be 16 and he would take light-meter readings as though shooting a film rated at ASA 16.

THE CHEATERS

If you are forgetful or simply don't want to be hassled with filter factors, just cut out a gelatin filter (the same as you are using over your lens) and tape it over the light gathering end of your exposure meter. In this way, the meter will automatically compensate for any light-absorbing by the lens filter and provide reasonably correct exposure settings.

". . . magnesium flash lamps. What a devilish device these were! A spark would ignite the magnesium, which would then explode with a blinding flash, after which a dense, acrid, white smoke would fill the air."

Aaron Sussman,
"The Amateur Photographer's Handbook"

Chapter IX.

ELECTRONIC SUNSHINE

Only recently has the underwater photographer really embraced the idea that the underwater kaleidoscope of color can really be captured on film, even at the deepest depths, with the subtle use of flash. Light from electronic strobe or flashbulbs allows the diver to photograph at virtually any time of day or night in the deepest and darkest of waters. The use of flash permits photographs which would be impossible in natural light. The intention is not to knock natural light photography. In fact, there are situations where it can't be beat. But if the diver attempts to photograph reef fish inside a coral cave or in the dark shadows of an overhanging coral ledge, he will learn, unhappily, there are simply some things that cannot be done without artificial light.

Under conditions of low visibility or in deep dark water, flash may indeed be the only way to get the photograph. In many cases, the lush colors of coral may be hidden behind dark shadows even in the clearest of waters. Even warm skin tones are frequently filtered out underwater, a problem which is easily corrected with fill-in flash.

FLASH VS. NO FLASH

Soon the neophyte subsea photographer discovers conflicting opinions exist among professional and expert about the manner in which underwa-

ter scenes should be photographed to insure optimum color rendition. The "no flash" element, the so-called purist, may feel that the underwater world must be photographed exactly as it appears to the diver's eyes. They argue that the diver sees his subjects in a world of subdued green or blue light, where all colors appear to divers and fishes alike as pale, hazy and unstriking!

At the other end of the spectrum are the die-hard "flash-all-the-time" proponents who, conversely, use artificial light with *every* photograph. As is true of most things in life, the truth lies somewhere between the extremes. Personally, I can't imagine doing much photographic work underwater without some source of added light. But it must be done subtly. Too many undersea photographers use flash like a sledge hammer giving the overall photograph a harsh glare. The artful undersea photographer is the one who uses the flash so delicately, it is difficult to tell whether the picture was exposed by natural light or flash. In this chapter, we shall consider the different light systems available to the underwater photographer and try to remove a bit of the mystery about them.

SYNCHRONIZATION

In flash photography, the strobe or flashbulb must ignite and produce its maximum intensity at the precise instant when the shutter is fully open. This exact timing or "synchronization" is absolutely fundamental to proper exposure. Some cameras can sync at only the slowest shutter speeds while others will sync with flash at any shutter speed. When using flashbulbs, for example, the right shutter speed for a given shot depends on your choice of flashbulbs. Different flashbulbs produce different intensities of light and, accordingly, produce different flash periods. As an example, a close-up picture can be made of a moving fish using 6B flashbulbs. A shutter speed as fast as 1/500th could be used to "freeze" the rapid motion of the fish. Such shutter speeds could be used with a 6B bulb. Other types of bulbs (M or MF bulbs, for example), would not work at the faster shutter speeds. It is most important that the photographer select a flashbulb which provides synchronization between shutter and maximum light intensity.

FOCAL PLANE SHUTTERS

Earlier, both the advantages and shortcomings of the focal plane shutter were described. Focal plane shutters only sync with electronic flash at the slowest shutter speeds. As we have seen, in focal plane shutters the film is exposed to light passing through a slit formed by overlapping curtains. As a result, the film is exposed in successive *stages.* In terms of natural light photography, the rule is: the shorter the exposure, the narrower the slit. The longer the exposure, the wider the slit.

The fact of the matter is, with electronic flash, the shutter speed has no bearing on the length of the exposure. With an electronic flash duration of approximately 1/1000th of a second, presuming conditions of little or no available light, the film will receive no more light if the shutter were to remain open for 1/30th of a second. Using a fast shutter speed because

of the super short "burn time" of a strobe, would only produce a narrow slit of exposed film. The width of the slit of exposed film corresponds to the width of the slit formed by the shutter curtains at the instant the flash ignited. This unhappy situation occurs with sufficient frequency to make the beginning photographer — and occasionally even the more experienced — all the more careful when checking shutter speed settings in the future. It takes approximately 1/50th of a second for the width of the slit to open larger than the film gate. In other words, 1/50th of a second before the shutter curtain has completely opened and exposed the entire film frame. It is obvious, then, a light with a "burn time" of only 1/1,000th of a second could only expose a *part* of the photograph. Most adjustable cameras are equipped with an "X" synchronization, which makes "instant" electrical contact with the strobe, causing it to reach and release peak intensity at the precise moment the shutter is fully open.

With respect to flashbulbs, it should be obvious that the intensity and duration of the flashbulb must be sufficient to match the travel of the focal plane shutter slit across the film plane. If not, the flashbulb will be burned out before the picture is fully exposed. Focal plane shutter cameras are additionally equipped with "FP" setting. Special "FP" (Fast Peak) flash bulbs quickly achieve maximum light intensity before the shutter opens and hold it for as long as the focal plane shutter remains open (1/50th of a second or 20 milliseconds).

Front shutter cameras are equipped with a "M" setting (Medium Peak) which is designed to trigger the flashbulb approximately 16 milliseconds sooner. The Medium Peak flashbulb also achieves peak intensity before the shutter opens, but has less than half the burn time of a FP bulb.

FRONT SHUTTER

The mechanism of the front shutter was described in detail earlier. Its greatest advantage, in flash photography, is its ability to expose the whole picture area *simultaneously*. As a result, it will expose film much faster than would a focal plane shutter. Front shutter cameras, correspondingly, use flashbulbs with considerably shorter "burn time."

Since shutter speed is synonymous with exposure time, it can be described as the length of time the shutter passes light to the film. Front shutter cameras usually have only two sync settings, "M" and "X". The "M" setting (Medium Peak) as mentioned earlier, delays the shutter opening long enough for the flashbulb to build up to peak intensity. "M" sync permits the use of most any flashbulb or flashcube at shutter speeds up to 1/500th of a second. The "X" setting is for sync with electronic strobe at virtually all shutter speeds. The strobe — when used with the front shutter — is not ignited until the shutter is fully open. This is possible because the strobe's light is both instantaneous and of very short duration.

ELECTRONIC FLASH

From the beginning of photographic history, photographers have searched and hoped for a so-called "repeating flashbulb", a bulb which could be used over and over again. In the frantic fifties, Doctor Harold Edgerton of the Massachusetts Institute of Technology developed and perfected the stroboscope — an electronic flash capable of making exposures up to the fantastic speed of a millionth of a second. Since then, every photograph made in the reaches of the deep ocean has been lighted by Doctor Edgerton's strobes.

HOW IT WORKS

The stroboscope or strobe produces a high intensity flash of light of extremely short life. So short, in fact, the flash duration of most underwater strobes is between 1/500th and 1/2,000th of a second. Basically, the strobe consists of a high voltage power supply, one or more capacitors, a triggering circuit and a flash tube. The function of the strobe is basically to convert high voltage direct current into light. For the larger underwater strobes, the high-voltage power supply is usually a standard 510 volt dry battery or a rechargeable nickel-cadmium

power pack. The capacitor(s) is charged by the high voltage batteries to certain limits and this electrical energy is stored by the capacitor until the strobe is flashed. The number of capacitors in the strobe is determined by the range of light outputs desired. Ordinally, if the strobe provides a range of 50, 100, or 150 watt seconds of light output, there are flash capacitors with 50, 100, and 150 watt seconds of energy inside the strobe. The triggering circuit discharges the capacitor when the camera shutter release is depressed.

The flash tube is actually a very tough, gas-filled glass lamp. The sealed tube is filled with Xenon and may be straight, coiled or "U"-shaped. Basically, when the camera shutter release is tripped, the electrical energy stored in the capacitor is rapidly applied between the electrodes on each end of the flash tube and the capacitor discharges abruptly into the flashtube. As the high intensity current passes through the flashtube, the Xenon gas glows brilliantly producing a very brief light impulse of extreme intensity.

LIGHT OUTPUT RATINGS

Before shopping for a strobe, it might be wise to have an understanding of how strobes are rated. Perhaps the most misleading term in light output ratings is the "watt second". There are a number of strobes on the market which are rated in "watt seconds". Manufacturers refer to them as a "200 watt second" strobe or a "50 watt second" strobe, for example. The strobes are usually quite good, but the potential buyer really has no idea from a watt second rating as to the real *light output* of the strobe.

The watt second is actually a measurement of the electrical energy which can be stored in the strobe capacitor. A true measurement of light output of a strobe must take into account the light field of the flash reflector, the reflector's light disbursement and efficiency and the electrical energy actually discharged into the flash tube (less the energy that is converted to heat and dissipated).

Perhaps a more accurate unit of measurement of a strobe's light output rating are beam candle power seconds (BCPS). The original Edgerton 50 watt second underwater strobe, for example, has a light output rated at 1,500 BCPS. The Sea Star III underwater strobe has power settings of 50 and 100 watt seconds. At 50 watt seconds it has a rated light output of

1250 BCPS and at 100 watt seconds, 2500 BCPS.

The most realistic measurement of light output, in my judgement, is the strobe's rated *guide number.* Once the strobe's guide number has been established by exposure test, any other exposures — in similar conditions — will be correct if the flash-to-subject distance is divided by the underwater guide number. As a result, a unit with a rated guide number of 100 would be twice as powerful as a unit with a rated guide number of 50.

The question is what do you want a strobe to do? The greater the subject-to-camera distances at which you photograph, the more powerful the strobe you will need. At long distances a 200 watt second strobe won't be too powerful. On the other hand, if macro-photography is your field almost any of the small strobe units will fill your needs admirably.

POWER SUPPLY

In general, there are three types of power supply used with strobe units. Small strobes may use conventional flash light batteries. Many use 510 volt or 300 volt standard dry batteries. An increasing number of underwater strobes are using rechargeable nickel cadmium battery packs. Whatever the power supply, it should provide, as an absolute minimum, sufficient power for one day's diving. And if it does

use rechargeable battery packs, they should be able to recharge fully overnight. If you intend to use a strobe quite a lot (meaning you're going to shoot pictures by the hundreds), it would be wise to investigate the rechargeable battery packs.

THE READY LIGHT

Each time the strobe is fired, the capacitor empties and must be recharged before the strobe will fire again. Better strobes are equipped with a small "ready" light that either emits a steady or flashing light when the capacitor is recharged and ready to be fired. This recycling time varies from unit to unit but usually takes between 1 and 6 seconds. The advantage of the ready light of course is that you don't release the camera shutter before the capacitor is fully charged and the strobe is "ready" to fire. A lot of wasted shots can be avoided by observing the ready light.

It is not without its shortcomings, however. Some strobes have an evil habit of showing a lit ready-light *before* the capacitor is fully charged. A recommended procedure is to wait a second or two after the ready-light comes on before shooting. Another problem with some strobes is that in bright natural light, it can be difficult to see if the ready light is lit. If your strobe displays this characteristic, shield the ready light from the natural light and get as close to it as you can.

LIGHT BEAM COVERAGE

One disadvantage common to most strobes designed for in-air photography is that they fail to produce a beam sufficiently broad to cover the field of the most popular wide angle lenses. Fortunately, the new generation of strobes designed specifically for underwater use feature dome ports and adjustable light beam coverage. This is particularly important if the photographer is using a lens like the super wide angle 15mm Nikonos lens or the 21mm Sea-Eye lens. These lenses cover such a wide field that conventional strobes can only cover a small part of the subject area. The Sea Star III, with a light beam coverage of 100°, covers a circle six (6) feet in diameter at a light-to-subject distance of 2½ feet. The Subsea Mark 150 has an

adjustable light coverage ranging from 90° to 150°! The undersea photographer is best advised to know the underwater coverage of the widest angle lens he uses underwater and use a strobe whose light beam coverage matches.

STROBE SHUTTER SPEEDS

Because the entire field of view is exposed simultaneously, pictures taken through a front shutter will be synchronized with electronic strobe regardless of shutter speed. Electronic flash will *not* synchronize with a focal plane shutter at all shutter speeds. Such shutters sync at 1/30 or 1/60 and, with some of the newer cameras, even at 1/125th of a second.

Shutter speed actually has little effect in exposing the film at considerable depth or any time or place there is little or no appreciable existing light. The flash duration of 1/500 or 1/1000 of a second is adequate for the job. If there is existing light illuminating the scene, however, the slow shutter speeds required by the focal plane shutters can cause double images or blurring on the film. This occurs because the high speed flash of the strobe exposes the film once. But due to the slow shutter speed (1/60 for the Nikonos) a second photographic image of the subject is formed by the strong natural light before the shutter closes. Consequently, the subject is exposed twice and the resulting photograph may very well show overlapping images which are particularly "fuzzy" if the subject was moving.

STROBE COLOR TEMPERATURE

The light emitted by the electronic strobe's Xenon-filled flashtube closely approximates that of daylight since the color temperature of each is in the 6000° K range. Strobe light does, however, tend to be a little blue.

STROBE VS. FLASHBULB

To begin with there really is no perfect lighting system. The strobe has its advantages and disadvantages as does the flashbulb. The strobe appears to be quite expensive initially, but a good BC flash gun is not cheap either. And flashbulbs, contrary to the popular misconception, are *not* cheap.

The Mark 50 strobe, for example, will ignite at least 2,000 flashes from a $12 battery. 2,000 flashbulbs would probably cost in excess of $400. If you are only an occasional underwater photographer, the investment in a strobe might be too expensive to be an advantage over flashbulbs. If you intend shooting hundreds of pictures each year, however, pure economics dictates that the strobe is the vastly better investment. What the photographer is really concerned with is the cost per flash.

Other advantages favor the electronic flash. The greatest nuisance with flashbulbs is that they must be carried around underwater and are bulky and buoyant. If the photographer doesn't carry enough bulbs down on the dive, he has the added worry of running out. And carrying a large number of buoyant flashbulbs around underwater can be a problem. Additionally, flashbulbs are fragile, break easily or may implode and flood at deeper depths. And, of course, they frequently misfire.

Still another disadvantage of flashbulbs is the time wasted changing bulbs and carrying the expended bulbs back to the surface. (Please take your bulbs up with you. It is really bad form to litter the sea with your flashbulbs.) Also, when you are changing bulbs, you must take your eyes off your subject and undersea subjects have a way of disappearing the moment you take your eyes from them.

Summarizing, flash guns are relatively inexpensive initially and there is an advantage to using different types of bulbs for different lighting effects. Over the long haul, however, the strobe will pay for itself many times over. The strobe is expensive initially, but by averaging that cost over a two year period the photographer soon sees that electronic flash underwater is his best buy.

Today's undersea strobes are extremely reliable, and though some pack a potentially dangerous voltage, they are well insulated and quite safe. While most of the larger strobes seem a little awkward in air, underwater they are well balanced and easy to handle. Another advantage of the strobe is that without a lot of extra equipment, one strobe can be used to provide lighting for two or more different cameras while underwater. The cam-

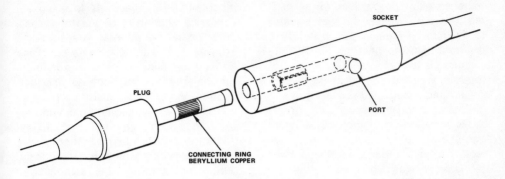

PLUG

SOCKET

PORT

CONNECTING RING
BERYLLIUM COPPER

The E.O. connector design is based on a cylindrical plug and socket with the the socket having an opening at the side. As mating occurs, water and other foreign matter are wiped out of the socket to provide a leak proof seal. It is pressure balanced and takes no more effort to plug and unplug at depth than at the surface

eras and strobe must simply be equipped with quick disconnect electrical fittings, like the Electro-Oceanic, E. O.-fitting.

THE FLASHBULB

As we have seen, in all but the shallowest depths, artificial light is nearly indispensable for underwater color photography. To be completely honest, I must confess to a wholehearted prejudice in favor of the electronic flash for a lot of reasons that make a great deal of sense. But I'll be the first to admit there is much to recommend the lowly flashbulb, particularly if you are only an occasional underwater photographer.

PRO

Obviously, the initial cost of an underwater flash gun is comparatively lower than an underwater strobe. It is light in weight and causes very little drag underwater. It is safe to handle with no dangerous voltages to worry about. And the variety of flashbulbs available does give the equipment a versatility in light intensities and color temperatures.

CON

Flashbulbs can obviously be used only once! As a result, flashbulbs get rather expensive if you shoot a lot of pictures. The larger flashbulbs have been known to implode under increasing water pressure at depth. Though I have never had a flashbulb implode by itself, I have cut my thumb severely while attempting to remove a recalcitrant flashbulb from its socket. After the bulb has ignited it is particularly weak and may well shatter in the photographer's fingers as it is removed. Conventional wet suit gloves or canvas work gloves offer no real protection at all since the glass fragments will pierce either with equal ease. Louis Marden of National Geographic has in the past used a special steel mesh glove made for meat cutters. If the larger flashbulbs are used, be sure that the flash socket has a bulb ejector. The miniature bulbs are really quite rugged by comparison.

The corrosion of the flash socket contacts is a constant problem as is the corrosion of the adaptors for miniature bulbs often used with the Nikonos flash. When the corrosion is bad enough the bulbs misfire and the result is a missed shot. Of course, the batteries can also go dead in the middle of a dive. Unless he has a tester to tell him how much punch is left in the batteries, the photographer's only recourse is to replace the batteries before he begins a photographic dive.

Carrying bulbs, recovering and changing them is probably the greatest annoyance. Changing bulbs takes the photographer's eyes off his subject. Carrying them around underwater is a hassle. Don't carry them in mesh bags. They are buoyant, excessively so, and usually end up tangled in something or wrapped around the diver's neck. Buy or make a slotted rubber tube that will fit over the flash arm into which bulbs can be snapped and be out of the way.

HOW THE BULB WORKS

Pick up a flashbulb and examine it closely. It is a closed bulb of very thin glass coated with clear lacquer inside and out and attached to a metal base. Some have no metal base but, instead, contacts which project outward from the bottom of the bulb. Inside the bulb is a combustible filler, usually a coil of thread-like zirconium

LACQUER COATING

OXYGEN-FILLED GLASS BULB

COMBUSTIBLE FILLER

TUNGSTEN FILAMENT

METAL BASE

ELECTRICAL CONTACT

(an aluminum alloy) and a thin tungsten filament coated with a primer powder.

The bulb is filled with oxygen at a pressure somewhat less than one atmosphere. The reason is to avoid an explosive shattering of the thin glass bulb when the internal pressure increases due to the explosive combustion of the filler. This also accounts for the internal and external lacquer coating. As the camera shutter release is tripped, a weak electrical impulse from the flash sync contact rapidly heats the tungsten filament thereby igniting the primer which spontaneously flares and torches the combustible filler.

Most conventional underwater flash guns ignite the flashbulb with a BC (battery capacitor) power pack. The BC power pack consists usually of a 22.5 volt dry battery, a capacitor and a resistor. When the flash gun is connected to the BC power supply, the battery charges the capacitor. The resistor in the circuit keeps the current too weak to ignite the flash bulb. When the shutter release is depressed, the resistor is by-passed and the capacitor discharges spontaneously into the flashbulb producing the brilliant flash.

CHOOSING THE RIGHT BULB

There are a number of considerations which determine which bulb is best for your camera. Perhaps the most important factor is that the flashbulb produce the greatest amount of light (peak brightness) during the brief time the shutter is open. Consequently, the camera's shutter speed is a prime consideration and there are different kinds of shutters, some faster than others.

The problem in selecting the right bulb arises because different types of flashbulbs vary considerably in the time it takes them to reach peak brightness. Unlike the "X" synchronization which, when the shutter is fully open, produces a "zero time delay" because electronic flash is so fast, flashbulbs take a while to reach peak brightness.

Focal plane flashbulb

THE FOCAL PLANE BULB

Focal plane shutters require special "FP" (flat peak) bulbs. Since the slit formed by the two curtains moving across the film plane exposes the film, the flashbulb must produce a peak intensity and hold that light constant until the slit completes its travel across the film plane. The focal plane bulbs (6B and 26B) ignite approximately 10 milliseconds before the shutter opens and hold the same light intensity for approximately 20 milliseconds.

THE AG (ALL GLASS) BULB

The tiny baseless flashbulbs pack a surprisingly good light output for their size, about the same as the light intensity produced by the larger M3 bulb. Because of their small size, a

AG-1 flashbulb

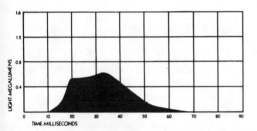

Consequently, flashbulbs must actually be ignited before the shutter opens. The "M" synchronization fires the flash 20 milliseconds before the shutter is fully open. (20 milliseconds transposes into 20/1,000ths of a second). Correspondingly, bulbs designed for "M" synchronization (M3B, 5B and 25B) peak in approximately 20 milliseconds. In other words, the flash is building up to peak brightness before the shutter opens. When the flash reaches maximum intensity, the shutter is fully open and the exposure is made. Synchronization is only important when shooting at shutter speeds faster than 1/30th. If the shutter speed is 1/30th of a second, the burn cycle of a flashbulb will be completed while the shutter is open. As a result, any "M" sync bulb will sync with any other camera regardless of the sync setting, provided the shutter speed is 1/30th of a second or slower.

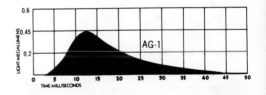

sizeable number can be carried with no significant buoyancy problems. The AG flashbulbs can be used at "X" or "F" sync at a shutter speed of 1/30th of a second or at "M" sync at any shutter speed. With the special Nikonos adapter, the AG bulb can be used with the Nikonos BC flash gun to sync with the focal plane shutter at some shutter speeds.

THE FLASHCUBE

The little flashcube does a very respectable job on close-up lighting assignments underwater. It is very compact holding, in effect, four tiny flashbulbs capable of four flash exposures

Flashcube

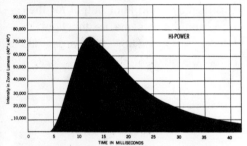

before the cube must be replaced. Special underwater flashcube holders (like the Ikelite "cube-flash") make flashcube lighting adaptable to virtually any camera. The synchronization characteristics of the flashcube are almost identical with those of the AG bulbs.

CLEAR OR BLUE?

The beginning underwater photographer would probably be best advised to shoot all his flash photographs with daylight film and blue bulbs. The designation for a blue bulb is the suffix "B". For example: AG-1*B*. If there is no "B" suffix, the blub is clear. Clear bulbs produce greater light intensity and, consequently, should be used for apparent flash-to-subject distances greater than 6 feet to maximize the reds and minimize the filtering effect of the water. Blue flashbulbs give better overall color balance at nearer

distances (flash-to-subject distances less than 6 feet) since clear bulbs tend to give a too bright light for these near distances.

POSITIONING THE ELECTRONIC SUNSHINE

A few of the less expensive commercial camera housings, as well as some misguided do-it-yourselfers, mount the flash right next to the camera lens. This may not be too bad a procedure when shooting "in-air" photographs but, as any experienced underwater photographer knows, the practice generally proves disastrous underwater.

BACKSCATTER

Perhaps one of the greatest differences between the "in-air" and underwater technique is simply the absence of any particulate which may surround the subject in air. In clear air or exceptionally clear water, for example, the light from the flash is transmitted to the subject and reflected back toward the lens without interruption producing a clear and crisply focused photograph. If the same photographs were attempted in a heavy snow storm or in slightly "dusty" water, the results would be hopelessly light-spotted, washed out, and out-of-focus. This effect is termed "backscatter" and is caused by the millions of light-reflecting particles which surround the subject. In the snow storm, the backscatter is caused by the snow flakes; in the water, by the multitude of microscopic organisms called plankton as well as bottom sediment in suspension.

As light from the flash travels toward the subject, it first strikes these particles lighting them brightly. It is this light from the thousands of different particles which is reflected into the camera's lens.

HAND HOLDING THE FLASH

One easy way to minimize the ef-fects of backscatter — at least to an acceptable degree — is to detach the flash and hand-hold it forward, above and well to the side of the subject, (approximately 45° from the camera). The object is to top-light the subject so that, if there is any particulate sus-pended between the light and the sub-ject, only the tops and edges will be illuminated. Even if these lighted edges are recorded by the camera, they will be far less objectionable than if they had been front lighted. There are other advantages to the hand-held flash technique. If the flash is detachable, the undersea photogra-pher is free to try a variety of light-ing techniques and angles.

FRONT LIGHTING

There may be a few good souls who are stuck with their fixed flash cube or flash bulb reflector. Fixed, that is, meaning attached directly to and close by the housing. Their pictures are obviously going to be front lighted and that's not too good. Front lighting can

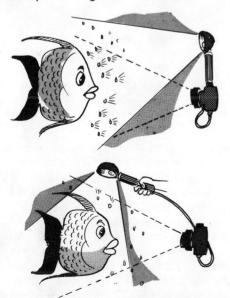

Minimizing backscatter

cause harsh shadowing and strong, "burned out" pictures. In the case of divers faces, if the flash is not reflected by the subject's mask, his face will probably appear chalky and lack detail. For immense improvement, the only solution is to get yourself some extra wire and a soldering gun. Take that flash off the housing.

BACK LIGHTING

Backlighting is a technique that can yield a beautiful and delicate lighting effect and yet is rarely attempted by new undersea photographers. It's really quite easy. Maneuvering the flash behind the subject may very well yield the most dramatic pictures in the photographer's file. Generally, with backlighting, the subject will appear as a dark silhouette against a bright background.

RIM LIGHTING

If the undersea photographer is sufficiently imaginative, there is hardly an end to the remarkable composition and dimension that can be attained through the artful placement of the flash. "Rim" lighting a subject highlights it's upper features while the lower are deeply shadowed, producing most dramatic results.

SIDE LIGHTING

Perhaps the most popular light positioning in underwater photography is side lighting which fully illuminates the subject on one side, while the other is cast in shadow. The obvious danger in side lighting divers' faces is that the shadowed side will be too dark. The most important rule, when hand-holding flash, is to be just as sure of where the flash is being aimed as of where the camera is pointing. It does take some practice and co-ordination. I hand-hold my camera housing as firmly against my face

plate as possible. This helps a great deal in steadying the camera. Unfortunately, with some camera housings, it is almost impossible to hold the camera steady and trip the shutter release with only one hand.

THE ADJUSTABLE FLASH ARM

Some housings, because of poor balance underwater or excessive bouyancy, tend to twist or turn making them difficult — if not impossible — to manage with one hand. For housings which are impossible to handle with one hand, the solution is an adjustable flash arm. There are several adjustable flash arm units which fasten to the housing currently on the accessory market. (The Oceanic Prod-

ucts ball-joint flash arm is an excellent example.) These fully articulated arms permit the diver to adjust the direction of the light beam toward the subject and yet free his hands to grip the camera firmly while focusing and squeezing the shutter release. Although these adjustable-position flash arms are designed primarily for electronic strobes, I'm sure with a little imagination one could be converted to accommodate a flashbulb head if

necessary. The Rolleimarin flash head provides some adjustment also and can direct the flash beam to cover distances from 12 inches away to 10 feet.

FLASH PARALLAX

One of the most agonizing moments in the life of an underwater photographer may occur as he studies some just developed, flash-exposed pictures. The moment is when he discovers that his aim was just a little off and, though the foreground or background are beautifully lighted, the subject is just an indistinguishable shadow. The beginning photographer is especially vulnerable when he begins hand-holding his flash. After composing the picture carefully through the viewfinder, he extends the flash and triggers the shutter release. If he hasn't been very careful aiming his flash, he may find it doesn't even hit the subject.

The problem is easily solved. It really is a simple matter of practicing with the strobe enough so you always know where the light beam will fall. Some photographers clamp a small divers light to the strobe so that the flashlight beam and the strobe beam are on the same axis. In this way, you can see exactly where your strobe light will fall. And the weak light projected by the flashlight is overpowered by the strobe's intensity and has no effect on the exposure.

MULTIPLE LIGHTS

Occasionally, the area you wish to photograph is simply too big to be covered by the light field of your flash. When shooting with an extreme wide angle lens, for example, one flash simply doesn't make it. But there is a way to illuminate the entire subject, and really get some exciting photographs.

The use of multiple lights is *not,* as the beginner might suspect, to increase the *intensity* of light. It is, instead, to increase the light field or to improve the picture composition by adding subtle lighting in areas which would be heavily shaded if only one flash were used. In this way, the subject can be given spectacular perspective and dimension. Exciting effects can be made by using the main light source on one side of the subject and weaker (fill-in) light on the other.

EXTENSION CORDS

There are several ways to achieve the multiple light technique underwater. You may elect to use additional flash guns or strobes connected to

FLASHLIGHT ⟶

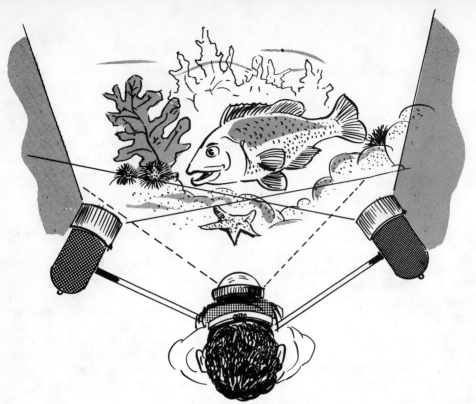

Multiple lights increase the light field

and triggered by the camera through extension cords. There are always certain problems attendant with the use of cords in underwater photography, however. No matter how carefully you position them, unless you are constantly on guard, those cords will show up prominently in your very best photographs. The only time I use a cord is when I can detach the strobe head and position it on the sea floor or have another diver hold it to avoid

Use an assistant to keep extension cords out of the field of view.

the "snow" or back-scatter problem when the water is loaded with suspended particulate.

SLAVE TECHNIQUE

The preferable method — in my judgement — is using the "slave-sensor", a light-directing switch which is triggered by the main light source. When the main light (key) fires, the slave senses it simultaneously igniting the secondary (fill) light source. The advantage of this arrangement is that the systems are independent of one another and, of course, no cords are necessary. There are slave units to trip either electronic strobe or flashbulb — or both. The beauty of the current wave of underwater strobes equipped with slaves is that they are virtually omni-directional. That is, they are capable of being ignited by a main light positioned almost anywhere. The relative angles of the strobe light fields needn't even intersect.

PHOTOGRAPHING A "FLASH"

A photograph of a diver's strobe "burning" invariably has photo class students asking, "How in the world did you ever catch the exact second when the other photographer triggered his strobe?" I usually mumble something about my "lightning reflexes" and let them think about it for a few minutes. With a "burn" time of 1/1,000 of a second, the photographer would literally have to be "faster than a speeding bullet". The shot is really only an example of the multiple light technique. The "slaved" strobe sees the main light and fires instantly.

CALCULATING EXPOSURES FOR MULTIPLE LIGHT PICTURES

The technique is really quite simple. Since you are probably aiming the lights at *different areas* approximately equally distant from the strobe and camera, you need only use the same lens opening you would have used with only one light. On the other hand, if two lights converge on roughly the same area, calculate your lens opening on the basis of one light and then close down another one half stop to allow for the additional light. Like calculating other underwater flash exposures, these methods are only guidelines and must be modified by test and practice.

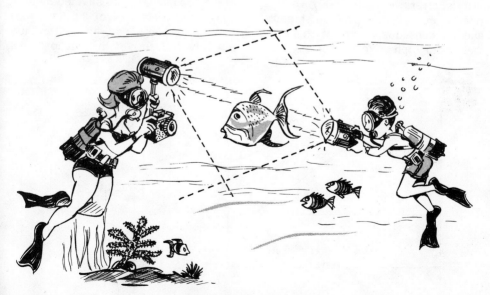

Strobe-Slave Technique

Whatever else you may do, be sure to keep accurate records of your lighting tests so that you can determine how the most desireable lighting effects were achieved.

INVERSE SQUARE LAW

"The intensity of light varies inversely as the square of the distance from its source." Probably the most critical factor in flash photography is the subject-to-flash distance. As indicated in the illustration, the amount of light which falls on the subject is inversely proportional to the square of the distance the flash must travel. A strobe fired from the camera position would cover an area at point A as shown by the shaded zone. If the light continued to point B, it would cover four times the area it did at point A. However, the light would now be only one fourth as intense as it was at point A. At point C the coverage would be nine times as great while the intensity would be only one ninth that at point A. Correspondingly, the coverage would be sixteen times as great at point D and the intensity only 1/16 that at point A.

It is clear from the study of the relative areas over which light spreads and its consequent loss of intensity that photographs exposed at point D,

for example, would require sixteen times the exposure as would a photograph made at point A. Correspondingly, photographs exposed at C and B would require nine times and four times the exposure of one made at point A.

GUIDE NUMBERS

One of the most grossly misunderstood terms in photography is the guide number. Since the amount of light which falls on a photographic subject depends upon its distance from the flash, it would seem a monumental task to determine exposure since the underwater photographer is constantly shooting at different subject-to-camera distances. Fortunately, the American Standards Association developed a formula with which camera and film manufacturers are able to calculate and publish *guide numbers* which greatly simplify the job of estimating flash exposures.

WHAT IS A GUIDE NUMBER?

The guide number is a measurement of the *effective* light output of the flash at a given shutter speed. The guide numbers are affected by the shape and reflectivity of the flash reflector, the film speed, as well as the intensity and size of the flashbulb.

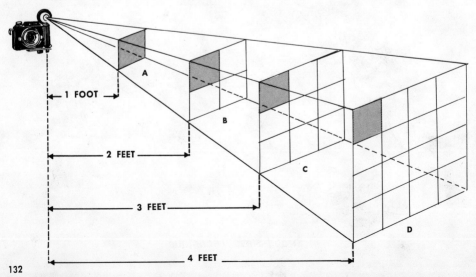

A
1 FOOT
B
2 FEET
C
3 FEET
D
4 FEET

WHERE DO YOU FIND IT?

The guide number is always found on the film data sheet furnished with the film. Your flash equipment or flashbulbs will also provide the appropriate guide number for your flash-shutter speed - film speed combination.

Once you have found your *in-air* guide number, it is a simple matter to determine the proper flash exposure. Since the camera determines the shutter speed you must use, (the Nikonos, for example, will synchronize with electronic flash at only 1/60th of a second), you need only determine the correct lens opening (f-stop). To do this, you need only divide the guide number by the distance in feet from the flash to the subject. The answer is your f-stop!

Example:
In-Air Guide number   110
Flash to Subject
Distance   10 feet
110 ÷ 10 = 11
Correct Lens Opening   f/11
Note: This method gives the correct lens openings for in-air photography and *not* underwater photography.

ONLY STARTING POINTS

It must be emphasized that the beginning photographer ought not place too much trust in the guide numbers. Guide numbers are based on average conditions and naturally do not take into account any variations in the shutter speeds of different cameras or flash equipment or your particular set of photographic conditions. Use the guide number as it was intended, as a starting point. Later, we'll describe a method of making a series of test exposures underwater to find the optimum guide number. It can be done as effectively for in-air photography.

⚡ **ELECTRONIC FLASH**

This table is for use with electronic flash units rated in beam candle-power seconds (BCPS). To determine the ƒ-number, divide the guide number for your flash unit by the distance in feet from the flash to your subject. If results are unsatisfactory, change the guide number as described under "Blue Flashbulbs."

GUIDE NUMBERS FOR ELECTRONIC FLASH

Output of Unit BCPS	350	500	700	1000	1400	2000	2800	4000	5600	8000
Guide Number	85	100	120	140	170	200	240	280	340	400

Kodak Tri-X Pan (ASA 400)

ELECTRONIC FLASH EXPOSURE GUIDE*

BCPS	350	500	650	1000	1600	2400	3200	4800	6400	12500	25000
GUIDE NUMBER	60	70	80	100	125	155	180	220	250	355	500
Watt-second	10	15	20	30	50	75	100	150	200	400	800

Electronic flash guide numbers are used the same way as flashbulb guide numbers.

Check the instructions supplied with the flash unit for BCPS or watt-second rating and filter recommendations.

GAF 200 slide film (ASA 200)

GUIDE NUMBERS FOR BLUE FLASHBULBS

Type of Reflector	Flashbulb	X Sync	M Synchronization			
		1/30	1/30	1/60	1/125	1/250
	Flashcube	50	36	36	28	22
	Hi-Power Cube	70	50	50	40	32
	AG-1B	36	26	26	22	18
	AG-1B	50	36	36	30	24
	M2B	45	NR	NR	NR	NR
*	AG-1B	70	50	50	45	36
	M2B	65	NR	NR	NR	NR
	M3B, 5B, 25B	70	70	60	50	42
	6B†, 26B†	NR	65	50	34	24
*	M3B, 5B, 25B	100	100	90	70	55
	6B†, 26B†	NR	95	70	50	34

*Polished bowl.   †Bulbs for focal-plane shutter.   NR—Not Recommended.

Kodachrome 25 (ASA 25)

NO SHORT CUTS

If you were to ask one hundred underwater photographers if they use guide numbers or exposure tables, a good percentage would answer in the negative. And they would argue convincingly against guide numbers citing variable factors as changing visibility, light levels, turbidity which make an infallible standard exposure table impossible. And though it is true, with experience, good photographers can "eyeball" an underwater scene and "guesstimate" the proper exposure setting with reasonable accuracy — the novice underwater photographer wouldn't have a prayer. Such skill comes only with experience and plenty of it.

In a way, though, the anti-guide number people have a point. Novice underwater photographers tend to look for easy, fool-proof settings that are infallible under any conditions and frequently get up-tight when they must calculate an accurate lens setting underwater. I couldn't begin to count the times I've been shooting on a reef and had a new photographer tap me on the shoulder and, by gestures, ask for exposure settings. No thought given to whether we are using matching film ASA or shutter speed or strobe intensity or flashbulb. He is looking for a shortcut to good flash exposures. Unfortunately, there are no shortcuts! Getting optimum flash exposures consistently is no big trick, either.

The so-called exposure calculators can only assign certain exposure settings to average underwater conditions. They do not take into account the fact that no two cameras or shutters or, for that matter, strobes or flash units are exactly the same. Such calculators, charts, or tables are only as good as the guide numbers, and consequently should only be considered as starting points. Each camera — flash — film combination must have its own distinct and individual guide number if it is to produce consistently acceptable results. The underwater photographer must be able to assign a particular setting to a given set of underwater conditions. Furthermore, he must be able to adjust this setting on the spot to compensate for the everchanging conditions which

exist underwater. The ability to accurately estimate exposures consistently goes a long way toward taking the underwater photographer out of the "beginner" category.

COLOR LOSS

One of the first lessons the beginning photographer learns is that the distance light must travel underwater can also cause a substantial loss of color. Even in natural light photography, this distance determines the degree of color loss. Reds, for example, are absorbed almost entirely in a distance of as little as 15 feet. At short distances, the color loss is not too significant. Therefore, the obvious solution to minimizing the effects of color absorption is to stay as close to the subject as possible. Flash, correspondingly, is directly affected by the distance it is held from the subject. If the flash is held close to the camera, the light from the flash must travel to the subject and return the same distance to the camera. In such a case, not only is there a substantial loss of color as the light travels from flash to subject — but the color loss is *doubled* since the light must travel the same distance from the subject back to the camera. Color loss can be reduced by moving the flash closer to the subject. If the flash is held close to the subject, only one-half the color absorption occurs since the light must only travel half the distance.

BUGGER FACTORS

As you probably have already surmised, the suggested guide numbers packaged with flash bulbs, and photo equipment are calculated for *in-air* use and are unusable underwater. However, a fairly easy to remember rule exists for transposing "in-air" guide numbers to underwater use. Basically, to determine an underwater guide number simply divide the "in-air"

guide number for your particular flash-film-camera combination by *three.*

EXAMPLE:

Flash to subject
distance 10 feet
In-air guide number 110
110 ÷ 3 = 36 2/3
Underwater guide number 36 2/3
Underwater guide number
(rounded) 37
37 ÷ 10 = 3.7
Correct underwater lens
opening f/3.7

The "bugger factor" refers to a conversion factor by which the in-air guide number is divided to determine the underwater guide number. This so-called "bugger factor" is arbitrarily fixed at 3. However, Doctor Hank Frey, physical oceanographer at N.Y.U., suggests for even greater accuracy that two bugger factors be used: Four (4) if the distance is 2½ feet or less and by 2.5 if the distance is greater than 3 feet.

Perhaps the best way to determine the "bugger factor" most suitable for your particular camera-flash-film combination is to make a series of test exposures underwater. After selecting your best test exposure (the pertinent data regarding which was carefully recorded), multiply the lens opening (f-stop) by the underwater distance for your underwater guide number. To determine the bugger factor, divide the underwater guide number into the in-air guide number.

EXAMPLE:

In-air guide number 110
Underwater guide number 37
110 ÷ 37 = 3
Bugger factor = 3

In either case, the underwater guide number is divided by the distance to determine the correct lens opening.

"TOTAL PATH" GUIDE NUMBERS

When calculating flash exposures where the flash and camera are not equally distant from the subject, you must use a total path guide number. Total path guide numbers, as the name implies, are based on the measurement of the "total path" or total light distance. That is, the sum of the flash-to-subject distance and the subject-to-camera distance. To calculate the correct exposure, first the total path *guide number* must be determined and doubled. For example, if the underwater guide number is 37, the total path guide number will be twice that or 2 x 37. The answer is 74. Now, divide the total path guide by the total light path to determine the correct lens opening.

EXAMPLE:

Flash-to-Subject distance =	2 ft.
Subject-to-Camera distance =	8 ft.
Underwater guide number =	37
Total path guide number =	74
2 ft + 8 ft =	10 ft.
74 ÷ 10 = 7.4 or	8 (rounded)
correct lens opening =	f/8

FINDING YOUR GUIDE NUMBER

The best "bugger factors" are only as good as their relationship to *your*-camera-flash-film combination. Since there are so many variable factors, your best bet is to construct an exposure table of your own. Use a swimming pool in which you have accurately measured and marked a fixed camera-to-subject distance. Have your diving model hold a slate on which is marked the f/stop and shutter speed if you're using flash bulbs. Since strobe guide numbers are the same for all shutter speeds because of the strobe's brief "burn" duration, it is not necessary to include shutter speed data on the slate. With a grease pencil, mark the underwater slate with the f/stop and shutter speed at which you shoot each picture. Now, at your fixed position, (try 3 feet of apparent distance) shoot a series of flash exposures, one at every f/stop. From these tests you can develop an exposure table or guide number that

should estimate open water exposures within plus or minus ½ f/stop. After the film has been processed, place the transparencies on a light box or sorting table where they can be viewed simultaneously. Find the one which appears to have the optimum exposure. The slate in the photograph will tell you what f/stop and shutter speed was used. Now that you have determined the f/stop for the best exposure for your camera-film combination, you can find the optimum underwater guide number by multiplying the f/stop by the subject-to-camera distance (in this case, an apparent distance of 3 feet). For example, if the optimum f/stop had been f/11 and the subject-to-camera distance 3 feet, the underwater guide number would be 33.

STILL ANOTHER WAY

Well-known underwater photographers, Jim and Cathy Church, carry the exposure tables one more interesting step. After establishing the optimum f-stop for a given distance, they suggest stops for other distances be calculated by the simple expedient of opening the lens one f-stop for each foot of longer camera-to-subject apparent distances and stopping down one for each apparent foot of shorter distances. For total light path pictures the change is one f-stop for each two feet. Note: In exceptionally clear water you may not have to increase exposure one stop for each additional foot of distance. In turbid water, you may have to increase by more.

Summarizing, all of the foregoing methods for determining flash exposure are time-proven and fairly reliable, but not one *guarantees* ideal exposure. No system can do that. There are simply too many variables to establish absolute or fool-proof rules. Once again, the best advice to the would-be subsea photographer is experiment. Find the system that works best for you and bracket your shots.

BRACKETING FLASH EXPOSURES

To be on the safe side, always bracket flash exposures by shooting additional exposures at least one f-stop below and above the estimated exposure under conditions of average water visibility. If the water is turbid, bracket toward the larger lens opening.

FAIL SAFE?

Nothing is fail safe, but one very reassuring practice has saved me a lot of sleepless nights. When I've switched to a new strobe, for example. (and it may be a carbon copy of one I've used for years) I still shoot a test roll as earlier outlined. Even the best of units will vary somewhat because of variances in capacitors or flashtubes. And this can be enough to throw your table off considerably. As a result, I shoot a lot of Ektachrome and carry an E-4 processing kit around with me. It's proven invaluable many times.

FOR MORE ACCURACY

By now you have probably surmised that guide numbers are not sacred cows. If your photographs are consistently over or underexposed, change the guide number. Guide numbers make no distinction between the differences in the reflectivity of different subjects. Light subjects reflect more light and may cause transparencies to be too light (overexposed). Conversely, dark subjects absorb more light and can lead to underexposed (too dark) photographs. These are judgements the underwater photographer must make on the spot. If a subject is light, stop the lens down ½ f-stop. If the subject is dark, open up by ½ f-stop. If the subject and its background are highly re-

flective, your guide number could be off as much as a full f-stop.

MAKING TAPE GUIDES

After you have determined the distances and f-stops at which you obtain your best exposures, make a series of plastic tape labels and stick

them on the strobe head for quick and easy exposures.

FLASH METER

To shed some light on a confusing issue — excuse the pun — there is no real shortcut to correct flash exposure underwater. And the flash meter, designed as it was to measure in-air flash intensity, is not a magical device which insures optimum exposure underwater. But a good flash meter can be a useful tool to the serious student of underwater photography. A cordless, flash meter can help determine flash exposures underwater and it can be an invaluable tool with which the strobe's guide number can be checked, or the light intensity of multiple flash measured, and a number of other tasks.

The flash meter most frequently used underwater is the incident light type. The Wein Meter, for example, measures the incident light falling on the subject. Consequently, the cordless-type meter must be placed at the subject position. The strobe is then

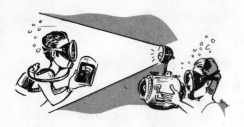

flashed at the meter. The meter automatically measures the intensity of the strobe's light and selects a lens opening to correspond to the film's ASA rating. It is important to understand, however, such meters are designed to measure strobe light intensity in *air*. The undersea photographer may discover the flash meter is consistently high or low by as much as a full f-stop underwater. As you learn the eccentricities of your meter, you will automatically compensate by opening up or stopping down a click or two as conditions dictate.

FILL-IN FLASH

Flash can also be used in soft and subtle ways that will leave your audience wondering whether or not you did indeed use flash. So many times beginning underwater photographers shoot otherwise beautifully-exposed, natural light photographs in which harsh dark shadows have blanked out the subject's face. And when shooting fish close-ups, the average photographer probably stops down to the smallest apertures to avoid "burning" the subject because of the nearness of the flash. As a consequence, most fish portraits look like they were shot on a night dive. The black background is a result of the small lens openings.

Natural light pictures generally lack the exciting color at depths much deeper than 15 or 20 feet since the intensity of available light is simply inadequate to bring out the warmth of these tones. What can be done to improve the color quality in this situation? Fill-in flash!

Fill-in flash can restore the vivid colors, eliminate harsh, dark shadows and the "night dive" quality of your photographs. Perhaps the most frequent mistake of underwater photographers using fill light is overpowering natural light with the flash. Since flash provides a much more intense light than sunlight, the background appears black. The good underwater photographer uses fill-in flash not only to restore true colors to the principle subject, but also to eliminate harsh black backgrounds and replace them with a more realistic and more appealing blue background.

HOW TO DO IT

First, with a light meter, determine the amount of natural light falling on the subject and select the optimum *daylight* exposure. Secondly, using the proper guide number for your flash, determine the optimum *flash* exposure. Third, compare the exposure settings! You want a flash exposure that gives slightly less exposure than does the natural light setting. In other words, you want the natural light to be your main light source, and the flash to lighten up the shadowed zones. Adjust the camera to correspond with the daylight exposure setting. Now, if the flash exposure indicates a smaller lens opening (f-stop) than does the natural light setting — cut down on the flash exposure by increasing the flash-to-subject distance or, in the case of variable power strobes, an easier way is to cut down on the light output. For example, an underwater photographer is taking pictures of his model in clear Jamaican waters. The natural light illuminates the reef and his model beautifully, but he is concerned with some heavy shadow areas. He is using a Nikonos and electronic flash. He must use a shutter speed of 1/60th, since the Nikonos only synchronizes with electronic flash at a shutter speed of 1/60th. Using Ektachrome X which has an

ASA of 64, he finds that his light meter indicates an aperture of f/5.6 for a natural light exposure. However, his flash exposure is f/8. He should set his aperture at f/5.6 but, to avoid over-exposing the subject, he must increase the flash-to-subject distance. In this case, a distance of roughly one foot would do the job.

AUTOMATIC ELECTRONIC FLASH

In many underwater circles, automatic strobe is viewed dimly to say the least. The earliest attempts at adapting automatic strobes to underwater use were largely unsuccessful because, the sensor, the heart of the automatic strobe system — that little black box which theoretically can compute the optimum exposure for a given lighting situation — was quite overwhelmed and confused by the world underwater.

In extremely clear water, the sensor indicated the proper exposure with sufficient accuracy to become believable. Unfortunately, in less than extreme visibility the sensor indicated exposures that were rarely acceptable. In the main, the problem was one of positioning. At first, sensors were mounted in the strobe heads instead of close to the camera lens where they are presently mounted. When mounted in the strobe head, the sensor could be fooled by the particulate suspended in the water. This suspended matter would bounce back light and give a false reading before the sensor had a chance to read the light actually reflected by the photographic subject. The light reflected by the subject therefore passed through the lens and struck the film with more or less intensity than planned and the image produced was over or under-exposed.

The simple solution consisted of merely relocating the sensor where it could most accurately measure the most important light — that about to expose the film. As a result, the camera mounted sensor yields a much better percentage of correct exposures.

UNUSUAL LIGHTING CONDITIONS

Everybody knows that lighting conditions underwater can be brutal. Picture a diver wearing a black wet suit, black hood and face-mask posed before the dark entrance to an underwater cave. The automatic sensor is not looking at the diver's face. It is reading the black areas around and behind. The result? Over-exposed pictures!

Automatic flash sensors do not really compensate for existing light. As a result, if flash is used as fill light with a focal plane shutter, the photograph is likely to be overexposed. The reason? At the slow shutter speeds (1/60th second for Nikonos) ambient light is exposing the photograph as well as the electronic flash. The result? Over-exposed pictures!

HOW IT WORKS

The heart of the automatic exposure system is the sensor, a small (1½" x 1½" x ¾") black box. When possible, the sensors should be placed in the camera housing so that only the light which actually enters the camera is measured and regulated. Since it is a self-contained camera itself, the Nikonos requires that the sensor be housed in its own small water-tight, pressure-proof housing. The sensor is connected to the "X" contact of the camera and to the strobe.

Next, the films ASA rating is set on the sensor's calculator dial. Regardless of the ASA, you may select an f/stop from a range of four automatic flash f/stops. By changing the f/stop on the sensor, the amount of light which reaches the sensor "eye" is varied. A range of lighting distances is programmed into the sensor and the unit is ready to fire.

Earlier the operation of a normal strobe light was described. An automatic strobe differs only in the light-

measuring sensor. With the data programmed into the sensor, it can measure the light reflected by the subject and instantaneously shut off or "quench" the light output from the flash-tube.

MOVIE LIGHTS

As in any type of underwater color photography, the name of the game is to restore color to our undersea subjects. But we want to restore true color! We do this by carefully selecting a light source whose color temperature balances that of our film. In underwater movie work, this can be done in several ways.

SURFACE SUPPLIED LIGHTS

Begin with a light weight gasoline-powered surface generator capable of producing at least 115 volts. Add two or more sealed beam lamps. These may range from 1,000 watt airplane landing lights to the relatively inexpensive General Electric Uniflood lamp. The 650 watt Uniflood is particularly well suited for underwater film making. It is sufficiently rugged to safely withstand the effects of pressure within the sport diver's range of

diving activity. As a result of the super efficient cooling of the lamp underwater, as compared to air, it's useful life may be extended underwater by as much as 30%. The color balanced Uniflood has a rated color temperature of approximately 3400° Kelvin and is available in three different beam angles: wide angle, medium, and narrow. While it would seem that the widest beam angle would be most suitable for underwater photography, it only requires a second's thought to understand that the wider the beam angle, the greater the backscatter. The medium beam angle has excellent lighting characteristics and when used in pairs provides surprisingly good coverage. Stretched between the portable generator vibrating in your boat and the Uniflood lights underwater there is a length of power cable through which the current must flow. This restrictive, but necessary tether is the major objection to the surface-supplied lighting system. The lamps must be soldered to the wire conductor (generally 12 gauge wire). The solder joints must also be carefully insulated to protect against electric shock. Perhaps the simplest method is to seal all the electrical connections in epoxy. Even so, while the generator is running, it is best to avoid touching metal in the boat. The great advantage of the surface-supplied lighting system is that the power is continuous until the generator runs out of gas.

MOUNTING THE LIGHTS

While some undersea film makers use assistants to hand-hold their lights, the average amateur cameraman doesn't have a string of assistants waiting patiently to carry his lights. For him, we recommend mounting the lights directly to a lightbar which is fastened to the camera housing. The positioning of the lights relative to the lens axis is important. The lights

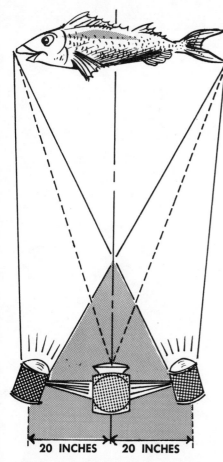

20 INCHES | **20 INCHES**

should be mounted approximately 20 inches from the center of the lens. While it is best to have some adjustment to light near or far objects, it is important to keep the lights in front of and approximately 45 degrees from the lens axis to minimize any light reflected back into the lens due to "back scattering."

SELF-CONTAINED MOVIE LIGHTS

A new generation of battery operated, self-contained movie lights has appeared on the scene. Although there are a number of different lamps available, the smaller units frequently use the 100 watt General Electric cinema lamp. This 6 volt sealed beam provides sufficient power when used at relatively close subject-to-camera

distances. In most cases, power is supplied through a rechargeable nickel-cadmium battery pack capable (when fully charged) of approximately

Farallon 350 watt movie light with rechargeable nickel cadmium battery pack, adjustable arm and charger.

12 minutes of running time. Larger units of up to 350 watts are also available. These, too, are powered by rechargeable nickel cadmium battery packs. The 350 watt lamps have a running time of approximately 16 minutes. The advantage of the self-contained lighting system is that the movements of the diver-cameraman are not restricted by any cable to the surface. He is completely self-contained and mobile.

Chapter X.

UNDERSEA IN MINIATURE

It has been said a photographer's pictures reveal his philosophy and his attitude toward life. While that concept is debatable, it is certainly true that the photographer's pictures reveal his ideas of what is important and interesting.

It has also been said that a photographer's creativity stems from his ability to select just the right shutter speed, the right aperture, the right composition, and the right focus in any given photographic circumstance. The truth is, of much greater importance is his ability to "see" a good photographic composition. All divers can talk for hours of the beauty of a particular coral reef, for example. How many have bothered to *really* investigate the miniature world living on that reef?

Years ago, I made many reef dives with an elderly gentleman who never swam more than 40 or 50 feet from the anchor line. Everything he wanted to see was confined to a 10' x 10' area. For him, one dive was hardly enough time to examine the detail of that area. I had become somewhat bored with the

reef, feeling as I did that I knew it intimately and had seen everything there was to see on it. It took an 80 year old neophyte diver to prove me wrong. I really only knew the obvious land marks and the overview. But I hadn't begun to know the microcosm of life which abounded on that reef.

Like too many other subsea photographers, I had been so psyched about using wide angle lenses, that the close-up possibilities underwater never occurred to me. I had seen too many bad photographs in which the subject, usually a tiny purple flower worm, was virtually lost in the center of an overwhelming background of blue. I was determined not to ever make the same mistake myself. I had already learned that when a wide angle lens is used behind a flat port at close-up range, the resultant photograph will record a subject image which will probably be lost on the screen when projected. If the Nikonos 35mm lens, for example, is focused on a close-up type subject at an apparent distance of 3 or 4 feet, the subject is reduced on film to about one twentieth of its actual size.

But close-up and macro-photography can add an entirely new dimension to the underwater photographer's prints or slide presentations. And subjects worthy of his camera exist even in the most unimposing of inland ponds.

One of the most exciting treatments in an underwater slide-presentation is a careful selection of macro-photographs, close-ups, medium and long shots which give the audience not only a detailed look at the elegant delicacy of tiny forms of sea life, but by increasing the angle of view in succeeding photographs, lends a sense of perspective and dimension to them. By including a diver in the long shot, size comparisons are quickly established.

CLOSE-UP PHOTOGRAPHY

The image of the photographic subject recorded on film grows larger as the camera-to-subject distance is reduced. Close-up photography is generally regarded as any subject photographed at a distance of three feet or closer. And since most normal lenses are capable of focusing down to this range, they can do acceptable close-up work.

MACRO-PHOTOGRAPHY

In ultra close-up photography, the term "reproduction ratio" is used to describe the size of the image recorded on film.

The Nikonos 35mm lens, as earlier explained, when used on an underwater subject at an approximate distance of 3½ feet, will produce a subject image on film reduced to about one-twentieth its actual size. Therefore, the image reproduction ratio would be 1:20, about average for a *normal* lens focused at that distance.

Remember, the standard Nikonos 35mm lens is not water-corrected. As a result, refraction underwater makes it the equivalent of a 50mm lens in air.

Macro-photography involves photographing subjects life-size or larger. That is to say the reproduction ratio is 1:1 or more.

To say that such large image reproductions offer an excitingly new challenge to the subsea photographer is a monumental understatement and at the same time somewhat misleading. The statement is true in that the results of macro-photography can be fantastic, showing incredibly crisp detail of the small area photographed. The photographer in all probability, will discover astounding detail in the photograph he hadn't even seen when making the picture. For the reef diver, the delicate coral polyps become screen-filling extravaganzas of most delicate design.

The inland diver will develop a greater awareness of the infinite variety of creatures and plant life which inhabit his favorite diving waters. When enlarged to heroic proportions on the screen, such macro-photographs can yield mind-blowing results. When photographed at a reproduction ratio of 1:1, the head of the lowly cray-fish becomes as intimidating as would a prehistoric pterodactyl. A quarter-sized cluster of algae becomes a swirling array of iridescent beauty.

The statement is somewhat misleading because it implies special photographic talents are required to shoot macro-photographs. Nothing could be further from the truth. Above all, macro-photography is doubtless the most fool-proof of any type of underwater photography. Anyone can take exciting, colorful macro-photographs underwater with virtually no previous training. And surprisingly, if you already own an underwater camera system, macro-photography can be a rather inexpensive way to expand your photographic capabilities. You can get started in underwater macro-photography in any number of ways.

WHAT EQUIPMENT IS NEEDED?

Should you already have an underwater camera, whether it be an inexpensive box camera in a plastic housing, a Nikonos, or a sophisticated Hasselblad in a machined aluminum housing, macro-photographs can be made with:
Close-up lenses (diopters)
Extension tubes
Macro-lenses
Telephoto lenses
Each has its specific function, advantages and disadvantages.

THE CLOSE-UP LENS

Undoubtedly, the Nikonos 35mm camera is the undisputed winner in the matter of availability of the greatest variety of accessory equipment for macro-photography. Its compact size is ideal for working into close quarters where the most interesting subjects always seem to be. Supplementary close-up lenses, diopters which are relatively inexpensive magnifying lenses, can be easily attached to the front of the camera lens and will permit focusing at distances much shorter than the lens by itself could focus. The term "diopter" is commonly used among opticians to express the refractive strength of eye glasses. They are really measuring the focal length of the eye glass lens.

In effect, the power of the diopter and the camera lens combine to produce a shorter focal length than that of the lens alone. As a result, it is now possible to focus at closer subject-to-camera distances. The shorter the focal length, the closer to the subject you can focus. For example, the minimum focusing distance for the standard 35mm Nikonos lens is 2.64 feet. By the addition of close-up lenses, the camera-to-subject distance can be reduced to only a few inches and still retain precise and accurate focus. Diopters are available in varying refractive powers from 1 through 10 and are classified as either positive or negative. (For example, 1+, 2+, or 1−, 2−.) Positive diopters tend to shorten the focal length of a lens allowing shorter focusing distances. Negative diopters *increase* the effective focal length of a lens, causing a telephoto effect. In general, the higher the diopter number, the greater the refractive power of the lens and the shorter its focal length. Also, the higher the number, the shorter the apparent subject-to-camera distance.

It is possible to "stack" as many as three diopters together to shoot at still closer distances. A 1+ and a 2+ diopter, for example, equal the refracting power of a 3+ diopter. When stacking diopters, always mount the stronger lens nearest the camera.

ADVANTAGES

Supplementary close-up lenses (diopters) are inexpensive and available for most any camera made today. There are even close-up lenses for Kodak Instamatic cameras providing the diver-photographer with a meager budget the opportunity to photograph in the subsea world of miniatures.

With the Nikonos camera, the close-up lens can be removed underwater thereby allowing full versatility of the camera lens. This can be a particularly important benefit when some exciting subject turns up unexpectedly. The close-up lenses can be quickly removed and the photographer is free to shoot at long, medium or close-up distances. It is a certainty if you are shooting with *camera and housing* set up for close-ups or macro shots, a love-sick whale or some other once-in-a-lifetime photographic opportunity will present itself. You're simply out of luck.

Another advantage of particular importance to those not blessed with the clearest diving water is that excellent macro-photographs can be made in the poorest visibility. Since such short subject-to-camera distances are involved, clear photographs can be made where the visibility is measured in inches.

Making sharp, colorful macro-photographs with close-up lenses is perhaps the easiest type of underwater photography. The camera's settings can be pre-set at the surface, requiring that the underwater photographer only compose the picture, frame it and trigger the shutter release. And unlike the macro-tube which requires a totally different exposure calculation, the close-up lens uses essentially the same exposure required by the standard lens itself.

DISADVANTAGES

All arguments to the contrary notwithstanding, when a simple, inexpensive diopter is placed in front of a high quality lens — it is inevitable that some loss of picture quality will occur. It seems a small price to pay, however, for the immeasurably increased versatility of the camera lens.

CLOSE-UP SYSTEMS FOR THE NIKONOS

NIKKOR NO. 2

Perhaps the least expensive way to get into the field of ultra close-ups is one suggested by Jim and Cathy Church. They simply use a NIKKOR NO. 2 close-up lens (which incidentally is not 2+ diopters as you might imagine, but corresponds instead with a value of 3+ diopters) with the 52mm filter adaptor ring and the W-NIKKOR 35mm lens. The image area is approximately 6″ x 8½″ when the measured camera-to-subject distance is 11 inches.

MICRO-LENS

Another popular close-up lens for the Nikonos camera is the micro-lens, a two-element, color-corrected lens

hermetically sealed in plexiglas and pressed into a stainless steel tube which is slipped over the Nikonos lens. The micro-lens provides *two* underwater focusing distances thereby increasing its usefulness over a range of close-up subjects. When the lens focus is set at infinity, the focus point is 8.4" from the front of the micro-lens. When set at its nearest focus (2.75 feet), the point of focus is 4" from the front of the micro-lens.

Generally speaking, the greater the refractive power of your close-up lens, the shorter the depth of field. The micro-lens provides a good depth of field for close-up photography. From as much as 4 inches at f/22 down to one inch at f/2.5. This is a rather important advantage since, in the short subject-to-camera distances of macrophotography, depth of field is so tremendously restricted.

As is true of all the supplemental close-up lens systems for the Nikonos, since there is no reason for them to be air tight, a water space is introduced between the close-up lens and camera lens. To avoid air bubbles in this space which could obscure the photograph, the common practice is to both attach and remove the close-up lens while underwater.

HYDRO PHOTO CLOSE-UP LENS

Hydro Photo produces three close-up lens systems for the standard Nikonos 35mm lens. The lenses are designated #1, #2, and #3 which refers, unfortunately, to the model number and *not* the diopter value. As a result the #3 lens produces the *least degree* of magnification and #1, the greatest. Just the opposite of the diopter ratings!

The magnifying lenses are sealed in clear acrylic and snap easily into the Nikonos filter adapter ring which in turn is screwed onto the Nikonos lens. The #1 and #2 lenses have two elements separated by a barrier of nitrogen which eliminates any fogging caused by condensation. This is no problem for the #3 lens since it has only one element. These lenses can also be "stacked" to further increase

the refracting power. The #3 lens covers a measured picture area of approximately 8" x 12", #2 about 4" x 6" and when using the #1 lens, 2¼" x 3¼".

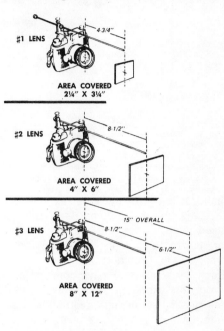

The #1 lens has a depth of field of approximately ¾" at f/22; #2 and #3, slightly more.

There are almost as many close-up lens systems produced for the 28mm Nikonos lens as for the standard 35mm (Green Things and Hydro Photo come first to mind). It is important that you buy the close-up lens designed for your specific lens or else undesirable vignetting (cropping of the format around the edges of the image) may occur.

NIKONOS CLOSE-UP LENS

With all the close-up lens systems produced for the Nikonos by outside manufacturers, it seems only fair that the Nikon people would design a close-up system of their very own. There is little doubt that the Nikonos close-up lens contains the best optics of all the close-up systems designed specifically for the Nikonos. On the other

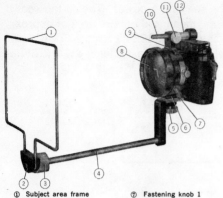

① Subject area frame
② Frame holder
③ Fastening knob 4
④ Supporting bar B
⑤ Fastening knob 3
⑥ Holder B
⑦ Fastening knob 1
⑧ Close-up lens
⑨ Holder A
⑩ Supporting rod A
⑪ Fastening knob 2
⑫ Safety device

THE PROBLEM OF FOCUS AND FRAMING

Most cameras suffer such enormous parallax error at close-up camera-to-subject distances as to make viewfinders or sportsfinders unusable for framing and composing the subject. The Nikonos is no exception. Consequently, the subsea photographer is without a means to accurately aim this camera and frame his subject.

To further compound the problem, we have an extremely shallow depth of field due to the close-up camera-to-subject distances. An error of as little as one-half inch in estimating the camera-to-subject distance would throw the photograph out of focus. If the subsea photographer is to have well-composed, sharply focused macro-photographs, he must have some way to accurately measure the camera-to-subject distance.

A few underwater photographers claim to be able to estimate close-up distances by "eye-ball" measurement . . . a practice which may work when operating with a depth of field of 3 or 4 inches. I'd like to check the sharpness of macro-photographs produced by "eyeball" estimate when the depth of field is down to ¾ of an inch.

Some close-up lens systems provide an aiming wand which is simply

hand, it is by far the most expensive.

The 2 group, 2 element lens can be used with either the 28mm, 35mm or 80mm lens and separate focal frames are provided for each lens. Each lens/close-up lens combination produces excellent photographs and the quality of the entire outfit is first rate. Whichever lens is used, the focus control must be set at infinity in order for the framer to be at the point of focus. Each framer is exactly 9.3

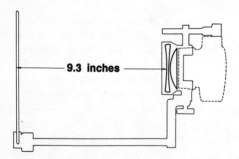

9.3 inches

inches from the optical center of the close-up lens. At this camera-to-subject distance, the subject area covered by each lens is as follows:

28mm	—	144 x 216mm	—	5 5/8″ x 6 7/16″
35mm	—	109 x 164mm	—	4 1/4″ x 6 7/16″
80mm	—	53 x 79mm	—	2 1/16″ x 3 1/8″

an adjustable wire probe secured to the Nikonos accessory shoe. The wand projects in front of the close-up lens to indicate the precise camera-to-subject distance.

Although the wand assures sharp focus, it only can establish the approximate center of the subject area. The accessory shoe which holds the probe is approximately 2½ inches above the optical center of the lens. By positioning the wand tip the same distance above the center of the subject, the picture area — with experience — can be closely approximated by eye.

Some close-up lenses are equipped with a focal framer, a device which not only indicates exact camera-to-subject distance for sharp focus, but also produces a border or frame around the entire picture area. By positioning the device directly over the macro-subject, exact framing and composition result. The framing device is not without its drawbacks. It is next to impossible to keep moving subjects inside the frame, for example. And both wand and focal frame tend to spook the fish. All in all though, the ability to outline the entire picture area tends to be a worthwhile trade-off for the small inconveniences attached to its use. It is particularly invaluable when your macro-subject is up inside a coral crevice, or for that matter, any tight spot too small to accommodate the photographer's head and shoulders.

THE EXTENSION TUBE

Still another popular device for underwater macro-photography is the extension tube. The extension tube is a rugged aluminum sleeve with carefully machined bayonet mounts at each end to mate with the Nikonos body and lens, and fitted with "0" rings to make it both pressure-proof and water-tight.

The extension tube increases lens focal length by moving the lens further from the film plane, thereby re-ducing the focused distance to just a few inches. With the extension tube installed between lens and camera, the lens can be moved much closer to the subject and a much larger image recorded on the film plane. Remember, the image size recorded by a close-up lens is determined by its reproduction ratio. The ratio between the actual subject size and the image size recorded on film is termed "reproduction ratio". If the image recorded on film is one-half the apparent size of the subject, the reproduction ratio is said to be 1:2. If the image recorded is one-third, the reproduction ratio is 1:3. A subject, one square inch in dimension when photographed through an extension tube with a 1:1 reproduction ratio, will produce an image on film of exactly the same dimensions. Remember, macro-photography is defined as a reproduction of images at a ratio of 1:1 or greater.

THE RIGHT REPRODUCTION RATIO

The degree of magnification you're after pretty much determines which extension tube you will want to use. And since they are relatively inexpensive, the serious macro-photographer should probably have at least two. The 3 to 1 extension tube fills the 35mm format with a picture area of about 3 inches, large enough to cover entire mini-creatures and still provide

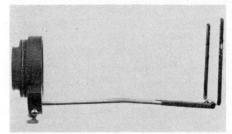

3 to 1 reproduction ratio (35mm lens)

good depth of field. And with patience and practice, even tiny reef fish can be photographed.

The 1 to 1 extension tube yields a

1 to 1 reproduction ratio

true macro-photograph reproducing actual image size on film, making an exciting ultra close-up view of even the smallest detail. The 2 to 1 exten-

2 to 1 reproduction ratio

sion tube provides a field of view approximately 2 inches. When in doubt of the picture area covered, check the framer.

Summarizing, there are a number of extension tubes available in various reproduction ratios. The longer the extension tube, the narrower the angle of view. Correspondingly, the larger the image size and the shorter the focused distance. Some, like certain close-up lenses, can be stacked to increase the image size. All are equipped with focal framers. If there is a significant difference between the close-up lens system and the extension tube, it is one of optics. Whereas the close-up lens basically magnifies the subject to gain a larger image size, the extension tube achieves ultra close-ups without the benefit of supplemental lenses. Some photographers feel that a higher quality image is gained with the extension tube because it uses only the camera lens. Close-up lens devotees, on the other hand, argue

that since the extension tube cannot be removed underwater, each dive must be limited to macro-photography at one set focal distance.

While there may be some overlapping, the close-up lens systems and extension tubes cover different focal ranges. Both can be invaluable in adding to the underwater photographer's range of capability.

FRAMERS AND FOCUS

In ultra close-up photography, the photographer is limited to a very shallow depth-of-field. Because of this narrow zone of focus, as little as ¼" with a 1:1 extension tube, it is clear the photographer had better be mighty accurate with his camera-to-subject distance. The lens must always be set at the shortest possible focus distance (2.75 feet for the 35mm lens and 2 feet for the 28mm lens). Any change from minimum distance will throw the picture out of focus. And as is also true of the close-up lens, at these short subject-to-camera distances, the viewfinder and sportsfinder — due to the parallax error — are of absolutely no help in framing or composing the picture. As a result, all extension tubes are fitted with wire focal frames which not only measure the focal distance precisely, but also skirt the picture area. The frame end is coated with flat black epoxy to eliminate the possibility of reflected light causing lens flare. The frame may be permanently attached to the extension tube projecting a precise focal distance in front of the lens, or it may be adjustable, locked in position by a thumb screw. If it is permanently fixed, any attempt to adjust it will change the focal distance and result in poor focus.

To insure correct focus, the framer must be carefully adjusted according to the manufacturer's instructions. To use the focal frame, simply compose

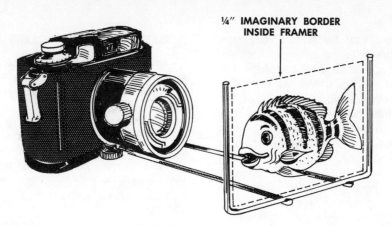

the picture area to within ¼" of the grid sides. The framing device is slightly larger than the picture area so that it will not appear in the photograph. The framer is positioned around the subject as close to the same plane as possible. The extremely shallow depth of field of the extension tube limits the choice of subjects to relatively flat objects. If the subject has greater depth than the tube's zone of focus, it is obvious part of the picture is going to be out of focus.

It is also important to check the alignment and subject-to-camera distance of the framer frequently while underwater. Also check the lens focus setting to be sure it hasn't been bumped and changed. It is possible to change either measurement or alignment unknowingly, throwing the photographs out of focus. Some photogra-

phers, file a nick to mark the frame position so that a quick check can be readily made. And remember, the smallest lens aperture will provide the greatest depth of field and you want all you can get. Use the f/22 iris setting all the time.

BUILDING YOUR OWN FOCAL FRAME

If you have built your own housing and wish to build a focal frame for it, you will find it is not at all difficult. First, you must determine the correct focal distance and the picture area

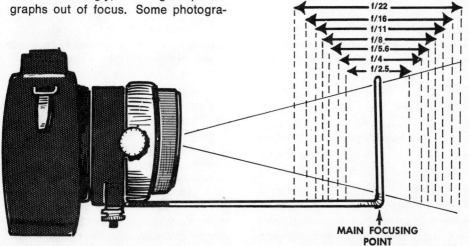

DEPTH OF FIELD

f/22
f/16
f/11
f/8
f/5.6
f/4
f/2.5

MAIN FOCUSING POINT

coverage at that distance. If your camera happens to be a single lens reflex, the distance and coverage are easy enough to determine with the viewfinder focusing screen. If not, it's only a little more work. First, remove the camera back and tape a piece of translucent film onto the film plane. Next, set the shutter speed at the (B) bulb or (T) time setting either of which will hold the shutter open. Now, with the close-up lens or extension tube attached and the camera in its housing, measure the correct camera-to-subject distance. This is the point at which the subject image appears in sharpest focus on the translucent film. This point can be determined easily by slowly moving the camera up and down a ruler held perpendicular to the well-illuminated subject. Where possible, clamp the ruler in place. Once you have the precise focal distance, the image area boundaries can also be determined.

Remember, these dimensions are the *in-air* subject-to-camera distance and picture area. Before you begin building your focal frame, these dimensions must be transposed to underwater measurements (apparent distances and sizes). The underwater measurement can be obtained by simply multiplying the in-air dimensions by 1.33, the refractive index of water. Or perhaps even better, carefully immerse the front port of the housing in a pan of water and adjust the camera and housing up or down to find the sharpest focus.

It is evident there is an awesome range of close-up and ultra close-up accessories available for the Nikonos camera. It is important to point out, however, there are other ways of recording the miniature undersea world on film. Some of the finest work in close-up and macro-photographic fields has been done with conventional cameras in underwater housings.

SINGLE LENS REFLEX CAMERAS

Certainly one of the finest close-up systems for underwater work is the single lens reflex and there are any number of top SLR's that fill the bill admirably. My personal favorite is the Nikon, primarily because of the over-sized prism reflex sportsfinder which shows the entire picture area, measuring about 1″ x 1 5/16″, right side up and unreversed, and the vast lens selection.

The Canon F-1 equipped with the Speed Finder is another excellent system. The oversized viewing screens allow quick focus, depth perception, and fast, easy composition . . . a distinct advantage over other SLR's which have comparatively small viewing screens. And since the subject is viewed exactly as the lens sees it, the through-the-lens viewing capability eliminates the problem of parallax. The photographer need only study the image on the viewing screen, compose the picture, adjust focus and trip the shutter. Better commercial housings accommodate a wide range of lenses. The Oceaneye 100, for example, will accept Nikkor lenses ranging from the 7.5mm fisheye to the 135mm telephoto.

SELECTING THE RIGHT LENS

One benefit of ultra close-up photography is that you don't have to spend extra money for a fast lens. A fast lens in close-up or ultra close-up photography is quite unnecessary. The underwater macro-photographer usually works on the other side of the f/stop scale; small lens openings. To achieve the desired depth of field, the smaller the aperture the better. To determine which lens to use, first decide which reproduction ratio (magnification) you desire. A number of photographers favor the 55mm Micro-Nikkor close-up lens. A reproduction ratio of 1:2 is produced by this fine

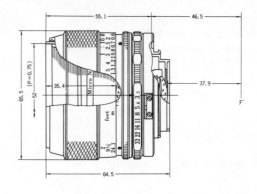

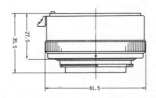
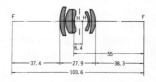

55mm Micro-Nikkor and M2 Ring

lens *without* diopters or extension tubes. With the short extension tube (M2 ring) provided with the lens, a reproduction ratio of 1:1 is produced.

The 105mm and 135mm Nikkor lenses have been used successfully underwater. However, the 105mm has a minimum focal distance of *only* four feet and the 135mm, about five and one-half. At these minimal focal distances, a subject 12 inches long would fill the film format. The obvious advantage is that the photographer can back off and still get good image size and sharply focused pictures. This can really be an asset when photographing spooky fish that duck out of view when the camera gets too close.

Obviously, for this type of magnification, the water must be crystal clear. With the addition of the M2 ring, the minimum focal distance of the 105mm lens is reduced to about 21 inches.

LARGE FORMAT SLRs

For ultra close-ups, large format SLRs like the Hasselblad, Bronica, or Rolleiflex SL66 can produce excellent photographs when equipped with suitable lenses and diopters. For the most part, they offer the same advantages as the 35mm SLRs. And, of course, the big advantage is that the ultra close-up image is reproduced on a large format (2¼″ x 2¼″ or 70mm) which makes for supremely well-detailed enlargements. Ideally, for close-up work the normal lens should be used behind a flat port.

The 80mm Hasselblad with the nor-

Hasselblad SLR Housing

mal lens and the 0.5 Proxar, for example, will focus down to about 16 inches (apparent distance) in water. To further reduce the focal distance and increase the reproduction ratio, a choice of diopters must be made. For ultra close-up photography of postage-stamp size, you need the real refracting power of perhaps 3+ or 4+ diopter.

TWIN LENS REFLEX

While there is certainly a resurgence in popularity of the twin lens Rolleiflex in the Rolleimarin housing, there are a number of talented underwater photographers for whom it has never been away. The impressive work of Doug Faulkner, Ludwig Sillner, and Jack McKenney, to name but a few Rollei devotees, is an indisputable testimonial to the quality and capability of the camera. The Rollei assures pin-point focus through a large viewing screen which produces a bright and extremely sharp image from center to corners. The Rollei is parallax-compensated for the close-up lenses designed for it. The Rollei offers two sets of close-up lenses for underwater photography, the Rolleinar I and II.

Remember, since this is a *twin* lens reflex, both the taking lens *and* the viewing lens must be supplemented with a close-up lens if the photographer is to see what the taking lens "sees". The Rolleinar II can provide a reproduction ratio of 1:4, covering a picture area of about 8-11/16" x 8-11/16" at a subject-to-camera distance of 12¼". Though hardly in the macro-photography category, this popular close-up lens is used extensively for outstanding close-ups of small marine life. Even stronger magnification is possible by "stacking" diopters.

The Rollei is a superb camera, despite its lack of lens interchangeability. In my judgement, the Rolleimarin housing is still one of the best ever engineered.

SUBJECT SELECTION

A whole new realm of exciting photographic subjects await your camera. The local quarry may produce minia-

ture creatures every bit as strange and exotic as those on the most remote coral reef. And because of the camera-to-subject distances of only a few inches, crisply focused, beautifully colored macro-photographs can be made in the poorest visibility. And this fascinating new miniature world of macro-life can be found where ever you dive, if you can only *see* it.

Seeing, of course, requires that the photographer train himself to locate worthy subjects. Now the subsea photographer must learn to look for an entirely different dimension of photographic subjects. These are subjects whose very presence will elude him unless he has studied them and learned where to search for them. Return to the books . . . and there are many fine, well-illustrated books from which to choose. Become familiar with the fascinating mini-creatures you wish to photograph. A new world will reveal itself to you! Not only tropical reefs, but pier pilings, rock jetties and quarry walls will disclose whole communities of incredibly diverse miniature plant and animal life. For the photographer who has trained himself to search carefully for his macro-subjects, the reward is most generous. He has entered the microcosmic world of nudibranch and anemone, the delicate and fragile state of lace coral and the rugged domain of never before discovered textured fossils. Having mastered the stationary subject matter, he must further expand his ability by photographing the miniature fish that inhabit every coral.

FILM

While close-up and ultra close-up photography can be done using high speed films and existing light, the results are rarely satisfactory. The best close-up and macro-photographic work is done with the slow emulsion, fine grain films and plenty of artificial light. Specifically which of these films you should use is largely a matter of individual preference, since many films in the ASA 25 to 64 range, while displaying different color characteristics and some more grainier than others, provide good results. Among the best are Kodachrome 25, Kodachrome 64, Ektachrome X, Agfachrome 64, Dynachrome 64 and GAF 64. My favorite close-up film is Kodachrome 25. Although it requires a lot of light, Kodachrome 25 produces the finest detail and the least grain of any film I've used. It is balanced for 5500 K, has excellent color resolution, is sensitive to the red end of the spectrum, and provides good contrast.

Agfachrome 64 is also balanced for 5500 K but is twice as fast at ASA 64 as Kodachrome 25 and consequently, requires less light. Agfachrome is tops for algae or kelp shots because it produces excellent greens. Due to its magenta cast and excellent rendition of warm colors, reds and yellows are quite striking.

My experiences with Kodachrome 64 and Ektachrome X in macro-photography have not been as exciting as with Kodachrome 25 or Agfachrome 64. Both display an overall greenish-blue cast which seems to rob the picture of some punch. But color appeal is a matter of preference and in macro-photography especially, I suggest you experiment with several films until you find one with the most appeal. While this appears to be in conflict with the earlier caution of selecting one film and mastering it before experimenting with others, I assure you it is not.

In macro-photography, because of the nearly automatic procedures and short camera-to-subject distances, exposures don't really vary much. As a result, you see precisely what a particular film can do within clearly defined limits. If you aren't pleased with the results of one film, try others until you find the one you like best.

LIGHTING AND EXPOSURE

The underwater macro-photographer rarely shoots with just natural light. If it must be done however, and it can, take accurate light meter readings and use the smallest f/stop possible, consistent with good exposure. But to get attractive, sharply focused and well-illuminated macro-photographs consistently, artificial light is a must.

Underwater flash or strobe enhances the macro-photograph, bringing out the brilliance of colors by establishing the correct color temperature balance between film and light source. Only with underwater strobe or flash is there sufficient intensity of light to use the smallest f/stops. Remember, the smaller the f/stop, the greater the depth of field! To make the most of the short depth of field, the f/stop should always be f/22 or smaller. Generally speaking, when using supplementary close-up lenses the proper exposure is determined as in normal picture taking. With the extension tubes, however, calculating exposure is just a little more involved. You recall, f/stop is determined by dividing focal length by lens opening. Since we increase focal length with extension tubes, we have a slower lens because its light passing ability is slower. Consequently, the f/stop indicated on the lens is not the true lens opening. Depending on the reproduction ratio of the lens-tube combination, it will be as much as a full stop or two smaller. Fortunately, this is a small problem which is easily corrected by decreasing the light source-to-subject distance. For example, a strobe held 12 inches from the subject gives optimum exposures for a macro-subject photographed with a 3 to 1 extension tube. Switching to a 1 to 1 extension tube, under the same conditions, the strobe should be held only 4 inches from the subject to yield the correct illumination.

In the same manner, exposures may be bracketed. Once exposure is set, do not change f/stops. Instead, vary the exposure by moving the light nearer or further from the macro-subject.

STROBE OR FLASHBULB

My personal preference is strobe and since we're dealing with such short subject-to-camera distances, even the inexpensive, low-powered units will do an excellent lighting job. If you must use flashbulbs, experiment with several types until you find the one that renders the most pleasing results. Use the smaller bulbs since most of the larger flash bulbs are too powerful for ultra close-up photography. For the Nikonos flash, M3B bulbs

The powerful M3B flashbulb

are the decided favorite for short distances. They are less expensive, stronger, and less likely to leak than the bigger bulbs. They are negatively buoyant and consequently, easier to handle underwater. The M3B bulb, however, is too small for the Nikonos flash socket so an adapter must be used. These adapters are inexpensive and can be found at most any photo store. The optimum exposure varies with the light source, the lens system and the light-to-camera distance. The following table will serve as a jumping-off point from which you can develop your own exposure table.

CLOSE-UP EXPOSURE TABLE

Camera-To-Subject Distance (Apparent)	Strobe (Watt Seconds)	Flash Bulb	Shutter Speed	Film Speed	F-Stop	Light-To-Subject Distance (Apparent)
3 feet	150	—	1/60th	ASA 64	F-11	3 feet
3 feet	100	—	1/60th	ASA 64	F-8	3 feet
3 feet	—	6B	1/125th	ASA 64	F-8	3 feet
2 feet	—	6B	1/125th	ASA 64	F-16	2 feet
2 feet	150	—	1/60th	ASA 64	F-22	2 feet
2 feet	100	—	1/60th	ASA 64	F-16	2 feet
12 inches	100	—	1/60th	ASA 64	F-22	12 inches
12 inches	50	—	1/60th	ASA 64	F-16	12 inches
12 inches	—	6B	1/125th	ASA 64	F-22	18 inches
12 inches	—	M3B	1/125th	ASA 64	F-22	12 inches
10 inches	—	AG-1	1/60th	ASA 64	F-16	10 inches
9 inches	—	FP	1/125th	ASA 64	F-16	9 inches
9 inches	—	MF	1/30th	ASA 64	F-16	9 inches
9 inches	100	—	1/60th	ASA 64	F-22	9 inches
9 inches	50	—	1/60th	ASA 64	F-16	9 inches
8 inches	—	M3B	1/60th	ASA 64	F-22	8 inches
7 inches	—	M3B	1/60th	ASA 64	F-16	12 inches
Extension Tubes						
3:1	150	—	1/60th	ASA 64	F-22	12 inches
3:1	—	26B	1/60th	ASA 64	F-22	12 inches
2:1	150	—	1/60th	ASA 64	F-22	9 inches
2:1	—	FP	1/60th	ASA 64	F-22	9 inches
1:1	—	FP	1/60th	ASA 64	F-22	6 inches
1:1	150	—	1/60th	ASA 64	F-22	6 inches

HOLDING THE FLASH

The position of the flash relative to the subject is quite important as is the distance between subject and flash. First, the flash should be hand held. By hand holding the flash, the photographer is free to experiment with different lighting angles to achieve different effects. Try side-lighting and back-lighting for exciting results. But watch those flat angles! They tend to foreshadow the subject, exposing only the side nearest the light. Since most shutter releases are tripped with the right hand, it follows that most macro-photographs are made with the flash hand-held in the left hand. It may be a problem if you're not left-handed . . . and perhaps even if you are. The angle at which the flash is held is critical, particularly if it doesn't happen to be aimed at the subject. When you are concentrating on framing your subject or composing a shot, it's easy to let the hand-held flash drift off a few degrees. At these short light-to-subject distances, the light may only partially illuminate the subject . . . or may miss completely!

To get good results consistently, position the flash above and slightly to the left of the subject. The correct flash-to-subject distance must be determined in order to avoid under or over-exposing the subject. Whether using flash bulbs or strobe, do not hold the flash too close to the subject or the picture will be burned out.

With the smaller strobes, the problem is not critical. For flash bulbs, however, the short distances involved could easily result in the subjects being over-lighted. There are a number of possible solutions. First, use only blue bulbs to reduce the intensity of the flash. Remove the flash reflector entirely or try covering the flash with a diffusing screen or even a handkerchief.

BACK SCATTER

When a flash is held too close to the lens and ignited, light from the flash is reflected back into the lens from particles suspended in the water between the subject and the lens. This problem is minimized in macro-photography. Because the lens is placed so close to the subject there is not much water, and consequently, not much particulate between camera lens and subject to cause the "snow" effect. Also, most macro-subjects are usually top or side-lit which further reduces the chances of scatter. As a result, clear, well-defined macro-photographs can be made even in dark, turbid water. However, it only makes good sense to be careful not to kick up the bottom and the less movement, the less likely the chances of stirring up the sediment and ruining the photograph.

SUMMARY

In short order you will discover that the position of your flash, the reflectivity of your subject and water clarity, are all variable factors which influence exposure. As you begin to experiment with different films, different flash angles, and different light-to-subject distances, you will soon find that getting first rate macro-photographs has become second nature.

". . . every photograph . . . is an attempt to penetrate and capture the unique, esthetic moment that singles itself out of the thousands of chance compositions, uncrystallized and insignificant that occur in the course of a day."

Lewis Mumford

Chapter XI.

GETTING IT ALL TOGETHER

Edward Weston once said that ". . . good composition is merely the strongest way of seeing things." And while there is much truth to his statement, it is equally true that one hundred photographers can view the same subject and each will come away with his own distinct "strongest way". So, while composition is generally presumed to mean the artistic arrangement of all the picture elements, each photographer "sees" the composition or arrangement of the elements in a distinct and highly personal way.

It can be argued with good reason that there are really two types of underwater photography, the scientific tool and the art form. Scientists, whose work requires the use of underwater photography, state frankly their needs are amply fulfilled if their pictures are well-exposed and crisply focused. They dismiss any thought of composition as being time wasting and unnecessary. Composition, they argue, is for the underwater photographer who has time to dabble in art forms. Nothing could be further from the truth. The fact of the matter is that composition is as fundamental to good photographic work as focus or exposure! And once the ability to compose good photographs consistently is developed, it doesn't take any longer and what a difference it makes.

The undersea photographer is limited only by his ability to recognize interesting subjects and put together the most harmonious organization of the picture elements. Every good photograph is not simply a picture; it is a photographic statement. It may tell a complete story, impart a thought, or simply portray beauty.

THE ELEMENTS OF COMPOSITION

To a great extent, the impact a photograph has on an audience is a result of thoughtful and skilled composition. In order to develop this all-important ability, the beginning subsea photographer must understand and employ each of the elements of photographic composition.

EMPHASIS

A good photograph should have an outstanding or dominant subject. There should be no question in the mind of the audience about the meaning of the photograph. If there is no dominant subject, the photograph has no meaning or purpose.

Far and away the greatest single mistake in photography is the failure of the photographer to move in close enough to his principal subject. All too frequently, otherwise perfectly good photographs are spoiled because the principal subject is lost among a welter of distracting features. In the foreground or background are subjects of lesser importance, all of which compete for the viewer's attention.

Always apply this universal commandment of good composition, "EMPHASIS: The Name Of The Game Is Fill The Frame!"

Occasionally, it is impractical or perhaps impossible to get close enough to the subject to fill the frame. The principal subject can still be unmistakably emphasized in the photograph, by *isolating* it which means basically keeping the composition simple and uncluttered. The subject can be "isolated" by filling the frame with it, either by actually moving in close or with a telephoto lens. The subject can also be lifted free of a confusing background or foreground by selecting the best point of view (the position from which the photograph is "seen" by the camera lens). Sometimes just shifting the camera position up or down a foot or so changes the composition radically.

Shooting upwards will frequently help to isolate the principal subject by cropping out confusing clutter and presenting the subject against a clean background. And there is no rule against shooting downwards, if a downward camera angle is the best point of view for a particular composition. Shooting from a higher camera angle is another way of emphasizing the subject by uncluttering the background. The subject can also be emphasized by using the strobe as the principal light source thereby casting heavy shadows over detracting foregrounds and backgrounds.

Still another method which can be successfully implemented to isolate and emphasize the subject is by critical or selective focus. By using the widest lens openings the depth of field is substantially reduced. The result is that the principal subject is crisply focused between a foreground and background which are in fuzzy focus.

THE CAMERA SEES EVERYTHING!

Another common mistake of the beginning photographer is forgetting that the human eye selectively emphasizes subjects. The camera lens, on the other hand, sees everything. If you get too excited while trying to photograph a large angelfish, for example, you probably won't notice the presence of a distracting background or foreground which will probably turn out as well-exposed and sharply focused as the angel fish in the developed film. While the human eye pinpoints the object of interest, isolating it from any surrounding clutter, the camera lens attributes equal value to all the objects within its field of view.

HARMONY

A well-composed photograph will first draw the viewer's eyes to the principal subject and then to lesser subjects of similar characteristics and thence . . . out of the photograph. When I view a good photograph, I know my eyes are being drawn into, around, and out of the picture exactly as the photographer intended. And it happens so subtlely, that the viewer doesn't even realize it. Harmony is the hallmark of good composition. It is the element which produces the feeling of unity and completeness. A good photograph is like a good book or good painting; each time you examine it, you receive pleasure from it.

PROPORTION

One of the most distressing misconceptions shared among neophyte photographers is the belief that subjects glued in the center of the format are well-composed. They rarely are. Almost without exception such pictures could have been vastly improved by the use of the so-called "Law of Thirds". Basically the Law of Thirds

"Law of thirds"

is an imaginary grid which divides the picture format into thirds. By re-positioning the principal subject at any of the four grid intersections, the photograph will have much more impact. This element of composition produces a division of the space covered by the photograph of the most eye-pleasing proportions. The technique is really not at all difficult. Looking through the sportsfinder or ground glass screen, simply imagine that the format is divided into thirds, horizontally and vertically.

BALANCE

Balance is the term which, when used in relation to the composition of a photograph, determines how well the photographer has thought out the intent of the photograph. A properly balanced photograph will have lesser subjects so positioned in the composition that they compliment and balance the principal subject without competing with it for the viewer's attention.

Sometimes a photograph can be balanced by using coral overhangs or cave entrances to frame the dominant subject. The technique not only frames and balances the picture, but even adds extra dimension. Before the photographer even swings the viewfinder up to his eye he should give thought to the *why?* of the photograph. What is the impression or the message he is trying to communicate? Good composition begins in the mind . . . *before* the viewfinder is brought up to the eye.

SHAPES, SHADOWS AND SYMMETRY

To a great degree, the composition of a photograph depends on the selection of the subject. A photograph of a manta ray in flight, for example, classically depicts grace and motion. The shape of the subject, to a great extent, sets the mood of the photograph.

Shadows can provide dramatic effects underwater. The wise subsea photographer will use them happily, carefully arranging the distribution of blacks and whites. Any good photographer knows that the viewer's eyes will be naturally attracted from dark areas to light areas. And the smaller the light area, the greater the attraction. Consequently, by arranging for the area of greatest contrast to be at the center of interest — the dominant subject, the photographer insures that the viewer's eyes are drawn to the exact spot he wants them.

A multitude of symmetrical shapes are actually lines which combine to form letters like T, V, Y, Z, N, L, or A. Photographs based on geometric composition usually lend a feeling of great strength and solidity.

MOODS

Compositions can be either dynamic or static. Dynamic compositions portray action, excitement and movement. Static compositions, conversely, depict non-moving subjects, coral sea scapes and the like. Static photographs, as a consequence, are usually gentle, peaceful and serene. Curved lines, for example, like O, C and S depict grace and flowing movement. The subject matter and the purpose of the photograph, to a large extent, set the mood. A good photograph can elicit happiness or sorrow from the viewer . . . as well as anger or love. The fact is, a good photograph is fully capable of drawing from the viewer most any human response. The good photographer is fully in charge of his talents and equipment and, therefore, capable of extracting any emotion he desires from the audience.

COLOR BALANCE

Composition must also consider the harmonious arrangement of *color* within the film format. Dashes of color add much zest to underwater photographs which are all too frequently portrayed in uniformily muted blues or greens. Avoid the use of colors where they might detract from the principal subject. Instead, use your colors to compliment or call attention to the subject. Color can help set a mood or tempo and establishes greater perspective. When properly balanced, it tends to unify all elements of the photograph giving even greater vitality. Balancing color simply means avoiding any excessive differences or clashes in color in your compositions. It is important to remember, however, that there are few hard and fast rules in underwater photography. The photographer should experiment with colors.

HAVE A PLAN

One inescapable fact of life is that a good photograph must have a purpose. The purpose may be to entertain or to inform. It may tell an entire story by itself or as one of a series of informative photographs. But if a picture has nothing to say, it may well be that it is pointless and the viewer will be left with the impression the photographer probably had one shot remaining on the roll and decided to shoot *something* so he could have the film processed.

Most amateur underwater photographers have no definite plan in mind when they start a dive. Instead, they hope to find interesting subjects along the way. And they certainly can. Photographic opportunities are everywhere — literally surrounding the underwater photographer. He is limited only by his ability to "see" the photographic compositions. Unfortunately, many beginning undersea photographers are blind to such opportunities. But picture blindness need be only a very temporary condition.

The aspiring subsea photographer has only to study the pictures in any of the undersea periodicals to get a feel for underwater subjects and how they can be composed. If you see a particularly impressive picture, try to duplicate it. Study it. Explore different lighting angles and change camera position frequently. Visualize how the subject might look from a different point of view. Do this enough and before you know it, you'll be creating photographs in a style that is distinctively your own.

Back to planning. Professional undersea cameramen, on the other hand, usually dive with a pretty well-defined job in mind. A lot of time can be wasted underwater waiting for something to happen. The professional can't afford the time. He anticipates every possible problem and arranges for contingencies.

MODEL RELEASE

Basically, the law of the land prevents a photographer from using the physical likeness of any person for commercial use without first obtaining his or her written consent. All magazine publishers require a model release whenever the subject's features are recognizable in a photograph. Whether you intend to sell your photographs or not, it's still a good idea to have the model sign a release.

The model release is a legal document which, strictly speaking, gives this permission to the photographer thereby protecting him from any legal action by the subject or the subject's legal guardian. A sample of a Model Release form can be found in the appendix.

SEQUENCE SHOOTING

Another way to bring an exciting new dimension to your slide presentation is through sequence shooting. Sequence shooting can produce an impression of flowing motion by showing the different stages of action through a series of photographs. For example, a photographer is shooting a diver being towed by a diver propulsion vehicle.

No. 1 slide could be a medium distance shot showing the diver and vehicle approaching . . .

No. 2 slide might show a close-up of diver and vehicle abreast of the camera . . .

No. 3 slide could be another medium distance shot showing the diver and scooter going away from the camera.

But don't limit yourself to three or four slides in a sequence. Shoot as many at different stages of the action as possible. Later, you'll be able to select the shots that best show the action. A battery-powered motor drive can be a definite asset in making a rapid series of photographs. With a well-designed housing, however, the subsea photographer should be able to advance the film — cock and trip the shutter — and advance the film again fast enough to catch most underwater action. Sequence shooting can also add drama and impact to a presentation by using sequences to tell a story. For example, if a macrophotograph of a brittle star is flashed on the screen, the audience has little or no sense of proportion relative to the size of the brittle star. Now, if a second slide showing a close-up of the underwater camera and the brittle star together is flashed on the screen, some sense of size is established. The third shot showing the camera, brittle star, and the diver's head and shoulders would establish a definite size relationship. A fourth (long distance) shot might show the vastness of the reef by dwarfing the diver against a background of coral. Projected on a screen, the sequence would take the audience underwater.

RETAKES

The data which he has carefully recorded in the log book is meaningless unless the photographer makes it work for him. Using the data he has extracted from previous experience, both good and bad, he should retake all pictures. When the photographs have been developed, which will he find most striking? What could he have done to make it even better? Does it need more light? Would composition be improved by changing camera positions? The point is, anyone can get lucky occasionally and trip the shutter to get an outstanding photograph without even knowing how. The serious underwater photographer, on the other hand, consistently shoots good pictures. And frequently, outstanding pictures. The talent to do this derives largely from taking lots of pictures and learning something from each one. No photograph, regardless of how bad it may seem to be, is worthless if one tidbit of knowledge can be distilled from it.

UNDERWATER HAZE

Haze is an everpresent problem of underwater photography presenting itself in varying degrees even in the clearest of waters. It can seriously degrade the quality of a photographic image by causing it to appear foggy and dull and generally lacking in crispness and contrast. The problem is the space of water separating the camera and subject. The poorer the visibility of the water, the greater the degrading of the photographic image.

Earlier, visibility was defined as the maximum distance (vertically or horizontally) at which an object can be clearly distinguished. Visibility, to a large degree, is determined by the amount of microscopic particulate suspended in the water. The greater the concentration, the more is light scattered, diffused, and absorbed — and the poorer the visibility. Most beginning photographers believe mistakenly that if an object is identifiable at an underwater distance of 100 feet, a photograph made at the same distance will show the subject as clearly. The truth is that human vision and camera vision are not the same. The camera lens will not produce a photographic image of the subject as clear and well defined as the eye sees it.

There are several remedial steps that can help the undersea photographer get good photographs under conditions of less than ideal visibility. First, eliminate as much of the water space between subject and camera as possible. Next, for good photographic results never photograph anything at a subject-to-camera distance of *more* than *one-fifth* (1/5) of the visibility. For example, if the visibility is 100 feet, limit your subject-to-camera distance to 20 feet. Haze can be further reduced by using a water-corrected wide angle lens which restores the in-air focal length of the lens. The photographer can, therefore, work even closer to his subject. Both model and photographer must stay well off the bottom so their fins do not stir up the sand and further reduce visibility. Finally, for sharper outlines, find a photographic point of view which separates the subject from the background.

SHOOTING

Nobody can tell you how many photographs you should shoot and taking a lot of pictures, in itself, is no guarantee you'll ever become a good photographer. The odds are, however, if you can learn from past mistakes, you're bound to improve.

The point is, balanced against the cost of getting to your dive site (particularly if the dive site is out-of-state or, even better, out of the country), film costs are very small indeed. I am amazed by people, professing to be underwater photography enthusiasts, who travel to some exotic island for a two week diving trip and expose only two or three rolls of film. I can't imagine any diver who is seriously interested in becoming a good underwater photographer surfacing from a photographic dive without exposing a full roll of film. If you're shooting 35mm, use 36 exposure rolls! Do shoot the whole roll on a given dive. If you surface with only five exposures left, you must change tanks and go back down. And not to shoot a full roll, but only to expose the remaining five shots. Changing film is always a hassle — especially on a rolling boat. Don't be frugal with film. If you see an exciting subject, SHOOT! SHOOT! SHOOT! Bracket your shots! Change camera angles! If something interesting happens by, I don't hesitate to fire off all 36 exposures in one continuous burst of the motor-driven camera. Be generous with your film; it will pay handsome dividends in the long run.

PICTURE SHARPNESS

The one subject on which most everyone agrees is that sharpness is vital to any good photograph. And attaining that sometimes elusive quality is not really difficult. It simply requires equal proportions of good photographic sense and common sense. First, when shooting natural light photographs under low light conditions use the films with the highest available ASA ratings. If the photographer uses slow films in low light conditions, it is doubtful that he will be able to hold the camera steady enough to get sharp pictures at the slow shutter speeds he'll be forced to use. Remember! The slower the shutter speed, the greater the risk of picture blurring. Also, the large lens openings required by low light levels reduce depth of field drastically, Shooting at less than a 1/125th shutter speed is not recommended.

Secondly, many beginning undersea photographers (and a few experienced ones who should know better) don't take the time to check their framing and focus. Proper framing is simply a matter of learning to use the viewfinder, sports finder, or reflex viewing system accurately. This translates into shooting pictures at various subject-to-camera distances and studying them. In this manner, the photographer learns to add or subtract the necessary corrections.

Focus, however, is another matter. To achieve accurate focus underwater, the photographer must be able to estimate distances with reasonable accuracy. Due to the refraction of light rays as they pass from water to air, the "apparent" subject-to-camera distance is actually ¾ of the actual distance. If you are estimating distance for a viewfinder camera like the Nikonos, you need only estimate the "apparent" distance and focus the lens at that distance. The lens, like your eye, is subject to the same refractive error. Therefore, it sees the same "apparent" distance. For example, if the actual subject-to-camera distance is four feet, the lens would be focused at the apparent distance, three feet. Remember, the larger the lens opening and the shorter the subject-to-camera distance, the more accurate must be the estimated distance.

Thirdly, learn to steady the camera and yourself underwater to minimize picture blurring movement. Some photographers prefer to plant themselves firmly on the bottom — in effect, making a tripod of themselves. A few even go to the extreme of wearing additional weight belts to hold them fast to the bottom and increase stability. This can be a most dangerous practice. NEVER, under any circumstances weight yourself excessively. If you must shoot in areas of excessive surge or current, use any underwater object, like coral or wreck or boulder to brace against, or hold yourself down. Many photographers will entwine their legs around bottom objects as an octopus might. However, I was once nipped by a large moray eel whom I had startled from a sound sleep by inadvertently seeking a steadying hand-hold on his nose while I composed a picture. Therefore, I feel I can state — with some authority — that before focusing your full attention on making a picture, check the bottom carefully before planting hands and feet anywhere.

If you need additional stability, have your buddy hold you down. If you must use extra weight belts, simply drape them across your shoulder so that they can be quickly thrown off in an emergency. Frankly, rutting around that close to the bottom is a bad idea. Fins tend to kick up the bottom and obscure visibility. If the surge or current is bad enough to warrant extra weight, you're taking a chance on jamming the front port of your housing (or your head, for that matter) into a coral head.

FOCUS BRACKETING

Another technique professionals use to insure a saleable photograph is focus bracketing. A shot is made at the estimated subject-to-camera distance. Then moving back, the photographer takes another at a distance approximately ½ foot greater than the estimated distance; moving closer and still another, ½ foot less. Another way to bracket focus is to set the distance at the estimated subject-to-camera distance. Then remaining in the same position, adjust the distance setting and take two more photographs; one about ½ foot more than your estimate and one ½ foot less.

LIGHT UP AND FOCUS

An underwater flashlight can be an indispensable tool when focusing a reflex camera in dark water — or, for that matter, making camera settings in dark water with any kind of camera. The flashlight can be mounted to the

housing so that its beam parallels the optical axis of the camera lens. The flash or electronic strobe will overpow-er the relatively weak light emitted by the flashlight so no adjustment need be made in determining the exposure.

BUOYANCY CONTROL

The best way to relax underwater so that you can steady the camera and gently squeeze off your shots is by controlling your buoyancy. Buoyancy can be regulated through a buoyancy compensator type vest or through breath control. The buoyancy compensating vest is explained elsewhere in this book and its values are obvious. Breath control can be used effectively to stabilize yourself in midwater. Presuming you and your photographic gear are reasonably close to neutral buoyancy, as well you should, you can literally balance yourself in the water long enough to snap the picture by simply holding your breath for a moment. Compose your photograph, take a breath and hold it only for the moment it takes to steady the camera and squeeze the shutter release.

> *CAUTION:* TO AVOID SERIOUS OVEREXPANSION OF THE LUNGS AND ATTENDANT LUNG BURST PROBLEMS, NEVER HOLD YOUR BREATH LONGER THAN A SECOND OR TWO. IF YOU BEGIN TO RISE, EXHALE IMMEDIATELY!

NATURAL LIGHT

Not all good underwater photographs are made with strobe lighting. A surprising number are made using only natural light. With flash or strobe as the sole light source, only a relatively small area can be illuminated and photographed. With natural light, however, great underwater panoramas can be photographed — the only limiting factor being visibility. The opportunities, composition-wise are virtually unlimited when shooting natural light pictures. Mood and special effect compositions will suggest themselves as underwater lighting changes in response to the sun's arc across the sky.

THE BEST TIME

From a lighting standpoint, anytime is the best time to take natural light pictures. So many underwater photographers refer to the hours between 10 AM and 2 PM as the best time of day for underwater natural light photography that beginning underwater photographers develop an almost obsessive clock-watching attitude. Certainly before 10 and after 2 the natural light is less intense, but exciting photographs can be made during these hours. I've passed over subjects at noon which were brilliantly lighted but disinteresting. Four hours later, the same reef was cast in soft shadow and produced a mood as one might feel tiptoeing through a cathedral. Remember, no hard and fast rules. Experiment!

SUN SILHOUETTES

A technique which is both artfully pleasing and very practical when natural light levels are too low for general photography is silhouetting your subject against the sun. This treatment outlines your subject in an almost three-dimensional manner enabling the underwater photographer to achieve a highly dramatic shot. As a general exposure rule for sun silhouettes — since you're pointing the camera directly at the sun and risking over-exposure — is to stop down approximately two full f-stops when shooting up at the surface . . . and bracket.

The most important consideration in any silhouette shot is the position of the subject relative to the camera.

Since the subject has no front light to identify it for the viewer, it must be clearly outlined so there will be no mistake as to its identity. For example, if our subject is a diver — he should be positioned with his arms and legs extended from his body so the audience can see arms, legs and head. If we want to show that he is a diver with a camera, the camera and flash should be clearly profiled. Experience and experimentation will teach you the positions for the most attractive silhouette shots.

FLASH SILHOUETTES

Almost the same technique can be employed substituting a strobe light for the sun. You will need an assistant to hand-hold the flash which should be equipped with as long an extension cord as practicable — about 12 feet works nicely. The assistant aims the flash back at the camera and the subject is positioned precisely between the flash and camera lens. The result is an exciting flash silhouette.

Be careful that the flash extension cord is not in the camera's angle of view.

The technique can also be done

with a slave tripped flash, either strobe or flashbulb. A little fill-in light from a second light source may make a silhouette shot even more dramatic by softly lighting the subject. The silhouette effect can easily be ruined, however, by over-generous application of fill light. Another way to artfully use a flash silhouette is to position the subject against a brightly lighted and attractive background. Another photographer, for example, can be silhouetted in the light of his own flash as *he* is shooting a picture. The resulting photograph will show the subject and his camera silhouetted sharply against the light of his own strobe which, incidentally, should really be illuminating an interesting underwater subject.

SUBJECTS

I can't help but chuckle every time I recall the following paragraph from Bill Stephens fine book, "Our World Underwater." He describes the frustrations of spending an entire day trying to get ". . . . . . one good picture of a school of fish in the foreground and a diver approaching from behind. When I'd get in position to photograph the fish, the diver would be in the wrong place. When the diver got in the right place, the fish would be gone. Generally this kind of thing goes on until (1) I'm out of air, (2) the other diver is out of air, (3) I'm out of film, (4) the camera has jammed, (5) the fish have given up and gone home, (6) the sun has gone behind a cloud, or (7) a storm has come up and threatens to blow the boat away."

Perhaps ever-so-slightly exaggerated, but every underwater photographer has had days like that. Underwater, photographic subjects are not nearly as cooperative as their above-water counterparts. To shoot good underwater photographs, one must first be able to select interesting subjects — a truism which presupposes the reason you are studying underwater photography is because you have already begun to "see" the multitudes of interesting subjects underwater. But if you have difficulty isolating interesting subjects from those which are drab and uninteresting, here are a few tips.

GET AN OVERVIEW

Learn as much about your dive site as you possibly can. When I dive a new spot, I always take a camera down with me in the event of something exciting happening. But my primary purpose is really to "scout the location". In other words, to get a good idea of the most attractive backgrounds, the highlights of the area, the quantity and type of marine life, and a multitude of other good reasons. I also make a point of diving with people familiar with the area, particularly those who share an interest in underwater photography. Such help is indispensable in determining the area's best photographic subjects. What marine life is likely to be found here? What are their patterns and behaviorisms? And not knowing anyone is no excuse. In a lifetime's experience, I've never known any people who, as a group, were as cooperative, helpful and friendly as people who work on or under the sea. Help is as near as the local dive shop, camera center, Coast Guard station, fishing fleet dock or marine biological station. Occasionally special local attractions like the seasonal migrations of pods of the California Grey Whale to Baja, California determine your subject matter for you. While it is definitely true that knowing what there is underwater to photograph helps the photographer to "see" the subject, it is equally true that much of the fun of underwater photography is stumbling on to an excitingly unexpected subject.

STILL LIFE AND SEASCAPES

Perhaps the best subject matter for the beginning underwater photographer is still life or seascapes since each allows plenty of time for the photographer to select his subject, determine exposure, compose the photograph, and shoot. The bottom of the underwater area where you most frequently dive — whether sea or ocean, lake or river — is loaded with interesting still-life subjects for your camera. Underwater seascapes are also a relatively easy beginning subject. But make no mistake. Seascapes are also an important aspect of undersea photography. No underwater slide presentation could be considered complete without a fair number of seascapes included. A seascape places the audience. In other words, it orients the viewer with the new world in which he is going to be entertained. Seascapes really challenge the photographer's imagination and creativity. Select the best points of view and shoot from each. Try to put a diver in the composition. He should be there to establish a sense of proportion — to show the immensity and expansiveness of the reef.

CLOSE-UP

Virtually all underwater life, plant or animal, lends itself well to close-up photograph and macro-photography in particular. The chapter entitled, UNDERSEA IN MINIATURE, treats this subject most thoroughly. The cardinal rule for this type of undersea photography should be: "KEEP IT SIMPLE!" The best still life shots have a main subject and a simple, uncluttered background. Get into the habit of looking over your subject and selecting the camera angle which best profiles your subject and separates it from the background.

FISH PORTRAITS

One type of underwater photography which can yield great dividends in pride and satisfaction are fish portraits. Even non-diving viewers emit very complimentary "ooooooooh's and aaaaah's" each time a colorful slide of a french angelfish is flashed on the screen.

But the novice underwater photographer soon learns that photographing fish has its own set of special techniques and that he must work a lot harder to get consistently good results in this demanding field. To begin with your photographic skills must be sufficiently developed that you can split your attention between the camera and a very wary subject. If you are seriously interested in developing this aspect of your photographic skill, you will do well to study the marine life in your area. Books, observation, discussions with fisheries personnel, will all help extend your knowledge and suggest interesting photographic opportunities to you.

FISH ARE FRIENDLY

Contrary to the popular beliefs held by non-divers, fish are quite curious and frequently have very distinct personalities. In the Bahamas, I photographed a particularly gregarious grouper named Harry. Harry had two very special weaknesses. He was very fond of having his chin scratched and he had developed a love, bordering on addiction, for the meat of the conch. So much did he love this delicacy with which he was rewarded for his modeling assignments, that if he could knock the quart-sized glass jar — in which the conch was carried — from my grasp, he could empty it in just under three seconds. The lesson was clear and I learned it quickly. "The way to a fish's heart is through his stomach."

I have subsequently used this technique successfully in salt water and fresh — on sea creatures ranging from shark to bass — from manatee to otter. Baits we have used range from conch to canned sardines (which are highly prized by barracuda, incidentally). Cheerios, the breakfast cereal, is loved by small fash but regretably gets soggy and tends to muck up the water. Sea urchins are plentiful and need only be crushed to attract vast numbers of reef fish. Conch passed through a meat grinder and carried in a glass jar seems to have universal appeal and apparently does not attract sharks.

Some photographers "chum" the waters to attract fish. Chumming simply means spreading a curtain of soupy concoction of blood and fish cut into small pieces through your diving area. The fish are attracted to the chum and are so excited about the food that they forget about the photographer. In fresh water, the ever-present clam is just about as effective as the conch is in sea water. Unfortunately, chumming is a less acceptable bait because the fish are uncontrolled and don't associate the food as a gift from the diver. Also chum is as highly regarded by shark as it is by the small, colorful reef fish. Whatever bait you decide to use, plant it behind a coral head out of the camera's view so that it doesn't appear in the photograph.

FISH HABITATS

Don't look for fish in large, open or exposed areas. All but the large pelagic fish feel rather vulnerable in the open and need cover and concealment to feel comfortable. To find fish, the photographer need only find cover and concealment. Shipwrecks, coral reefs, piers and pilings, kelp and weed beds all provide a host of dark recesses, caves, niches in which the fish may go to hide when threatened.

GETTING CLOSE

Feeding them is the first and, many times, the only step the photographer need take to get close enough to the fish to fill the frame. However, the diver must keep in mind that his very size, in proportion to that of the fish, is intimidating. Add to this the great cyclopean eye, the frightening bubbles bursting at short intervals from his regulator, the diver's quick, jerky movements and the startling flash of blinding light from his strobe. It's no wonder the fish are so easily spooked. You will find in short order, certain fish like the grouper become so fearless after being fed, that the photographer may on occasion be forced to push them out of the way in order to photograph other subjects. Other fish, particularly the small reef dwellers, will sorely tax the photographer's patience. He may well waste a whole dive without getting a good picture of the more neurotic subjects.

THE WAITING GAME

Don't chase the fish! They can swim faster and farther than you can. Besides, from that position you can only get the least interesting angle on the subject. Play the waiting game. After you have scattered the food, relax your breathing and settle down into a comfortable and inconspicuous position. This position should be selected with a mind to a suitable background and foreground with which to frame your fish portrait. You will find in short order that fish are driven by an insatiable curiosity. After a short time, you will probably be inundated with curious fish.

Make all your movements with exaggerated slowness. Any sudden movement will cause the fish to bolt and it may take some time before their confidence can be restored. Whenever you find a particularly fertile area, continue to dive that spot as frequently as you can. The fish will become so accustomed to you, in a short time you will actually have them eating out of your hand.

NATURE'S CAMOUFLAGE

To become a successful fish photographer, you must first be able to see the fish and isolate it from its natural background. And this particular talent is not nearly as easy to acquire as it might seem. Many fish — the grouper, flounder, and ray come quickly to mind — are masters of disguise. The underwater photographer must be a consumate investigator. He must examine anything that looks unusual or out-of-place. He must learn to recognize camouflage and he must learn never to touch anything of which he isn't absolutely sure. Scorpion fish and stonefish blend very well with their surroundings, too. The sea creatures may change color or markings or they may simply hide. They may change positions or conceal themselves under sand. But generally, they blend so well with their background, that it requires training and experience to ferret them out.

DIVERS AS SUBJECTS

While fish portraits and seascapes can be beautiful and dramatic, audiences tend to get most excited over photographs which show divers doing their thing particularly if the action is in concert with sharks, porpoises, seals or — for that matter — most any animal. Non-divers may find it somewhat difficult to fully identify with a seascape or a fish portrait. The non-diver has never been there and there is no diver in the scene with whom he can relate. But flash a slide of a diver on the screen and our non-diver, can not only sense the weight-

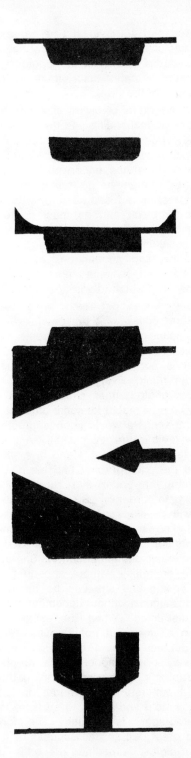

The underwater photographer must learn to recognize camouflage. Can you find the word?

lessness of the diver, but he can also appreciate the size of the coral heads, shipwrecks or fish in the photograph because he can measure them against the size of the diver.

Photographs of divers in action are the most challenging and the most fun of all types of underwater photography. It is also the most frustrating. Consider the plight of the underwater photographer. When he is taking people pictures, he is faced not only with his own problems but he must contend with the model's ear problems, rate of air consumption, distractions, mask clearing, and on and on. . . . And he has only a limited amount of air (time) with which to get these pictures.

In order to get really good diver pictures *consistently* (anyone can have an occasional lucky accident) you must have a truly dedicated model. That is not nearly as easy as most would think. Every would-be underwater photographer should spend a day being a model for some other photographer. He would soon appreciate how tedious the job can be. A good model is indispensable and in a short time the photographer and his model develop an underwater rapport that seems to border on ESP. A good model will develop good "picture sense" and knows what the photographer wants her to do almost before he asks. She anticipates his direction. She can pose gracefully without appearing to be posing and she can be attentive for his signals without becoming bored or distracted. When she exhales, it is in a small but continuous stream of bubbles instead of short, heavy bursts. A good model shares the photographer's enthusiasm for getting good pictures. If his model decides she is cold and wants to surface, the photographer is through. Therefore, to a great degree, the success of the diver-picture expedition depends on the model.

Don't make the mistake of thinking that you can use fellow underwater photographers as models. They are only interested in taking their own shots and after a moment or two of dutifully looking cross-eyed into your lens, they're gone off to their own devices. And it's best that they do. If you follow them around, hoping to get a decent shot, you'll only end up with lots of shots of backsides. And as a final reason, underwater photographers, regardless of how nattily attired they demand their models to be, are usually the rattiest-looking bunch on the reef.

There is nothing more frustrating for a photographer than blowing a great shot because the model didn't understand the hand signals or what she was expected to do. The more people there are in a scene, the more difficult the job of communicating with them. Since they cannot vocalize underwater, the photographer and his model must rely heavily on hand signals. But hand signals are only as effective as their mutual understanding of them.

The best insurance against confusion and mistakes underwater is a pre-dive briefing wherein the photographer and model discuss the various shots or sequences on the schedule. Indeed, when time permits, it is most helpful to "walk through" the shot at the surface showing the approximate model and camera positions and the effect the photographer wishes to achieve. But don't even think of starting the dive until everybody fully understands not only *who* is supposed to do *what,* but *why* she is expected to do it and *when, where,* and *how* she is expected to do it. When the undersea photographer is shooting sea creatures, he takes what he can get. When he makes people pictures, there is no acceptable reason for not being "right on".

STAGING

If you believe that each great diver-action picture you see published was an example of an underwater photographer just happening on the scene at the right instant and click, a super photograph . . . well, you're wrong. Most super photographs are carefully planned beforehand. The photographer and the model discuss the staged poses and the model may even act it out at the surface while the photographer finds the best camera angle. In just a few rolls of film, you will discover which camera angles produce the most flattering results and you and your model can work in concert to further improve on those angles. For a head-on type shot, the model should look just over the photographer's shoulder and never directly into the lens. A quarter-turn or quarter profile is also not bad. In a full profile close-up, however, the model's mouth protrudes unseemingly to grip the scuba mouthpiece.

Even when shooting natural light people pictures, I recommend using fill flash to light up the face and avoid the heavy shadow normally found inside the mask. Hand-hold the flash above and to the side to avoid any flash reflection from the mask lens. If you have no flash, position the model so that she faces the sun. In this way, the ambient light will illuminate the inside of the mask. Still facing the sun, another position will cause the mask lens to reflect the light. Select an attractive background for your subject instead of just shooting her against blue water.

Above all, have your subject doing something — exploring a shipwreck, focusing a camera on a large fish, or any of dozens of things that suggest action to the audience. The tank and regulator themselves suggest action by enabling the model to hang motionless in midwater exhaling a flow of bubbles, which immediately signal *movement* and *authenticity* to the viewer's mind. The movement of bubbles can be frozen by using a shutter speed of 1/125 or faster. Good photographs can be made of a snorkeling diver but the tank, regulator and bubbles add a touch of excitement. The air supply also allows time for the model to change backgrounds and set up shots and eliminates the need to surface continually to breathe.

DRESSING THE DIVER

If your interest in undersea photography is scientific or purely mechanical, you probably couldn't care less how the diving models look underwater. If your interests, however tend toward the graphic aspect of photography, you'd better be concerned. I've seen possibly thousands of otherwise beautiful photographs ruined because the subject-diver was dressed in sweat socks, or rusty-paint-chipped scuba tank or flowered pajamas or . . . the list goes on. In the old days, a well-exposed, colorful photograph was a treat and nobody seemed to mind that the model wore a dirty T-shirt, and cut-off levis, and had harness ends sticking out all over. Those days are over forever. Now, diver-models must be attractively dressed. Check the model's tank and back-pack. Are they neatly painted (preferably in yellow or orange) or are they scratched and rusty? Is the harness frayed? Snaps or buckles missing? Are the straps too long? Do the ends dangle unattractively? The remedy should be obvious. Paint the tank. Repair the harness, fit it to the model and trim off the excess. Is the model wearing a wet suit? Are the armpits and crotch ripped? Are there holes in the knees and elbows? Are the zippers in need of repair? Does it fit well? Does it have an attractive colored nylon exterior or is it black? Black wet suits are murder, photographically speaking, because they absorb rather than reflect light and generally cause the diver to be lost in the picture. Wet suits with colorful nylon exteriors — particularly red — make quite a difference. If the budget can't handle a new wet suit, brighten up the old black suit with an artful application of light blue or yellow seam tape. Color makes a difference in fins, mask and snorkel as well. Equip the model with yellow, light blue, or any light-colored fins, mask, and snorkel in preference to black, which doesn't stand out well at all. And don't let the model wear those awful-looking canvas work gloves. They are really practical but they don't photograph well. Have the model go bare-handed instead. The hand itself is a great deal more attractive.

PHOTOGRAPHY AT NIGHT

Night diving, one of the most delightful forms of diving, can truly extend the undersea photographer's range of activity. Find a likely reef and dive it extensively during the daylight hours in order to completely familiarize yourself with its landmarks. Select, photograph and mark certain coral forms for later study and photographing at night. Equip yourselves with one of the helmet-type lights that can be worn on the head, thereby freeing the hands for camera and strobe.

The world underwater comes alive at night. But contrary to popular belief, there are some reef dwellers that do sleep at night. The parrot fish, normally quite skittish during daylight hours, becomes so docile at night that he may be held in the diver's hands. Corals, which appeared stone dead when marked and photographed during daylight, come excitingly alive at night. The polyps, which are tightly closed by day, expand and extend their delicate tentacles to trap the plankton floating near. Exciting new challenges await your camera at night. One caution should be added. Although this rule applies to daylight diving, it is particularly important at night.

Never corner any large fish or sea creature in a confined area from which his only route of escape is through you. It is perfectly natural for a group of divers to spread out and surround an animal discovered on the bottom and shine their lights down on him. If, at that moment, somebody starts firing off a strobe in the animal's face, it will surely panic and try to escape. If a large enough space is not provided, it will try to make its own. I saw this very situation occur once in a fresh water lake. A group of divers had surrounded a large muskie. The result was that the large fish smashed head-on into the chest of one diver; ricocheted into another; and slapped the mask from the third before he made good his escape.

LIGHTING EMPHASIS

By imaginative use of strobe or flashbulb the viewer's attention can be shifted to any part of the picture composition the photographer may wish to emphasize. To emphasize a fore-

ground subject, hand-hold the strobe so that the subject is lighted from overhead. Conversely, if the principal subject is in the background, the flash should be held above and to the side to concentrate the light on the main subject and avoid illuminating a distracting foreground.

On the other hand, very handsome pictures can be made by thoughtful and clever use of the foreground as a frame for the principal subject. Almost anything can serve as an interesting frame, a porthole of a shipwreck, a kelp bed, a coral outcropping, a cave entrance. For a super effect, position the flashgun between the foreground and the principal subject. You can have an assistant handhold it or simply lay it on the bottom aimed toward the subject. The result will be a beautifully exposed main subject framed by a foreground which appears as a silhouette in the photograph.

MULTIPLE CAMERA DIVES

It is axiomatic in underwater photography that when the undersea photographer commences a dive with his camera rigged for macro-photography, a forty foot whale will give birth to quintuplets five feet from his lens. The point is, regardless how sophisticated his camera — the underwater photographer is committed to a particular style of photography because he generally has only one lens and one type of film on a given dive.

The more involved one becomes in underwater photography, the more necessary it becomes to take two cameras underwater. It is clear in order to cover most underwater subjects one camera should be equipped with a close-up type lens and the other with a wide or even super wide lens. There are a number of systems which can provide a good range of photogra-

interchanged while underwater. The coverage of these lenses ranges from 3″ x 4½″ for the diopters up to a field 160° for the fisheye. The only disadvantage to this system is that the photographer is still limited to one film type and only 36 exposures per dive.

Several firms are currently manufacturing a special bracket which accommodates two Nikonos cameras with single or double strobes. The advantages, obviously, are doubled film capacity, different films speeds and types, in addition to the lens versatility already mentioned. The photographer may use an extension tube on one camera and a super wide angle lens on the other.

The truth is the Nikonos can be mounted on and used in conjunction with virtually any camera and housing made. Some photographers have even "stacked" the Nikonos on top of the venerable "Rollei" thereby supplementing the Rolleimarin's close-up capability with (depending on the lens selected) the Nikonos' wide angle coverage.

THE RIP-OFF

In case you haven't heard there is a universal rule among thieves. "If you see photographic equipment lying around loose, steal it. You can always find a buyer." The most frustrating thing about having a camera stolen is that the thief generally sells the item for one-tenth of its value. Most people would be willing to buy it back at that price. Now for some rules to help you retain ownership:

1. *Never turn your back on your camera for a second!* I have a

phic coverage. The series of close-up, wide-angle and fisheye lenses produced by Aqua-Craft, Inc., for example, really extend the capability of the Nikonos camera in that all these supplementary lenses can be slipped over the standard Nikonos lenses and friend who placed his Nikonos and strobe on a counter as he signed the register at a Bahamian hotel. When he finished signing in, camera and strobe were gone . . . forever.

2. Take down the serial number of every piece of photographic gear you own: cameras, lenses, meters, strobes, and keep several copies of this list in different safe places. (You will also need this list for Customs on trips out of the country.)

3. Buy or borrow a small engraving tool and engrave identifying information on your equipment.

4. Insure your equipment.

CLOSING THOUGHTS

It is unlikely that the subsea photographer will encounter precisely the same conditions underwater on two consecutive days. Therefore, all the material presented in this book — though time-tested and proven — must be considered solely as a guide-line and a jumping-off place. This jumping-off place is the point from which you should begin your own experimentation. There are no universal formulae which can insure prize-winning results. Instead, there is trial and error. In the beginning, mostly error. But with practice and perseverance, more and more good shots. If you've a mind to be a really good undersea photographer, you'd best plan on shooting lots of film. Study! Study the sea. Study its creatures. And study undersea photographs that impress you. Ask yourself how the photographer composed a shot. How could he have improved the composition? Couldn't his lighting have been improved? Now, try to duplicate it. No! Try to better it. Many people emphasize the importance of mastering one film type before moving on to another. I quite agree. But don't be afraid to try something new. To be a creative, artful photographer you must at all costs avoid the "sameness syndrome". That is, taking the same kind of pictures that everyone else shoots. Be an originator.

Note:

Please make it a practice to always extend the courtesy of asking permission before photographing another human being, regardless of the country or his economic situation. A few inconsiderate tourists have generated a great deal of bitterness around the world by not offering this simple courtesy. Occasionally, one gets a camera broken . . . or a jaw.

THE LAST CAUTION

The undersea world is filled with mystery, excitement and beauty. It is easy to become so fascinated with your surroundings that you forget to pay attention to currents and depths and generally what is happening around you. Don't swim off and forget about your diving buddy. Develop your diving skills to such a fine degree that you can focus your attention on photography. And lastly, carefully maintain and wear a good inflatable vest. I can best emphasize the point by paraphrasing the old aerobatics instructor who said of the parachute, "If you need it and haven't got it, you'll never need it again."

"When you acquire a housing for your movie camera, you will, hopefully, become thoroughly familiar with both camera and housing before you take them underwater."

"I keep six honest serving-men . . . they taught me all I knew. Their names are What and Why and When . . . and How and Where and Who. I send them over land and sea; I send them east and west; but after they have worked for me, I give them all a rest."

Rudyard Kipling

Chapter XII.

MOVIE MAGIC

The still photographer must use all his imagination and skill to develop a complete story in a single photograph. The underwater movie maker, on the other hand, has the advantage of a series of photographs taken in rapid succession to give an impression, when projected, of continuous motion. But the story told by this series of photographs must have logical development . . . in the film maker's vernacular, continuity. It must have an introduction, a body, and an ending,

DIVERS AND CAMERAS TAKE 1

and the film story must progress smoothly from scene to scene.

The good movie uses all Kipling's serving- men. The complete story can only be told when the questions of what, why, when, how, where, and who are answered.

Film making presents an endless challenge to the photographer's imagination, and he is indeed limited *only* by his imagination. Ours is, without question, a visual society. And no other media can tell as complete a story in as short a capsule of time as the motion picture.

HOW IT WORKS

The movie camera shoots a series of small photographs (frames) on a long ribbon of film. When these frames are projected on a screen at a speed of 18 frames per second (for Super 8 film), the viewer's eye cannot detect that these are distinctly separate photographs. Instead, he sees an illusion of continuous, uninterrupted motion. This is how the movie camera works.

The *unexposed* film is pulled off the feed (film supply reel) by the sprocket which feeds it into the film gate. (The sprocket in this camera is driven by a spring motor.) In the film gate, the film

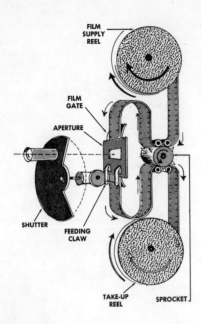

FILM SUPPLY REEL

FILM GATE

APERTURE

SHUTTER

FEEDING CLAW

TAKE-UP REEL

SPROCKET

is pressed flat against the aperture by a pressure plate and exposed. The film is pulled down by the feeding claw, *frame by frame,* past the aperture for each frame exposure. The feeding claw hooks the film by its perforations and pulls it down. The number of times per second that the film is pulled down determines the filming speed. For example, standard filming speed for silent 16mm film is 16 frames per second.

Although the sprocket turns continuously, the film is held stationary for as long as necessary to complete the exposures. There is a finely synchronized interaction between the feeding claw, which pulls the film through the film gate intermittently, and the sprocket, which turns continuously. This interaction proceeds smoothly because of the loops formed by the film. These loops provide the slack which, while allowing the film to spindle continuously off the supply reel and onto the take-up reel, also insures the intermittent frame by frame action of the claw.

Meanwhile, the shutter rotates to cover the film gate and prevent light from striking the film as a frame is

pulled down into the gate. When the next frame is in position, the open section of the rotating disc shutter is positioned in front of the film frame to allow the reflected light to pass through the shutter and strike the film.

PLANNING

Every film maker hopes the audience will enjoy his movie. The measure of a film's success, however, depends on the audience's response. Were they receptive and enthusiastic or bored to tears? And the success of a film depends not only, as you might expect, on the actual production but on the painstaking planning and attention to detail which must precede any worthwhile film project. In the not-too-distant past, to become an instant success in underwater movie making one merely had to find some clear water, colorful reef fish and awesome looking coral and shoot lots of film. But the initial fascination with the underwater world lingered but briefly. Today's sophisticated television viewer is routinely treated to spectacular underwater specials. He expects a great deal more.

In order to be a successful film, be it 100 feet of vacation movies on Super 8 or a sophisticated television documentary, it must have audience appeal. Even an amateur film maker, with the most meager of budgets, should aspire to produce the most appealing film he can. And it all begins, not with a series of disconnected or unrelated underwater random shots, but by building a film as you would tell a story . . . with a beginning, a middle, and an ending. In between, the good film maker will include an interesting series of events which complement the film.

PLANNING CARDS

It should be clear that good films are carefully thought out and reflect a good deal of planning. Perhaps the least painful method of transposing ideas into something more tangible is through planning cards. All right, you already have some vague ideas for a movie taking shape in your mind's eye. Get a stack of 4" x 6" index cards and on each make a rough sketch of an idea you wish to communicate on

film. Below the sketch, pencil in an explanation of the shot's relationship to the film.

First, just make up a planning card for each of the important stages of your movie. As the story line develops, more ideas will be generated and consequently, more cards made up. Eventually the entire film, shot for shot, will be on individual cards. As each card is made up, it should be thumbtacked onto a cork board (planning board) and the cards arranged into a logical development of the story. It is surprisingly easy to visualize a film when you can scan the planning board. It is a simple matter, as well as a lot of fun, to rearrange the planning cards . . . adding cards as necessary or discarding the extraneous. The planning cards do far more than simply outline the film story; they can also help the film maker to visualize the filming procedures.

SUBJECTIVE TECHNIQUE

The planning card sketch indicates the subject's position in the frame as well as the camera set-up for the shot. The position of the camera, relative to the subject, determines how the audience will view the film. In *subjective* film making, the scene is shot as though through the eyes of the subject. By filming from the subject's point of view, the audience is drawn into the scene and becomes a participant in the action.

OBJECTIVE TECHNIQUE

The objective technique, conversely, brings the scene to the audience. The viewer does not participate in the action but sees it instead as an observer.

It is always recommended that the underwater film maker prepare at least a basic shooting script. Even while filming, however, he will find that he must think each sequence through. At the same time, he must always be prepared to film the unexpected. If he should stumble onto some exciting subject matter, the good film maker will forget the script and film the new subject. He has learned that if he shoots enough exciting footage, he can build a film around it. So if there is action, shoot plenty of film while you have the opportunity. Shoot from many different angles and think of how the footage can be developed into a story.

CINEMA VERITÉ

Because it is filmed directly from life without elaborate staging (without making a production out of it, as the saying goes) cinema verité is called direct cinema. This technique is employed in the overwhelming majority

of underwater films. The camera simply follows the subject around, filming it from life. After the film is processed and the footage previewed, then — and only then — is the script written. This technique may at first glance seem a little backward. Its proponents argue logically that no one ever knows exactly what the camera will find underwater and since it is impossible to predict what will happen next, what better technique than cinema verité?

SHOOTING SCRIPT TECHNIQUE

Most professional films made for theatre release begin with a rather strongly defined idea. The film story is written from which a shooting script is developed. Each shot needed to illustrate the story is taken from the shooting script. The advantages of shooting from a script are numerous. The script enables the cameraman to account for the "takes" completed and those yet to be filmed. The script can also specify how a particular scene is to be filmed. If a shooting script is used, there is generally no off-the-cuff filming.

This shouldn't imply the cameraman misses any opportunities. Sometimes an unexpected bonus swims by that turns out to be the best shot in the production.

DEVELOPING THE SCRIPT

Although most amateur underwater films can be made directly from the planning cards, a formalized script is most helpful when the film-maker plans to add narration and musical background. When developing the script, be it after the actual filming or before, the film-maker must be certain each note of music, every sound effect and all words of narrative have a useful purpose and add something to the scene.

The following is an example of a typical script for an underwater film:

SHOOTING SCRIPT—"DIVERS AND CAMERAS"

SHOT	CAMERA	MUSIC/SOUND EFFECTS	VOICE
1	L.S.—Divers making strobe photographs on coral wall	Soft Guitar—Bubbles —Strobes Firing	Narrator: "Welcome to the underwater world of Divers and Cameras!"
2	M.S.—Underwater photographer carefully aiming his camera and hand-held strobe	" " —Bubbles	"Here — deep underwater — on a Caribbean coral reef the undersea photographer is really in tune with life . . ."
3	C.U.—QUEEN Angel fish swimming slowly before camera	" " —Bubbles	"photographically recording the incredibly beautiful reef fish . . ."
4	C.U.—Freeze frame on Queen Angel fish	" " —Strobe Firing	"and discovering vivid colors do exist even in the 'twilight zone' of the deep reef."

(a sample section of shooting script)

CAMERA-TO-SUBJECT DISTANCES

The surest way to start an audience yawning and looking for the nearest exit is to film all scenes at the same camera-to-subject distance, particularly long distances. Any subject worth filming should be shot from different camera-to-subject distances as well as different subject-to-camera angles.

Different distances smooth the transition from one scene to the next, lend variety, and stimulate interest. More importantly, this technique enables the film maker to direct audience attention to only that which he wishes it to see.

Basically, camera-to-subject distances can be described as long shots, medium shots, close-up shots or extreme close-up shots . . . terms relative to the size of the subject being filmed.

LONG SHOT (LS)

The long shot places the scene. It establishes the audience's orientation to the subject's surroundings. In underwater movies this is a particularly important shot since audiences may be composed largely of non-divers who are unfamiliar with the underwater environment. And as such, it is important that this establishing shot be long enough for the viewer to get the "feel" of the scene and the locale.

MEDIUM SHOT (MS)

The medium shot is usually the bread and butter shot in underwater photography. It brings the main subject into focus and fills the frame. The audience's view is immediately centered where the film maker wants it . . . on the principal element of the scene.

CLOSE-UP SHOT (CU)

In the close-up shot the camera-to-subject distances is so short that only one small element of the entire scene fills the film frame. As a result, the scene is completely dominated by the detail of that single element.

EXTREME CLOSE-UP SHOT (ECU)

Extreme close-up work is only just beginning to catch on in underwater movie photography. In extreme close-up photography, the film maker may be required to add supplemental lenses (diopters) to the camera's standard lens in order to focus down to the short subject-to-camera distances involved. ECU can provide a most impressive view of the delicate and intricate miniature creatures which live in the sea.

CAMERA ANGLES

Always position the camera at an angle to your subject rather than directly in front where it can only record the subject as flat, without depth or perspective. On the other hand, swim a little to the left or right and above or below the subject and suddenly, the film shows more life and dimension.

There is almost nothing more distressing than a long sequence filmed from one position without interruption or change of camera angle. But, worse yet is the sequence during which the camera motor runs down and filming is renewed from exactly the same angle.

Each shot should be treated as an individual visual idea. Use your imagination and try different filming angles. Change back and forth to add variety to the movie. Above all, the changes in camera-to-subject distances or camera angles should be made as smoothly as possible. Such changes, when properly executed, will pass completely unnoticed by the audience. It is clear that the angle at which the camera views the subject goes a long way toward improving or degrading the scene.

EYE LEVEL ANGLE

For the eye level effect, the camera is usually held parallel to the sea floor to show a perspective of the subject, much as the eye would normally see it.

BIRD'S EYE ANGLE

In high-angle shots, the camera is aimed *down* toward the subject. Slight downward angles are acceptable in underwater movie making and frequently attractive. Extreme downward angles, however, are taboo since they tend to give false and confusing impressions of perspective and subject. High angles can be particularly helpful when photographing other divers.

WORM'S EYE VIEW

For low angle shots, the camera is aimed up at the subject. These shots are especially useful for separating the principal subject from a cluttered background. Generally speaking, a low angle shot will be more interesting to an audience than an eye-level shot of the same subject. And low angle shots are easy to make. Simply place the camera on the sea floor, being particularly careful not to kick up any silt which could obscure the film. The diver, when operating directly under a boat, can plant himself firmly on the bottom by placing an additional weight belt on his lap.

SELECTING THE RIGHT LENS

Having determined the correct subject size and camera-to-subject distance for a given shot, the cameraman must now select the lens which will give him the desired image size from the distance selected. To do this, he must first know the capabilities and limitations of each of the lenses he intends to use.

Obviously, all lenses do not produce the same picture. The average wide-angle lens for 16mm cameras has a focal length of 10 to 17mm, while an 8mm movie camera would use a 6.5mm wide angle lens to produce essentially the same effect. A so-called normal lens for the 8mm camera would have an average focal length of 12.5mm, while the focal length of the "normal" 16mm lens would be twice that, or 25mm.

It is interesting to note that the angle of view of movie camera lenses is about one half that of equivalent still camera lenses. The viewer can take the time to casually examine a still photograph. The image in movies is on the screen for such a short time, however, the viewer could never scan the entire image if it were full coverage. The important thing is to know the capabilities and limitations of each of your lenses. Knowing this, selecting the right lens to give you the best story-telling shot is easy.

WIDE ANGLE LENS

The wide angle lens, as we have already learned, is most popular with underwater still photographers. And it is probably equally popular with the undersea movie maker. The shorter the focal length of the lens, the closer the photographer can move to the subject, and the less will be the loss of contrast and quality of the film. The great disadvantage of the wide angle lens is that although it does include much more of the scene, it also makes the subject appear smaller and more distant. The advantage of the wide angle lens stems from its great depth of field. Foreground and background elements can be in acceptable focus when the principal subject is sharply focused.

NORMAL LENS

The normal lens "sees" the scene much as the human eye views it. That is to say, normal perspective is retained over all elements of the photograph — the principal subject, the foreground and the background. The normal lens when used behind a flat port becomes a moderate telephoto and can be a highly effective instrument for filming sequences of fish behavior, for example.

TELEPHOTO LENS

Telephoto lenses are becoming increasingly popular in underwater still photography, particularly in fish portraiture where the fish are usually timid and do not allow the photographer to move in close enough to fill the frame with a normal lens. There is every reason to believe that before long some inquisitive movie maker will experiment with telephoto lenses and develop an exciting new underwater movie technique.

The telephoto lens has shortcomings however. For obvious reasons, the water must be exceptionally clear. In addition to enlarging the subject and bringing it closer, it also includes much less of the background and foreground. And the depth of field

is foreshortened considerably. Consequently, subject-to-camera distances must be precisely determined to keep the subject in sharp focus.

ZOOM LENS

The majority of the current wave of Super 8 movie cameras are packaged with a zoom lens as standard equipment and most of them are really excellent lenses. Termed by some as a "variable focal length lens", the zoom lens has a moveable set of lens elements which — in effect — provide for a continuously changeable range of focal lengths. For example, an 8mm camera zoom lens might have a focal length range of 8mm to 48mm. A popular focal length range in 16mm format is 12mm to 120mm. The cameraman obviously has a wide range of image magnifications from which to choose. The unique capability of this lens to "zoom in" on the subject or "zoom out" away from it without changing camera position makes for some rather spectacular effects.

On the other hand, it is hard to over-emphasize the need to limit the use of the zoom as most new film makers (and some who should know better) tend to zoom the audience to death.

DEVELOP YOUR STYLE

Whether you aspire to be the greatest film-maker of all time or simply wish to improve your home movies, you have an opportunity to create something distinctly unique . . . your personal style. Style is the common connecting thread interwoven through the sequences of visual commentary. It is style which unifies them into an exciting film.

Style is the sum of many things. Among these are outlook and concentration, confidence and attitude. The film maker's personal style begins with an editorial statement. The manner in which the cinematographer films his subjects reflects his personal feelings and attitude towards them. Secondly, style is evidenced in the manner in which the camera is used to display the subject. While the filming techniques of others can be copied or imitated, style develops naturally. There are many books which profess to teach technique but nothing can teach style! The film maker can only hope to develop his own. With each roll of film he shoots, the conscientious movie maker will see a marked improvement in the quality of his work. By carefully analyzing the results he will separate the good from the bad. In this manner, he will develop those techniques which work well for him and discard those which are unnatural. Developing his style thusly, the cinematographer will find that each film project holds promise of newer and more exciting discoveries.

SCENE LENGTH

Understand the nature of the movie camera before exposing the first bit of footage. A movie camera is *not* a still camera, so don't try to economize by taking two or three second sequences. The action simply won't be on the screen long enough for the audience to absorb. And a film of such short sequences will become quite maddening. In the beginning, at least, make your scenes on the average of 12 seconds long. With practice, you will find you can count off 12 seconds very accurately. Twelve seconds probably seems a bit long, but it usually takes the audience that long to orient itself to the underwater scene. No two scenes will be of the same length . . . and that's fine. We wouldn't want them to be. As you gain experience you will find that the scene and the subject dictate the scene length. For example, suppose you should find

an angel fish swimming toward you. You pan with it as it passes before you and follow it until it swims into the darkness of a small cave in the reef. You have just filmed an entire sequence, the length of which was established by the action. And it probably would have been a long scene. On the other hand, a shy eel which might just poke his head out of his lair only to quickly disappear again would undoubtedly justify a brief shot. Experience will aid you in determining the most suitable scene length. In the meantime, if the scenes are too long, you can simply snip out a bit of film. But . . . if you've cut the scene off too early in the camera, you've got nothing but a wasted piece of film that might have been an excellent sequence.

ACTION

There is nothing more rewarding than a well-produced underwater movie that relives every breath-taking moment of a memorable dive. Still photographs, wonderful though they may be, lack the punch and the excitement of movement — the personal feelings sparked by the animated marine life and the vicarious thrill enjoyed by the audience as they glide with the cameraman through crystal water and coral reefs. But good movies don't just happen. A satisfying film is the result of careful planning, composition and imagination. Above all, movies excite where still photographs cannot. Movies show movement . . . *ACTION.* If you want to show static scenes, use a still camera.

CONTINUITY

Movies are simply stories told in film and everybody knows that a story has a beginning, a main body, and an ending.

A good story develops logically and smoothly, step by step or, more appropriately, scene by scene. And *continuity* is a word that summarizes it nicely.

An excellent example of a common break in continuity is the typical sudden cut from a surface sequence of divers on a boat deck preparing for a dive to a scene showing the divers underwater. Above water sequences are important to the overall film and lend a touch of realism with which even the non-divers in the audience can identify. The transition from above water to under water should not leave the viewer asking himself how the devil he got underwater! Instead, it should be part of a continuous, easy flow of action that is neither abrupt nor startling.

CONNECTING SHOTS

Connecting shots are simply shots which connect or link together important elements of the story in a smooth and continuous manner so no break in the action is noticeable. Instead of the abrupt change from surface to underwater, the film maker could have filmed the divers making water entries from the boat and then repeated the shot with the camera now underwater pointing up toward the surface at the point where the divers would hit the water. These connecting shots, properly edited into the action, would preserve the story continuity and make for a vastly more professional film. Another interesting technique for the same situation would have the cameraman in the water shooting up at the divers on the boat with the camera held above the water. Then, as the divers made their entries, the camera would slowly submerge and descend with them. In this manner, the entire connecting sequence could be filmed from one camera position.

CHECK DIRECTION OF MOVEMENT

In professional films, when an underwater photographer is stalking a fish, for example, and the fish close-up shows the fish swimming across the screen from left to right, it is a certainty — in the next shot — the photographer will likewise be swimming across the screen from left to right. In poorly planned and edited films, it is just as likely that while the fish swims from left to right, the photographer will cross the screen looking for the fish in the opposite direction. In amateur films it is not uncommon to see the action moving constantly in different directions.

MATCHING ACTION

Another typical mistake is to film anything interesting or exciting and leave it in the edited film whether it fits or not. I am immediately reminded of a beautifully exposed and colorful film made in the Florida Keys. In one scene, a diver approaches carrying a spear gun. He stops, takes aim and fires. In the very next scene a group of divers are busily investigating some treasure they have found beneath the sand! You are left wondering what in the world the spearfisherman was shooting at. It would have been far better to edit out the spearfishing scene, regardless of how well it was done photographically, if it was distracting or as incomplete a sequence as this obviously was.

Matching action also refers to the continuity of action as the camera moves closer to the principal element of the shot. For example, if you were filming a diver feeding a grouper, you would probably take a long shot to establish the scene and then move closer for a medium shot to identify the diver and the grouper, the principal elements.

As the camera moves from one shot to another, the film maker should attempt to make the next shot appear to flow continuously from the preceding shot, rather than a series of jerky, stilted shots of the same subject. This is done most easily by making a definite change of the camera-to-subject angle each time the camera-to-subject distance is decreased. In effect, this eliminates any abrupt change and makes the action appear smooth and continuous.

THE FOLLOW SHOT

In underwater movie making, the follow shot is used extensively. It is continuous shot in which the camera follows behind the movement of the action, keeping the subject in the same relative position in the viewfinder. The follow shot is used frequently when filming fish, for example.

CUTAWAYS

Cutaway shots are highly important in movie making. They are used to depict a subordinate action which is happening at the same time as the main action. For example, while filming a spearfisherman shooting a fish, a shark suddenly swims into the scene and swallows the wounded fish. An ideal cutaway would be a close-up of the expression on the spearfisherman's face.

Cutaways, then, interrupt the main action of the film to show a secondary action which enhances the film story.

SEQUENCES

Perhaps we have gone off too fast without defining all our terms. First, the word "shot" refers to the amount of film footage exposed during a single run of the camera. A "sequence" is the term used to describe a series of "shots" or "takes" which collectively have a common story or theme. A "film" is composed of a series of sequences which follow one another in logical succession to the story's conclusion.

In theory, at least, it is possible to "edit in the camera" or construct a film of sequences shot in chronological order. A more practical technique is to shoot the film out of sequence and edit the out-of-phase sequences into their proper order later.

Most underwater scenes begin with a long shot to establish locale and occasionally conclude with a long shot . . . of, for example, divers ascending to the surface. It is clear, therefore, that sequences can be started, ended or changed by varying the camera angle or the camera-to-subject distance.

TECHNIQUES

Like virtually everything else in life, underwater movie making has its own set of tricks of the trade. And your film will begin to take on a professional look when you can skillfully make these techniques work for you.

PANNING

"Panning" refers to the technique of swinging the camera in a *slow,* wide arc to shoot a scene too broad to be included from a straight-ahead, static camera position. A sweeping panorama is a good example. A "pan" is also frequently used to follow the action of a subject moving across the scene. A pan may be a vertical movement of the camera or horizontal.

Like most filming techniques, panning is all too easily overdone. Use the pan shot judiciously, but do use it. The pan plays an important role in underwater photography. When well done, it immediately familiarizes the audience with the expansiveness of the diving area and promotes a sense of vastness. It shows the audience where the action will be taking place.

A pan shot of a long, coral reef would begin with a fixed shot for several seconds and then a *slow, smooth,* and *steady* movement, either horizontally or vertically, to an important element of interest and held there for several seconds. Generally speaking, the greater the area to be panned, the slower should be the sweep of the camera.

The two most important "don'ts" in panning are:

1) Don't swing the camera too quickly!

and

2) Don't reverse directions when panning!

These two rules are broken so frequently, they are probably responsible for a good percentage of the groans heard whenever home movies are suggested. Reversed direction and fast, jerky pans frequently give the audience a case of acute seasickness.

Actually, because of the increased density of water, pan shots are easier underwater than in air, for the heavier medium tends to support the camera and cushion it against the diver's unsteadiness.

ZOOM IN — ZOOM OUT

Zoom scenes can be accomplished, appropriately enough, with a zoom lens. This variable focal length lens has the capability of moving in towards (zoom in) or away from (zoom out) the subject without changing the camera's position.

Zoom scenes can also be filmed underwater without a zoom lens. The underwater cameraman need only swim in slowly or float in toward the principal element. Better yet, he need only be a little above and to the side of the subject to glide down toward it, effectively simulating a zoom in.

There is only one caution for me to add: *Hold the camera steady!* The natural swimming movement tends to shake the camera, but with practice the cameraman can attain a surprising degree of stability underwater.

Years ago, in order to dampen camera movement, I attached a two foot long aluminum wing to my Bolex housing. I'm sure its effect was largely psychological. Lamar Boren wears fins with a very small blade area, preferring to control his position underwater through breath control. He thereby eliminates any problems caused by long fin blades. Because of the ever-present threat of serious lung overexpansion this procedure is definitely *NOT* recommended for beginning underwater photographers.

Zoom out scenes, unfortunately, are a bit more difficult. The underwater cameraman is required to swim backwards away from the subject during the filming. In addition to being clumsier, there is also the strong possibility of ruining the footage by filming his own fins.

SWIM-THROUGH

The swim-through describes the filming technique in which the camera is held in a fixed position (by tripod or simply by bracing or weighting yourself as firmly as possible) while the subject swims across the optical path of the camera lens. For the best effect the model should swim diagonally across the scene rather than at a right angle to the camera position. Ideally, a swim-through begins before the subject enters the viewfinder and continues for several seconds after he has swum out of the frame.

STEADY

The underwater world may very well be unfamiliar to the audience. As a result, you should make your underwater shots a little longer than your surface shots to give the audience time to orient itself with the underwater scene. Naturally, the longer the shot, the more important it is that the camera be held as steady as possible to avoid those fuzzy shots which bounce spasmodi-

cally around the screen and make everyone ill. The underwater cameraman can brace himself on the bottom when heavily weighted. Some photographers intentionally weight their belts excessively, offsetting the negative buoyancy with a buoyancy-compensating inflatable vest. When positioned over the right spot, the excess air is vented and the photographer becomes negatively buoyant.

An alternate method is to brace the housing on the sea floor or any reasonably solid object. Probably the best way to insure camera steadiness is to use a tripod. Most underwater photographers prefer to be mobile and portable and, consequently, shun the restrictive tripod. Other film makers use the tripod extensively underwater, particularly when shooting extreme close-ups.

DOLLY SHOTS

"The film maker", it has been said, "should make sequences, not pot shots!" "If a scene isn't worth three shots, it isn't worth shooting."

What all this means is that the really creative film maker mixes into a film long shots, medium shots, close-ups, zooms, swim-throughs, pans and . . . dolly shots. A "dolly" in movie language refers to the vehicle which moves the camera and cameraman smoothly toward or away from the sub-

"In reality, a dolly can be most anything."

ject during the filming of a scene. In reality, a dolly can be most anything. While filming a documentary in Canada, I used a railroad handcar which filled the bill most admirably . . . and at no cost.

On a Hollywood sound stage, a dolly could be the epitome of engineering, a vehicle costing hundreds of thousands, capable of telescoping camera and operator high above the set or changing direction and angle so swiftly and smoothly that hardly a whisper of movement can be detected.

The underwater film-maker can accomplish the same photographic effect with no added equipment for the diver is, in effect, his own dolly. By moving upward, downward, forward, backward, diagonally or in whichever direction his imagination leads him, the undersea cameraman is free to "dolly" his camera in any dimension.

There is this rule of thumb to consider relative to any of the techniques we have discussed or will discuss. All camera techniques are good when used for their intended purpose. Like seasoning on roast beef, the techniques should only flavor and compliment. Occasionally a film maker gets hung up on a pet technique forgetting that nobody comes to dinner for the seasoning. They come for the roast. Use these techniques artfully and sparingly, and you will be well rewarded.

FADE

An interesting and quite simple way to begin or end a sequence is the "fade". A "fade-in" opens a scene and a "fade out" closes it. To do a fade-in, first determine the f/stop for the proper amount of exposure. However, the smallest f/stop is used as shooting begins. The cameraman then "opens up" the lens until he is shooting at the pre-selected f/stop. The screen is dark as the scene begins but rapidly grows lighter until the optimum exposure is reached. The fade should be a brief visual effect and not linger on the screen. Fade-outs are simply reversed in procedure.

THE PROBLEM OF PARALLAX

Picture a beautifully exposed, sharply focused, excitingly colorful underwater scene! Now add a diver! But the diver's head is cut off the screen. Frustrating, isn't it?

As we have already seen, the small viewfinder on the camera, the mask, and housing all combine to make the camera's viewfinder virtually unuseable underwater. When you acquire a housing for your movie camera, you will, hopefully, become thoroughly familiar with both camera and housing *before* you take them underwater. The first time underwater, take an experimental roll at a series of different camera-to-subject distances. Make careful notation of the distances used. When projected, you will see if you are framing your subject correctly. If not, you will know how to correct it. With most cameras, parallax is rarely a problem in the medium to long distance range. It is usually when the camera is moved up for close-up work that parallax error becomes a serious problem. The problem can only be overcome through knowledge of your equipment, practice, experience and concentration. If you are fortunate enough to have a camera and housing which are set up for through-the-lens viewing, you ought to have absolutely no framing or parallax problems. In the more likely event that you are using a sportsfinder or viewfinder sighting device you will just have to practice and experiment. At camera-to-subject distances of less than three or four feet, you'll have to be particularly careful.

GENERAL RULES

The differences between professional and amateur films are monumental and yet these differences aren't always as obvious as they might seem. For example, the amateur may very well have interesting subjects and good equipment. In other words, he may have all the ingredients to put together a fine movie, except the techniques. Professionals work quickly and efficiently. The secret to their smooth operation is organization and technique.

Before you even lift the camera, picture in your mind what it is you want the shot to show. Don't just look at the scene. *See it!* Try to visualize a scene as it will look to an audience. In other words, "see" and compose the scene, placing the subjects where they will be displayed to best advantage.

Underwater movies generally require lots of light and the best way to film a scene (in natural light photography) is with the subjects front

lighted. The sun should pass over the cameraman's shoulder. Don't be afraid to use lots of film. If you expect to be a good photographer, you better be prepared to shoot film. Make many different shots. Cut-aways and inserts will add detail and punch up interest when edited into the film later. Shoot the same subject from different angles and different distances. Long shots are great for overviews; close-ups for detail.

Always use a light meter, preferably a direct-reading meter, to measure exact levels of light. Mount it on your housing. Experiment with different positions until you find one that allows you to determine the optimum f/stop without shifting your eyes too far from the view finder. With experience, the f/stop can be determined from the meter and the aperture adjusted even during a traveling shot.

If you're not fortunate enough to have an electrically driven camera, get in the habit of rewinding the motor immediately after every shot. There is nothing more exasperating than having the camera run down in the middle of an exciting shot. By the time the camera is rewound, the action has usually disappeared from view. However if the subject is still close by, resume shooting from another angle. This will minimize the interruption and the audience probably won't even notice.

Finally, save all unused footage. You will eventually use it as fill-in for another film.

Shoot scenes from many different angles and utilize as much of the environment — corals, boulders, marine life, wrecks — as possible for background or framing your subject.

EXPOSURE

Everything mentioned earlier about determining exposure for still photography underwater generally applies for movie cameras as well. And since there are so many variables to contend with, an exposure meter is an absolute must. Or you might wish to try one of the new cameras that offer fully automatic exposure control. These cameras are perfect for the casual film-maker who occasionally wants to put together a little film for his own enjoyment. The serious student of undersea film making will do better to learn with an adjustable camera to better prepare for more sophisticated equipment. There is no question, however, that cameras with automatic exposure control make film making a lot easier for the beginner. For example, he needn't worry about changing f/stops as he swims from shaded area to bright sunny area. The camera compensates quickly and automatically.

SELECTING THE RIGHT CAMERA

All right, you've got the desire and we'll presume that you can build or buy a housing for most any camera. To get started, you must have a camera. So what's it going to be?

8 MM . . . ?

If you already own a good 8mm camera and you can't afford anything else, by all means use it. However, the only reason that 8mm is still around is because of the large number of privately owned cameras. The film manufacturers are not about to stop making 8mm film.

If you're only shopping, however, that's a different story. When compared to the present generation of Super 8 cameras, the poor old 8mm just doesn't make it. With 8mm cameras, for example, you can only expose 25 feet of film at a time. Then you must surface, open the housing, turn the film (roll or magazine) over, and close the housing. Actually, 8mm film stock is special 16mm film. It is run through the camera twice, exposing only one half of the film width as it passes through the camera. Then the film must be turned over and run through again to expose the other half. After the film has been processed, the laboratory slits the film into two halves and joins the strips, forming a 50 foot length of 8mm movie film.

When projected side by side with Super 8, the old 8mm format looks small and fuzzy by comparison. And lastly, most 8mm cameras are powered by spring motors which require frequent winding. Of course, while it produces a film image only half the size of the 16mm format, 8mm costs only a fraction of 16mm. On the other hand, 8mm film is really suitable only for home movie enjoyment. Due to its small size and poor projection characteristics, it is definitely unacceptable where a large image must be projected.

SUPER 8 vs 16 MM

Without question, the two most popular film formats are Super 8 and

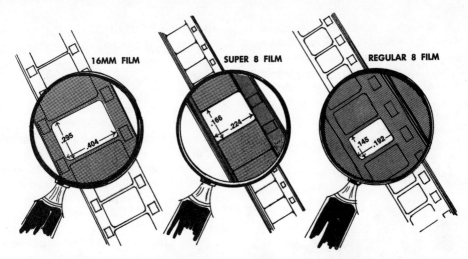

16MM FILM SUPER 8 FILM REGULAR 8 FILM

Comparison of film formats (dimensions in inches)

16mm. Although the techniques of filming, editing and production are virtually the same, from the underwater film maker's point of view there are definite advantages and disadvantages to each.

Regardless of the format of the camera, there are two things to keep in mind. First and foremost, the smaller Super 8 cameras are easy to handle and relatively inexpensive to buy and operate (about 1/5 the cost of 16mm). The 16mm format is still generally considered, however, the smallest professional film format, notwithstanding some excellent experiments being conducted by the networks with the Super 8 format.

SUPER 8

Perhaps the greatest advance in amateur movie making is the development of the Super 8 film format which has all but obsoleted the venerable 8mm format. The Super 8 format is larger, producing an image 50% larger than 8mm. Consequently, Super 8 can be projected larger, with less loss of detail, for a greater audience than regular 8mm.

Most Super 8 cameras feature electric motor drive, thereby eliminating the need to wind after each shot. And running down in the middle of a shot is

forever eliminated. With Super 8 the film maker can shoot off an entire 50 foot roll of film in one 3½ minute continuous run, if he's so inclined. The alkaline batteries have enough juice to run through 25 film cartridges before they need changing.

Most of the new generation of Super 8 cameras also have automatic exposure control. A light-measuring cell in the camera calculates the intensity of light on the subject and automatically adjusts the lens to the correct f-stop. Many of the better Super 8 cameras are also equipped with a power zoom lens which further increases the camera's versatility underwater.

An added advantage of Super 8 over regular 8mm is that the Super 8 cartridge exposes 50 feet of film without

Cinemar Super 8 housing

being turned over. But good equipment costs money. A Super 8 camera featuring automatic exposure control, power zoom, electric motor drive in a good housing will range from $350 to $600. There are so many top Super 8 cameras, it would really be hard to single out one. Still, for the money, it would be hard to imagine a better bargain than one of the new low-light cameras protected by a molded Ikelite housing. These revolutionary

Kodak XL camera and Ikelite housing

cameras (Kodak's XL-55 is but one example) seem to have it all: fast f/1.2 lens, great depth of field (from 2 feet to infinity underwater), electric motor drive, automatic exposure control, power zoom, and simple snap-in film cartridges for easy loading. Add to this the revolutionary 230° shutter which yields 40% more exposure than conventional shutters and Ektachrome 160 movie film and the film-maker can shoot available light movies at depths where light levels were previously considered too low for filming without artificial light.

For example, when used together, the XL camera and Ektachrome 160 film provide the film maker with as much as 4½ f/stops over conventional Super 8 camera and film combinations. And since they are fully automatic, they allow for one-button operation underwater.

The final choice ultimately depends on how much you can afford and what you're going to do with the film. If you want to record your dives to entertain friends and family, Super 8 is your best bet.

SUPER 8 "TALKIES"

Probably the most exciting development in Super 8 technology is the Kodak Ektasound movie camera. It combines all the features of the revolutionary XL camera with an integrated recorder. The amateur film maker equipped with the Kodak Ektasound can shoot sound on film synchronized with the action at a cost that won't bust his pocketbook. (The fixed-focus lens Kodak Ektasound 130 is less than $190.) And it's almost as fool-proof as shooting silent movies.

The only additional step required is to plug in the mike. Kodak presently

Kodak Ektasound Camera

offers two Super 8 films with magnetic striping: Ektachrome 160 and Kodachrome II. The new camera will also accept conventional (silent) Super 8 cartridges. Processing costs are identical to silent Super 8 film cartridges. At least one manufacturer (Ikelite) is marketing a housing for the Kodak Ektasound cameras.

16 MM

But supposing your ambitions are greater? If you aspire to lecture professionally or participate in film competitions, television or even theatre release, then your choice must be the

16mm film format. Despite the experiments being conducted by the television industry with the Super 8 format, the 16mm film is still considered the smallest acceptable professional film gauge.

The variety of 16mm movie equipment available is staggering. But then, so are the prices this equipment brings. A 16mm camera-housing system equipped with the same features as described for the Super 8 system (automatic exposure control, reflex viewing, power zoom, electric motor drive, mounted in a top quality housing) would carry a price tag of $3,500 to $12,000.

Of course, there are less costly ways to get into the 16mm scene. My first venture into 16mm movie work began with a creaky, antiquated Bolex liberated from a Chicago pawn shop for less than $50. The Plexiglas housing cost more than the camera. But projecting that first roll of processed film told the whole story. The larger 16mm format projected a huge, well defined image such as I had never seen before in years of filming in 8mm.

There is much to recommend the 16mm format: variety of lenses, accessory equipment, film stocks, professional laboratory services, special effects and printing services that are

unlimited. Much of the professional underwater film work in the past has been done with the 16mm or 35mm Arriflex. But among other cameras with a 400 foot film capacity the Eclair and Bolex are enjoying an increasing popularity. The French Beaulieu is still another favorite of 16mm devotees. And finally, in the spring-wound, 100 foot film capacity cameras, a good

Long-time favorite of underwater movie makers, the venerable Bolex in its rugged aluminum housing

many divers favor the Bolex, the popular Kodak K-100 and the Bell and Howell 70DR model. All these cameras are practical and economical and are easily accommodated by underwater housings.

As I'm rather lazy by nature, it sometimes seems as though I've spent the better part of an underwater lifetime

MAKO housing for the Arriflex camera designed and manufactured by Jordan Klein

Kodak K-100

cranking up the rewind on spring motors. The K-100 provides a 40-foot film run on a single winding, but while nice to have, few cameramen ever expose 40-foot long shots. It's not the length of the film run that bugs me, it's the tedious rewinding! Most spring motor-drive cameras will accept electric drive units. Unfortunately, because of the heavy ni-cad batteries needed to supply the power, the housings tend to be bulky and heavy. But the convenience of the electric drive is well worth the extra effort.

Now that you're all excited about 16mm and ready to run out and buy a camera, let me acquaint you with the economic facts of life. Shooting 16mm cannot be done inexpensively! Cameras, lenses and accessory equipment aside, it costs roughly 4 or 5 times as much to buy, shoot and process 10 minutes of 16mm film as would 10 minutes of Super 8. Keep in mind to get the same amount of running time, you must shoot twice as much 16mm as Super 8 film. If you are serious about getting into underwater moviemaking and your knowledge and skill are limited, break in and make your beginner's mistakes in Super 8. Then, when you're ready to step up to 16mm format, the transition will be easier and a lot less expensive.

FOCUS

Generally in movie cameras, there are focusing lenses and non-focusing or fixed-focus lenses. Fixed focus lenses are usually fixed by the manufacturer at a surface subject-to-camera distance of approximately 15 feet for a normal lens. A focusing lens, however, must be set to the correct distance in order to be in sharp focus. If your lens is a focusing lens and your housing has a focusing control, then you focus at the "apparent" distance or ¾ of the actual or measured distance.

But focusing needn't be a big has-sle. Wide angle lenses have great depth of field, remember? The wider the angle, the greater the depth of field. Frequently with a wide angle lens, the depth of field is so great that focusing is not required at all. The need for a housing focusing control is therefore eliminated. Simply preset your distance to 6 or 7 feet before mounting the camera in the housing. At the average underwater working range of subject-to-camera distances, you will always be in sharp focus. For example, the Yvar 16mm lens is in acceptable focus from less than 3 feet to infinity covering the usual range of long shots through medium close-ups. The ever-popular 10mm Switar lens used extensively on Bolex and K-100s provides an astounding depth of field from only inches in front of the lens to infinity.

FILMING SPEED

Filming speed in film making is not a means of adjusting exposure time as shutter speed frequently is in still photography, although it can be. Instead, it is a way of changing the pace of the action. For example, most Super 8 cameras record normal silent action at a rate of 18 frames per second (fps). However, by exceeding the normal 18 fps by a ratio of 2:1 (36 fps) or 4:1 (72 fps) the projected image moves only one half or one quarter as fast as the original motion. While some interesting effects can be filmed in slow motion underwater, they tend to be overdone and pointless. In any event, Super 8 cameras record silent movies at a speed of 18 fps. And 16mm silent film is shot at 16 fps. Professional sound speed is 24 frames per second. So, if you are considering adding commercial sound to your film, it must be shot at 24 fps. It might be interesting to note that in changing from a filming speed of 16 fps to 24 fps, film use increases 50 per cent!

Finally, most exposure meters require that you convert filming speed (frames per second) to equivalent shutter speeds. While there is a little variance from camera to camera, at 64 frames per second most movie cameras provide a frame exposure of 1/120th to 1/140th of a second. At 32 fps, 1/60th to 1/70th of a second. At 24 fps, 1/45th of a second. At 16 fps, 1/30th to 1/35th of a second. And at 8 fps, 1/17th to 1/20th of a second.

FINISHING THE JOB

You have planned. You have toiled. You have shot your footage. Now you come to that great moment of truth. It is time to edit!

Editing is the term film makers use to describe the process of sorting through, sorting out, and assembling the best of your footage into the best possible story.

SHOOTING RATIO

Determine the ratio of the number of feet of movie film exposed in making a film to the number of feet of film actually used in the final edited version and you have the shooting ratio. In the average television documentary, for example, the film crew will shoot at a ratio of 40:1. That is to say, for every 100 feet of 16mm film (shot at 24 fps for a running time of less than 3 minutes) *4,000 feet* of film was exposed!

An even more interesting example are those super one-hour underwater specials you see on the TV networks. An average of *150,000 feet* of film is exposed to be edited down to a final *1,800 feet*! Think about that when you're daydreaming about hitting big-time TV.

More importantly, don't become so enamored of your footage that you can't bear to cut any of it out of the film. You must be brutally critical of your own footage. If a shot is worth-less, get rid of it. A few poor shots can bring down the whole film. Cull out the superfluous, the excess, the tedious and the duplications, even if they are technically perfect. It's a lot better to cut the excess and have a snappy, fast-moving short movie that leaves the audience clamoring for more, than to have a boring, dragging epic that will have the ones who are still awake begging for mercy.

Editing can be a matter of simply attaching one shot behind another with splicing tapes or it can be a really artistic endeavor in which the editor creates in the film a vibrance, a mood, pace or tempo on which the entire audience hangs. If, at this point, you've elected to go 16mm, you've already discovered that 16mm editing equipment is also proportionally more expensive than 8mm or Super 8. But, thanks to the large size of the film, it is also much easier to edit.

THE EDITOR'S BENCH

Most any *clean* table will do. Try to work close to an uncluttered wall space so you can use masking tape to momentarily set aside a scene by taping it to the wall. You'll need a good film editor. Get the best you can afford; you'll be using it a lot. And keep it clean and covered when not in use. When your films have been processed, check them through the film editor. Cull out any bad footage (the little that you'll have).

While you were filming you didn't take the shots in any particular order. Now it is time to rough edit and arrange the shots into a logical story development. This will be especially easy if you have been shooting from a script. You really only need, in addition to your film editor, two (2) film rewinds, a *good* splicer, and film cement. The editor should wear light cotton gloves (preferably white to show dirt) anytime the film is being handled. The gloves will reduce the risk of scratching, finger printing or otherwise damaging the film. When the film has undergone rough editing, you may want to try projecting it to get the feel and pace of your film. Take careful notes of running times and scenes that will require additional editing.

GENERAL RULES

Keep the scenes only as long as necessary. After viewing the establishing shots, the audience will be quick to pick up on the action in any one scene. Concentrate on using your underwater scenes. You're making an *underwater* film! Surface shots should be used as required for continuity, but they should not overpower the underwater scenes. The good film maker overlaps his action, whenever possible, so that when he edits there will be enough overlap to precisely match the action from scene to scene.

There is also the problem of color compatability between different shots in the same sequence. In other words, if you have a scene of divers exploring a colorful reef surrounded by pale green water, you should not cut away to a shark in deep, dark blue water. It just doesn't make it.

It is clear then, the purpose of editing is to weave a multitude of shots into a meaningful story which has visual importance, impact, logical development and a smooth flow. And keep in mind, most any film can be enhanced with the addition of a narrative and musical background.

MUSICAL BACKGROUND

If you have just finished watching the edited version of your film for the tenth time and you're feeling down because, despite all the pretty shots and careful editing, it seems to be lacking something, *try a little music!* You'll be amazed at how much more

professional the film will be with just a little music to fit the mood or set a tempo. The music should complement the scene, not dominate it.

With a little imagination, you can elevate a cute underwater sequence to a moment of unforgettable hilarity. Jack McKenney, editor of *Skin Diver* magazine, some years ago did a short film called "Quarry Diving" which regularly pops up at film festivals all over the country. There is, in that film, a chase sequence of a baby duck attempting to elude Jack and his camera. Most of the sequence shows the poor duckling from the rear, webbed feet paddling feverishly to escape Jack's ruthless pursuit. To this great chase scene, hilarious by itself, Jack scored a masterful stroke of matching the right music to the action. He selected "The Storm" from the William Tell Overture, which the older readers will remember as the "Lone Ranger's" theme song. Needless to say, the audience howls! I've seen it several times and I begin to smile now just thinking about it.

For the amateur film maker, any good tape recorder will record the music you wish to use as background. Indeed, several Super 8 systems currently offer "home-sound" movie projectors with which inexpensive magnetic sound can be added to the film while you view it in the projector. In effect, the projector is also a tape recorder. Sound is recorded on a special magnetic edging applied to the film and can be played back in perfect synchronization with the film.

On the other side of the spectrum is the professional, optical sound track which must be laid on the film by a laboratory . . . a must if the film is intended for distribution. And when the film maker goes to that expense, his musical background can get rather expensive. One film maker I know recently completed a commercial 20-minute underwater film and decided he wanted an original musical score. Between scoring, orchestra and recording studio fees, the cost of the finished 20-minute film was well over $10,000.

THE NARRATIVE

Most film lecturers prefer to use the live narrative. The musical background and sound effects are recorded on magnetic tape and played on a tape recorder while the narrative is done live. In contrast, films that are to be entered in film competitions have narrative, musical background and sound effects on the same tape. With the exception of a few well-done art films, most underwater films — due to the fact the general public is only vaguely familiar with the underwater world — require some sort of narrative. A narrative only helps the film to tell its story. Therefore, the narrative must naturally play a role subordinate to the film. In other words, a good film maker doesn't fill a 30-minute film with 30 minutes of narrative. Some film makers, however, do get a bit uneasy when a few seconds go by without any talking. The narrative should occupy only as much time as necessary without adding a lot of needless jabber that only detracts from the film rather than compliments it.

On the other hand, the narrative is important to the success of the film. And it deserves as much consideration, thought and effort as the filming and editing. All elements of the film — the story, the filming, the editing, the music, the narrative — must fit together and blend smoothly if the film is to be a success.

The narrative can only be written after the film has had its final edit. And then, the film maker must lend drama and excitement to the narrative! He must reach for the element that "hooks" the audience, that holds their attention . . . whatever that may be.

NARRATIVE FOR THE SAKE OF TALKING

Don't describe for the audience things they can see on the screen. Nothing annoys an audience more than the film-lecturer who says, ". . . the multi-colored reef fish were beautiful." The audience can *see* that the beautiful reef fish sport different colors. Instead, tell them about something they can't see. For example, try describing the behavior patterns of the beautiful fish.

TIMING IS EVERYTHING

The part of the narrative describing a particular sequence should end when the sequence ends, if not before. The narrator should never describe a sequence before it appears or continue after it has left the screen. That only serves to confuse the audience.

SOUND EFFECTS

One great benefit of the live narrative is that in presenting it from a carefully timed and interadjusted script and film, the lecturer projects a much more intimate relationship with the audience than he would with a taped narrative. The lecturer also has the advantage of complete control over the volume of music, as well as the sound effects which he activates from timing cues in the script.

Some sound effects can really enhance a film when used effectively. The metallic tinkle of bubbles escaping from a regulator, for example, can really punch up the audience excitement. There are a number of professional sound studios which offer a wide range of sound effects that could enrich your next film. Sound effects

liven up the film and add impact to the on-screen or off-screen action. Two studios you could contact are: Elektra Records, 51 West 51st Street, New York, N. Y. 10019 and Folkway Records, 165 West 46th Street, New York, N. Y. 10036. Folkway even has an interesting album on the sounds of sea animals including, among others, the recorded sounds of parrot fish, manatee, porpoise and drumfish. Strangely enough, it's called "Sounds of Sea Animals." And remember sound, whether it be narrative, music or sound effects, must be unobtrusive. Sound must belong in a scene — enhancing it — and not stealing attention from it.

SUMMARY

Well, Cecil B., you have just read a great deal about movie making and are anxious to get a camera and begin your film making career in earnest.

Before you begin, let's review just a few points of importance. We have discussed the planning and the techniques of actually shooting the film,

and we have studied the techniques of editing and adding musical background and sound effects. It is obvious that all these facets must be given great and equal attention if the film is to be anything more than just another of the "ho-hum" underwater flicks.

And to those put-down artists who would have you believe that you can't make an underwater movie unless you travel to some remote Pacific atoll, forget them!

Wherever you live, nearby is a body of water holding a multitude of exciting subjects and your choice is limited only by your imagination. Once you start, you'll be amazed at how rapidly you progress. Certainly, experience is the best teacher — but you needn't shoot movies for a lifetime to develop your own style. Study the books listed in the appendix, shoot lots and lots of film, and learn from your mistakes. You will soon be among the elite in a small, but rapidly growing, corps of artists finding immense satisfaction creating films.

"When the last individual of a race of living things breathes no more, another heaven and another earth must pass before such a one can be again."
William Beebe

Photo by Jim Tallon

Joe Strykowski and friend

ABOUT THE AUTHOR

Joe Strykowski is the producer-host of the television series "Man and Sea".

His camera has been his passport to diving adventure around the world. He is a formidable film-maker and his underwater and vanishing wildlife film work has received wide television coverage.

Since his first published work appeared in a national magazine at age 14, he has been writer, correspondent, editor and photo-journalist whose photographs and stories have appeared in scores of periodicals.

A former working diver, he is also a well-qualified engineer having worked on the development of much new underwater equipment, most recently as project engineer in the development of a complete saturation diving complex.

Joe Strykowski was one of the pioneers of diving safety and his credentials are numerous. He was one of the very first instructors to be nationally certified and the divers he has introduced to the underwater world number in the thousands.

Joe is a board member of the Marine Technology Society, National YMCA Scuba Committee and the Gillette Scuba Safety Association and serves as a diver training consultant

to the underseas industry. Joe is a member of the American Society of Mechanical Engineers, Outdoor Writers Association of America and

the American Society for Oceanography.

It is from this diversified underwater background that Joe Strykowski has provided the material and proven methods included in this book.

MODEL RELEASE

For value received, the receipt of which from ....
.... is acknowledged, and without further
consideration, I hereby expressly grant to said ....
.... the absolute right and permission to photograph me and copyright and/or publish or use any photographs taken
of me at .... on .... 19.........
for art, advertising or any other lawful whatsoever, or as my physical
likeness may appear in any still camera photograph and/or motion
picture film, in and in connection with the exhibition, theatrically, on
television or otherwise, of any motion picture in which the same may
be used or incorporated, and also in the advertising and/or publiciz-
ing of any such motion picture, but not limited to television or theatrical
motion pictures.

Accepted by subject .... date ....

Parent or Legal Guardian if subject is under 21 ....

Model .... Witness ....

Address .... Address ....

Signature .... Signature ....

SUGGESTED READING

Church, Jim and Cathy, "Beginning Underwater Photography", Jim and Cathy Church — Gilroy, California

Church, Ron, "Beginner's Guide to Photography Underwater", Ron Church Productions — LaJolla, California

Clark, John, "Basic Underwater Photography", Petersen Publishing — Los Angeles, California

Cross, E. R., "Underwater Photography and Television", Exposition Press — New York, New York

Frey, Hank and Tzimoulis, Paul, "Camera Below", Association Press — New York, New York

Greenberg, Jerry, "Underwater Photography Simplified", Seahawk Press — Coral Gables, Florida

Mertens, Lawrence, "In-Water Photography", Wiley Interscience — New York, New York

Montanus, Neil, "Underwater Photography", The Fifth Here's How, Eastman Kodak — Rochester, New York

Pincus, Edward, "Guide to Filmmaking", Signet — New York, New York

Rebikoff, Dimitri and Cherney, Paul, "Guide to Underwater Photography", Amphoto — New York, New York

Roberts, Fred, "Nikonos Photography — The Camera and System", F. M. Roberts Enterprises — Dana Point, California

Schenk, Hilbert and Kendall, Henry, "Underwater Photography", Cornell Maritime Press — Cambridge, Maryland

Starck, Walter and Brundza, Paul, "The Art of Underwater Photography", Amphoto — New York, New York

Strykowski, Joe, "Diving For Fun", Dacor — Northfield, Illinois

Note:

Without a doubt, the Eastman Kodak Company has compiled the most extensive bibliography on underwater photography ever put together. You can get a copy of Kodak Pamphlet No. P-124, "Bibliography on Underwater Photography and Photogrammetry" and the updating supplement P-124A by sending your request to:

Department 412 — L
Eastman Kodak Company
Rochester, New York 14650

MAGAZINES

Skin Diver, 5900 Hollywood Boulevard, Los Angeles, California 90028

Dive Magazine, P. O. Box 7765, Long Beach, California 90807

Aquarius, 1757 Long Beach Blvd., Long Beach, California 90813

The Underwater Photographer, Drawer 608, Dana Point, California 92629

Modern Photography, P. O. Box 14117, Cincinnati, Ohio 45214

Popular Photography, P. O. Box 2775, Boulder, Colorado 80302

Super-8 Filmmaker, 10 Pelham Parkway, Pelham Manor, New York 10803

Filmmaker's Newsletter, P. O. Box 115, Ward Hill, Massachusetts 01830

American Cinematographer, 1782 North Orange Drive, Hollywood, California 90028

ACKNOWLEDGMENTS

Sincere thanks to the following manufacturers who provided the photographs and artwork of their products:

Aqua-Craft, Inc.
Eastman Kodak Company
Electro Oceanics, Inc.
Farrallon Industries
GAF Corporation
Giddings/Felgen, Inc.
Harry Gocho Enterprises, Inc.
  (Distributor of Sekonic Meters)
Hydro-Photo, Lee Grobe
Ikelite Underwater Systems
Micro Lens III, Ken Sprouls
Mitchell Photogrammetry, Inc.
  (Oceaneye Housing)
Oceanic Products
Paillard, Incorporated
  (Distributor of Hasselblad and
  Bolex Cameras)
Rollei of America, Inc.
Seacor, Inc.
Sea Research & Development, Inc.
Subsea Products, Inc.

And special thanks to Bryce Blore of Nikon Inc. (Subsidiary of Ehrenreich Photo-Optical Industries, Inc.)

INDEX

Night photography, 174
Nikonos close-up systems, 146-152
  Extension tube, 149
  Hydro-Photo, 147
  Micro Lens, 146, 147
  Nikkor No. 2, 146
  Nikonos close-up, 147, 148
Nikonos II 35mm, 29, 35, 36, 39, 69
Nitrogen Narcosis, 12

O

"O" rings, 50, 56
Opportunities, 6

P

Panatomic X, 103, 116
Panning, 83
Parallax error, 35-38, 53, 129, 192
Peak action, 82
Planning, 162
  movies, 180-181
Plus X Pan, 104
Presentations, 7
Pressure, 9, 10
Prism, 64, 65

R

Reflection, 18, 22
Refraction, 19, 23, 24
Reproduction ratio, 149, 150
Retakes, 163
Rollei, 37, 154
Rolleimarin, 37, 154
Royal-X Pan, 104

S

Safety, 5, 6, 11, 12, 15, 166, 177, 178
Salinity, 14, 15
Scattering, 26
Scene Length 187
Sequence Shooting, 163
Sharpness, 100, 165
Shooting, 164
Shooting Ratio, 199
Shooting Script, 182, 183
Shutter, 78
  front, 78, 79, 119
  focal plane, 80, 81, 118
  speed, 79, 80

speed/aperture relationship, 85, 86
synchronization, 117, 118
Silhouettes
  flash, 167, 168
  sun, 167
Slave sensor, 131
Sound, 13
Sound Effects, 201, 202
Specific Gravity, 10
Spectrum, 17, 18
Sports Finder, 35, 38, 53
Still Life & Seascapes, 169
"Stop Action", 81
  blurred motion, 82
  "freezing" motion, 82
Strobes, 119-121
  automatic, 139
  color temperature, 122
  function, 119
  light beam coverage, 121
  light output ratings, 120
  power supply, 120, 121
  ready light, 121
  shutter speeds, 121, 122
Style, 186-187
Subjects, 168-172
Subject-to-Camera-Distance, 75
  movies, 184
Sun (angle), 22, 23
Sun Light, 21
Surface Conditions, 21, 22

T

Thermocline, 13
Timing, 81
Tripods, 11
Tri-X Pan, 104
Type 2485 High Speed Recording Film,
  104

V

Valsalva Maneuver, 9
Vest, buoyancy compensating, 11
Viewfinder, 35, 39
Visibility, 27, 164

W

Water Resistance, 14
Waves, 21, 22
Wet Suit Compression, 10